W9-CTW-794

Market-Driven Journalism

For Marsh, who taught me
how to love with my ears

Market-Driven Journalism: Let the Citizen Beware?

John H. McManus

SAGE PUBLICATIONS
International Educational and Professional Publisher
Thousand Oaks   London   New Delhi

For information address:

 SAGE Publications, Inc.
2455 Teller Road
Thousand Oaks, California 91320

SAGE Publications Ltd.
6 Bonhill Street
London EC2A 4PU
United Kingdom

SAGE Publications India Pvt. Ltd.
M-32 Market
Greater Kailash I
New Delhi 110 048 India

Printed in the United States of America

Library of Congress Cataloging-in-Publication Data

McManus, John H.
    Market-driven journalism: Let the citizen beware? / John H.
McManus
        p. cm.
    Includes bibliographical references and index.
    ISBN 0-8049-5252-X. — ISBN 0-8039-5253-8 (pbk.)
        1. Television broadcasting of news—Economic aspects—United
States. 2. Television—Production and direction. I. Title.
PN4748.T7M36 1994
070.1'95'0973—dc20   93-49517

94 95 96 97 98   10 9 8 7 6 5 4 3 2 1

Sage Production Editor: Astrid Virding

Contents

Acknowledgments

I had lots of help with this book and the research that preceded it. At Stanford, Professors Jeremy Cohen and Clifford Nass were both supporters and crucial problem solvers. Professors Steve Chaffee, Don Roberts, Elie Abel, and Henry Breitrose helped shape my thinking during the dissertation. I also enjoyed the assistance and friendship of six John S. Knight Fellows, who faithfully met with me over several months of their Stanford sabbaticals to review newscast tapes: Mike Greenberg, Allen Short, Mark Jaffee, Mike Smith, Karen Steele, and Shinji Otsuki. Jim Risser, director of the Knight program at Stanford was also a great help. Robert Coen, senior vice president at McCann-Erickson in New York, graciously provided advertising data and projections. The A. C. Nielsen Co., the National Association of Broadcasters, the Times Mirror Center for The People and The Press, and the Freedom Forum Media Studies Center also provided statistical and other materials without charge.

Early drafts of the book profited immeasurably from the keen minds and insightful editing of Professor D. Charles Whitney at The University of Texas, Austin, and Professors Laurie Mason and Don Dodson, at Santa Clara University. Guido H. Stempel III, distinguished professor at the E. W. Scripps School of Journalism at Ohio University, added many helpful notes. Professors Larry Iannaccone, Ed McQuarrie, Mark Seabright, and Meyer Statman of Santa Clara University's Business School offered lots of help with economics as did Professor Stephen Lacy of Michigan State University. Brian Adams, an adjunct professor of broadcast journalism at Santa Clara offered helpful advice, as did Anne Chalfant and Dr. Steven Lee of Santa Clara's Communication Department. Elwood Mills of the Media Center at Santa Clara provided the graphics. Priti Khare and Branden Mello, both students at Santa Clara, tracked down research articles and assisted with the bibliography. At Sage, Sophy Craze shepherded the project, Kristin Bergstad saved me from an embarrassing number of mechanical errors, and Astrid Virding oversaw production. Meanwhile at home, I benefitted from the constant support of Laura, Jack, Adam, my mother Kay, and Aunts Mary and Helen.

Last, and perhaps most importantly, I would like to thank the news directors and television journalists who made my research such a joy. They took a chance in letting an outsider sit in on their daily efforts to produce the news. And they were extraordinarily generous with their time in the midst of a frantic profession. I hope this book justifies their investment and trust in me.

This book is dedicated, with all my love, to the memory of the Reverend Marcia Renee Lapp.

Introduction

Rather than begin with an overfamiliar quote from an eminent dead guy like Jefferson or Lippmann about the importance of a trustworthy supply of news in a society that seeks to govern itself, I'd like to begin with a fresh, if homely, metaphor. In democratic theory, news media are supposed to act as society's headlights. As we travel through time, they illuminate what's before us. If they work properly—and we don't fall asleep at the wheel—society may not only avoid driving off a cliff, it may avoid dead ends and steer around some pitfalls. Good journalism can't smooth the path into the future, but it can help us find less bumpy routes.

For at least 45 years, media watchers have been warning that society is moving faster and faster and that every society sharing the planet depends more on others than in the past. No longer can a farmer survive by knowing only what his or her father knew. The same holds in nearly every other business too. Not only is a computer obsolete soon after it hits the market, so are cars, all sorts of medical technology, drugs, legal and financial techniques, even tomatoes. Less noticed is the obsolescence of social institutions, government policies, and theories explaining how society works.

The "shelf life" of knowledge has never been shorter. And with competition from a global economy forcing farmers in Iowa to take into account harvests in the Ukraine, and auto-makers in Dearborn, MI, to consider manufacturing wages in Monterrey, Mexico, the volume and distance over which that knowledge must travel have vastly increased. The importance of up-to-date information—of news—has never been greater. Society's headlights have to shine farther and more broadly than ever before and their beams must be bright enough for us to see our options and their consequences clearly.

As the need for illumination of current issues and events has grown, Americans have been changing their media habits. Many are moving away from printed sources of news toward televised sources. The corporations that produce news have been changing too—redesigning society's headlights. Partly leading and partly responding to shifting public demand, media firms are now beginning to rely more and more on what is perhaps the nation's most trusted instrument for satisfying social needs and wants—the marketplace.

"Introducing market forces." "Letting the market decide." "Taking advantage of the creativity of the market." "Putting the productivity of the market to work." Such is the rhetoric of national reforms in what used to be the Soviet Union and throughout Eastern Europe. In our own society, the marketplace is seen as a cure for problems with the public schools, with our health care system, with our farms. In recent years, factory work has moved into a global marketplace and knowledge work may soon follow as satellites and "data highways" permit engineers in India to write software once produced in California's "Silicon Valley."

This book examines the application of market logic to news and—because of its growing importance—particularly to broadcast news. By replacing the journalist with the consumer as the "gatekeeper" of what becomes news and replacing the standards of journalism with the rigors of the market, will the news media provide society greater illumination? Or will we see a new era of "yellow" journalism designed to sell itself at the expense of informing the public enough to make wise civic choices?

I invite you to think along with me through the following pages. I promise a dispassionate and relatively jargon-free investigation of what happens when market thinking—essentially microeconomics—shapes production of news. You won't need a degree in economics or ever to have set foot in a newsroom to enjoy the adventure. And at the other end, I'll suggest how you might be able to influence the quality of the journalism you get.

When academics launch books, it is incumbent upon them to cite "gaps" in our current knowledge into which their manuscript may be thrust. Here goes. Although market-driven journalism is spreading like a sniffle through a day-care center, little has been written about it. No analysis has yet to subject to a newsroom test the logic promoters of the trend boast will reinvigorate journalism. In fact, using economic theory to understand how newsrooms are organized, and how events and issues are selected and reported, is novel—even controversial. This is so despite the wide currency of the criticism that news media care only about "the bottom line." Finally, this book offers a new theory of commercial news production—the first to incorporate the idea that media firms compete in markets, not just for readers or viewers, but for advertisers, sources, and investors. Such a theory may help predict what will become news and what will remain obscure at a time when much of the news industry is moving to replace journalistic judgment with market judgment.

Now for some warnings. This book attempts to explain a change in the way news is produced. It aims at building theory. A friend of mine used to keep a cartoon on his office door. It showed a nerdy little guy with thick glasses and paper-straw arms sitting down to arm wrestle an enormous scowling brute. On the nearly empty T-shirt of the nerd was the word "Theory." And on the brute's bulging shirt? "Reality." Particularly in social science, theory is often overmatched. Nevertheless, I'll adjust my glasses and do my best in the hope that others will improve upon this beginning. One other warning. I want to be clear that microeconomic theory represents *only one* way to understand what's happening to journalism. Given that most of the news we consume is produced by profit-seeking businesses, however, it's one important piece of the puzzle. But it's not the whole picture.

Most of the data in this book originated in my dissertation research at Stanford University. Subsequently, I have supplemented it with the work of other news researchers. The dissertation began in early 1986 and concluded a year later. More recent studies suggest that since 1987 the situation in both print and television newsrooms has changed only in that news departments are now trying to do more with fewer resources. Since 1987, market forces have picked up considerable momentum.

Method

This book is divided about evenly into theory and research. The theoretical parts concern local news production in both local television and newspapers. The original data, however, was gathered for broadcast only, for reasons explained in Chapter 1.

To collect this data I visited four television stations located in the western United States, each affiliated with a major network. Two of the stations, one used as a pilot, and one in the formal study, were located in a very large market—the primary area reached by the station's signal. The market is one of the nation's 10 largest. A third station was located in a large market, between the 10th and 25th largest; and a fourth station was in a mid-sized market, between the 50th and 100th largest. No stations were selected in smaller markets because the great majority of American households are located in the 100 largest markets. I spent the better part of a month at each station, concentrating my visits on midweek days when staffing and news production were at their highest levels. Looking for routine news production, I avoided "sweeps" months when each station's audience popularity ratings are estimated for the purpose of setting advertising rates. I also chose non-summer months to avoid short-staffing due to vacations.

In each market but the largest, I chose the station whose premier early evening newscast was the second most popular. In the largest market, I chose the most and least popular stations, although they differed by less than three Nielsen percentage points at the time. My purpose was to find the most typical stations, those in which ratings presumably were important but perhaps not all-consuming, and to cover the spectrum of popularity. Each of the stations agreed to give me free rein of the newsroom provided I agreed not to divulge their identity or that of staffers.

At each station I used two research strategies. To gather quantitative data, I flooded the newsrooms with five sets of questionnaires and videotaped a nearly random set of newscasts. The questionnaires measured the mechanics of news production and the logic underlying it. The videotapes were subjected to content analysis by two expert panels of journalists. To collect qualitative information, I shadowed reporters, producers, and assignment editors, asking them to "think out loud" about how they were approaching their tasks. This yielded scores of case studies. I also interviewed news directors, who supervise newsrooms, general managers, who oversee the overall performance of the stations, and advertising managers. In each city, I also interviewed the publisher of the largest metropolitan newspaper to discover a contrasting view of what the major local issues were.

In general I followed the theory-building tactics of Barney Glaser and Anselm Strauss[1] in what they call the Constant Comparison Method. The approach is iterative. Research begins with a theory explaining some behavior that's available from past scholarship. The researcher tries to find the most likely point of breakdown of the theory and collects data there. The theory is amended over time with its weakest link continually subjected to test. When it has passed all of the "devil's advocate" tests that the researcher can devise, the resulting theory may be offered to others.

I began with the theory that news production followed the norms, or standards, of journalism as set out in ethical codes written by the Radio-Television News Directors, the American Society of Newspaper Editors, the Society of Professional Journalists, and the Associated Press Managing Editors. Each of these codes makes essentially the same claim: The primary purpose of news is to empower the public by maximizing its understanding of those current issues and events that most shape its environment. Each day I would place myself in position to test the components of this ethic. As I went along I modified this theory of responsible journalism to account for new data. In general, I tried to give local television news the benefit of all doubts. Where I couldn't follow every reporter at a station, I chose those managers considered most able and accompanied them on what seemed to me the most significant topics. Throughout the visits, I tried to adopt a neutral persona, someone who knew something about journalism from 6 years as a newspaper reporter, but was naive about television news.

Note

1. Glaser & Strauss, 1967.

1

The Rise of Market-Driven Journalism

A profound change is sweeping American newsrooms, print and broadcast alike. Even though profit-seeking business has been the enabling foundation of journalism here ever since entrepreneurs succeeded political parties as operators of the press 150 years ago, it has usually been kept in the basement. Now the business of selling news is being invited upstairs, into the temple.

As newspapers, television stations, even the networks, have been sold by the families of those entrepreneurs to investors on Wall Street, more and more of the nation's news is being produced by corporations whose stockholders seek to maximize return on their investment. Newsrooms have begun to reflect the direction of managers with MBAs rather than green eyeshades. The reader or viewer is now a "customer." The news is a "product." The circulation or signal area is now a "market." As business logic begins to permeate the newsroom and journalism is crafted to serve the market, will it provide a clearer picture of the world upon which we can act? Or as news becomes more explicitly a commodity, will it lose its informational value?

An Idiot Culture?

For journalism purists, the trend toward letting the logic of the marketplace into the newsroom is defilement, a blasphemy. Listen to Carl Bernstein, one of the reporters who broke open the Watergate scandal that eventually unseated Richard Nixon from the presidency. Bernstein blames the market orientation of modern journalism for creating an "idiot culture":

> For more than 15 years we have been moving away from real journalism toward the creation of a sleazoid info-tainment culture in which the lines between Oprah [Winfrey] and Phil [Donohue] and Geraldo [Rivera] and Diane [Sawyer]

and even Ted [Koppel], between the *New York Post* and *Newsday,* are too often indistinguishable.

In this new culture of journalistic titillation, we teach our readers and our viewers that the trivial is significant, that the lurid and loopy are more important than real news.[1]

Listen to legendary former CBS anchor Walter Cronkite:

> With television's competition for people's attention—and hence for the advertising dollar—many more newspapers have tried to compete by becoming more entertaining and reducing their news coverage to barely more information than television itself provides. We are filling the airways with more words and pictures and grinding out newspapers in record numbers, and yet to the average news consumer we are imparting less information of importance.
>
> We are producing a population of political, economic, scientific ignoramuses at a point in time when a lot more knowledge rather than less is needed for the survival of democracy.[2]

Media critics, such as Ben Bagdikian of the University of California at Berkeley, write that market journalism gathers an audience not to inform it, but to sell it to advertisers. A few large, powerful corporations win and the public loses.[3]

But for a growing majority of newspaper publishers and station general managers—those who run local print and broadcast journalism—market journalism[4] represents a breath of fresh air, a chance for a win-win situation. They argue that market forces possess the potential to reinvigorate an American journalism that was too serious, sanctimonious, and often just plain boring. The "professional" journalism of Bernstein's era, the marketers contend, has lost its attraction among Americans, particularly those under 35 years old. John Walter, managing editor of *The Atlanta Journal and Constitution,* explained:

> Somewhere in the late 1960s, what I call the stuff-pot factor took over. Stories lengthened. Attitudes toward stories changed. And we, the institution, became so convinced of our mission to save the world and comment soberly on it that we veered away from what we had.
>
> We've been dulling newspapers up. Now we're returning to the "I didn't know that" factor, where news is anything that will capture your interest and make you turn to the next page because you don't know what wonder and revelation will be cast upon you.[5]

In a recent discussion of the future of news at Columbia University's Freedom Forum, Harvard University Law School researcher Anne Wells Branscomb said:

Looking back in history we see that some of the most influential pieces of literature have been great novels that entertained their readers. One [current] example of the intertwining of education and entertainment is "Sesame Street," a program that has found a way to be both educational and entertaining. Entertainment, or "infotainment" is really the right direction to go in terms of raising the level of comprehension of the population.[6]

Academic defenders of the move toward market logic, such as Philip Meyer of the University of North Carolina, argue that the market contains adequate safeguards against abuse while providing the opportunity to serve readers and viewers better than ever before.[7] The market should protect democracy because it is, by nature, a democratic mechanism based on free choices by buyers and sellers operating as they—rather than a professional elite of journalists—see fit. Just as the unfettered market brings consumers better computers and cars and corn at lower prices, it brings us livelier news that responds to our needs and wants, or perishes in the competition.

Perhaps more important than any of these claims for market journalism—and certainly more ominous—is the argument that it is inevitable. According to Michael Fancher, executive editor of *The Seattle Times* and a leading spokesperson for the approach, a successful editor must integrate the business and news subdivisions and become a "marketing expert":

> Some editors resist getting involved in the business side of newspapering, fearful they will be tainted by filthy lucre. I believe those editors are doomed. Sooner or later their journalistic options will be proscribed by someone else's bottom line.[8]

Market journalists like Fancher contend that the media environment of the 1990s has become too competitive to support media firms pursuing traditional journalism with its separation of the "church" of news-gathering and "state" of advertising sales, production, and distribution. Certainly the media environment has grown much more competitive. Metropolitan and suburban newspapers, local broadcast stations, scores—and soon hundreds—of cable channels, one—possibly two—new and three older networks, direct mail advertising notices and "shoppers," all are battling each other for the attention of consumers with less leisure time than a decade ago,[9] and fighting for a share of a stagnating or slow growing pool of advertising dollars.[10]

What's at Stake?

Whether conducted behind academic ivy and stone or the smoked glass of a corporate headquarters, two elements of this debate over market journalism are striking: (1) The diametrical opposition of advocates and opponents; and (2) The agreement on both sides that what's at stake is democracy, specifically the survival of a public knowledgeable enough about current issues and events to govern itself. Despite the high stakes and the acrimony of the debate, there has yet to be a theory-based analysis of the trend toward journalism that serves the market, much less of its implications for society.[11] This book represents a first attempt to fill that gap.

My purpose is to combine what we know of how markets work—starting with Adam Smith—with a set of studies I and others have conducted about how newsrooms work. Between the theory and the evidence we can analyze whether the critics or the advocates of market journalism have the stronger case, or if neither, under which conditions each better realizes journalism's goal of public service. Throughout this book, I will try to show that such an analysis is important, not just for journalism but for society. As Walter Lippmann wrote 70 years ago, people act, not on reality, but on the "pictures in their heads," however unreal those images may be.[12] Like it or not, the pictures of the world beyond our own sensory experience come to most Americans through the news media. Even if we don't watch, read, or listen to the news, our views are affected by news media because most of those who inform us have also had to depend on the media. If the news presents us illusions or leaves out important parts of the story, or if it distracts us from reality,[13] the consequences can be serious. An ill- or misinformed public can elect irresponsible representatives and be led into tragic policies.

Market Theory and Journalism

Whether operating in local television, newspapers, radio, news magazines, or network TV, at the heart of market journalism is the logic of the marketplace. As the name implies, a marketplace is where people come to buy and sell goods and services. Markets are said to increase everyone's happiness because no one would engage in an exchange unless he or she valued what was gained more than what was given up. After the trade, everyone should be better off.[14]

When they operate properly, markets—whether they be for groceries, automobiles, computers, or hogbellies—should possess certain advantages over other systems of providing the public with goods and services. Among the most important are these six related characteristics:

- *Quality and value are defined by consumers, rather than producers or government:* Sales should depend on characteristics that *consumers* value. Their wishes, not those of the producers or third parties, must be satisfied.

- *Responsiveness to consumers:* Sales depend upon consumer demand. Rational consumers will reward producers of those products consumers value most highly by purchasing them. Consumers will discipline other producers by spurning their offerings. Quality products and services, as defined by consumers, will drive inferior commodities from the market.

- *Self-correction:* If the market doesn't offer what consumers want, new producers may enter. Markets are also flexible. As society's needs and wants change, producers must change as well or face replacement.

- *Constant motivation to excel:* Because producers compete with each other to meet consumers' needs and desires, there is constant pressure to produce new and improved goods and services at stable or lower cost and thus expand one's share of the market.

- *Efficient allocation of society's resources:* Producers of what consumers most value will gain more of a society's scarce resources as their products sell. Fewer resources will flow to producers of less valued products.

- *Freedom of choice:* Consumers are free to pick among products offered. There is no coercion to buy one over another. All producers are similarly free to offer products in the market.

The advantages of the market should apply particularly well to commercially produced news. That's because in the United States most news media trade in four markets at the same time. The most familiar is the *market for audience* in which firms may sell a certain number of newspapers or capture a certain share of television viewership. But other transactions are occurring also. Shares of the media firm may be bought and sold on the *stock market*. The media firm also sells audience attention in an *advertising market*. Finally, the firm trades in a market for newsworthy information, a *market for sources*. It barters access to the public to news sources in return for information needed to fill the paper or newscast. Most corporations trade in only three markets simultaneously: with the stock market, with suppliers of raw products, and with consumers.

If each of these markets operates properly, news ought to be an outstanding commodity. Consumers ought to give their allegiance to the firm providing the highest quality news. That firm then has the largest share of consumer attention to sell to advertisers, so it can command the highest price. And the wide attention the firm draws ought to give it clout with news sources, such as politicians, civic leaders, and business people, who want access to the public. Finally, that firm's stock is likely to command a premium price because it generates high returns. Sale of stock in turn provides the firm additional money for expanding or upgrading.[15]

For both printed and broadcast news, the commodity system seems ideal. In print, a third party—the advertiser—subsidizes part of the cost of producing the news.[16] In broadcasting, advertisers pay the entire cost. In both cases, society benefits because the news is made available to the public at less than its true cost. Further, the news firm does not depend economically on the patronage of government or a single private funding institution, either of which might interfere with the news' integrity through bias or censorship.

Finding Sites to Analyze

If we are to test the promise of this market theory of news production against its actual performance—as we shall in Chapters 4 through 8—we need to find media firms operating under market logic. The more established that logic, the better the test will be. To discover optimal test sites, we must briefly review the history of marketing's marriage with journalism.

Because the modern concept of market-driven journalism is relatively new, little has been written about it. But two media scholars, Daniel Hallin and Craig Allen, both suggest that the trend began in the late 1960s in local television news.[17] Local stations began to discover that originating their own newscasts could both satisfy Federal Communications Commission requirements for public service and generate large profits if the news was designed by media researchers, so-called show doctors, to appeal to large numbers of viewers. Unlike newspapers, few traditions of journalism bound the production of local television news. Stations were free to reinvent it. The result was a different kind of news, much more responsive to popular demand than the traditional journalism newspapers were peddling. Market journalism was to become successful beyond their imagination.

As recently as the mid-1980s, the three networks and many newspapers still pursued a traditional style of doing news, providing the public an alternative to the approach of local television news. But as local television news grew in popularity and profitability while media carrying more traditional journalism receded, executives at media firms from *The New York Times* to CBS News to the local daily paper began a profound reassessment of what constitutes news and how it should be gathered and reported. These executives may not have consciously borrowed from local television's popular and inexpensive way of doing news, but they either initiated or accelerated trends that moved their news-gathering and reporting closer to the model of the newer medium.

CHANGES IN NEWSPAPERS

Seymour Topping, director of editorial development at the New York Times Company and chairman of New Directions for News, a think tank at the University of Missouri, said the viewing and reading trends have caused "a restructuring of the newspaper industry and its whole approach to readership."[18]

Adopting a sensitivity to audience ratings similar to that of local television news, newspapers have diminished the traditional role of "professional" journalists as arbiters of which events and issues are newsworthy. Managers are telling journalists to let the public decide what becomes news by paying attention to what kinds of reports are most highly valued in the marketplace.[19]

In a national survey of editors, Carl Sessions Stepp found:

> a dramatic shift around the nation. In what some view as better serving the readers and others see as pacifying them, newspapers large and small are reshaping their notions of news, giving readers far more influence over content and play. It's a calculated move away from the "we'll-decide-what's-news" mentality that traditionally prevailed in newsrooms.[20]

As a result, print also has followed local television's expansion of the definition of news beyond the traditional emphasis on government and politics to include whatever is interesting. Stepp wrote that newspapers are now moving "to embrace such topics as parenting or hobbies or shopping, and a willingness to billboard such subjects on the front page—often at the expense of government news." Newspapers have also shortened stories, permitting readers to approximate the rapid pace of local television news.[21]

A more obvious change in print has been the trend toward more vivid and graphic presentation. Led by *USA Today,* the newspaper sold in a stand designed to look like a television set, newspapers across the country have become more visually oriented. Leo Bogart, then executive vice president of the Newspaper Advertising Bureau, wrote that "many editors appear to have been convinced . . . that more and bigger photographs, and more 'features' and 'personality journalism' were necessary counters to the visual and entertainment elements of TV."[22]

CHANGES IN NETWORK NEWS

In the mid-1980s all three major networks went through ownership changes that in each case led to a substantial reduction of reporters, photographers, producers, archivists, technicians, even entire news bureaus.[23] Under new ownership, network news also became more attuned to the demands of viewers.[24] With fewer reporters and bureaus, network television leaned more on other organizations to uncover the news than before. Network stories became briefer, visuals and emotion became more important story elements, even at CBS, "the *New York Times*" of networks.[25]

Television journalist Bill Moyers quit CBS about that time. As a defender of traditional journalism he deplored replacing professional news judgments with market demands:

> Managers [at CBS News] . . . yielded to the encroachment of entertainment values from within. Not only were those values invited in, they were exalted. The line between entertainment and news was steadily blurred. Our center of gravity shifted from the standards and practices of the news business to show business. In meeting after meeting, "Entertainment Tonight" was touted as the model—visual images containing a high emotional quotient that are passed on to the viewer unfiltered and unexamined.
>
> Instead of the role of gathering, weighing, sorting and explaining the flux of events and issues, we began to be influenced by the desire first to please the audience. The object was to "hook" them by pretending that this was not news at all.[26]

Professor Hallin, who recently documented the decline in the length of network "sound bites"—taped quotes from sources—from 43 seconds in 1968 to 9 seconds in 1988, credits local television news with significant influence on network news production:

> The change [of news from a money-losing obligation to a profit opportunity] started in local news. By the early part of the [1970s] local stations had discovered that news could make a great deal of money.
>
> The local television industry is intensely competitive, with at least three stations competing head to head in most markets, and it is not surprising that this was a period of considerable innovation in the structure of news programs as stations battled for ratings. Consultants were brought in to recommend more effective ways of maintaining audience attention. And their recommendations typically pointed in the direction of a more tightly structured and fast-paced presentation of the news. Though there are no systematic data on the lengths of sound bites in local TV news in this period, it is likely that it was the local stations that led the way in shortening them.[27]

With fewer bureaus around the nation, network news divisions are relying more on local stations and other outside sources to cover stories or supply video for network news.[28] The networks also have been adopting some of the cost-conscious news-gathering techniques established at the local level. One example is the occasional practice of "handing off" stories. Rather than having a crew, consisting of a reporter and photographer, gather, edit, write, and produce a story, the task can be segmented to save money. At the local level, just a photographer may travel to an event. Network news has begun to use local photographers who are self-employed or work for another organization, to shoot footage of some event. The network reporter then prepares a story from the video without undergoing the cost of actually visiting the site of the story and directing news-gathering (and of course without knowing if the video collected is an accurate representation of events).[29]

It overgeneralizes, of course, to say that all commercially produced news will soon resemble local television news. The trend is in that direction. But there are important differences of technology, regulation, competition, and scope of coverage that will continue to differentiate newspapers and network news from the local 6 or 10 o'clock news. The new similarities, however, are important to notice. According to a 1991 Harvard University study of local and national election coverage, journalism is changing direction.

> The marketing-based approach represents a significant change for the journalist. It represents no less than the erosion of a central professional ethic that has been in place, with varying degrees of effectiveness, for more than 30 years.
>
> As television news divisions succumb more and more to market factors in deciding what to cover as news, historians may well look back on the last three decades as the golden age of objective non-commercialized news.[30]

Analyzing Local Television News

Partly because it has been longest established there, the best place to study market journalism is within local television newsrooms. Although it is important to look at the phenomenon across several media, only the theoretical chapters of the book will do so. I have chosen to concentrate this analysis on local newscasts because I believe local television has become the dominant force in the American news industry today and because it is the least studied of the three major news media[31]—the other two being newspapers and network newscasts.

Because local newscasts have been more slurred than studied, most academics and others have missed how important the new medium has become. Consider that local television is:

THE FASTEST GROWING NEWS MEDIUM

Over the past 30 years, local television news has grown faster than any other segment of the U.S. news industry. In 1960, there were only 515 commercial television stations, many with no local newscast. By 1990, the number of stations originating programming had almost doubled.[32] Of those, approximately 740 now produce their own daily newscasts.[33] This means that virtually every non-wilderness region of the United States lies in the signal area of one or more local newscasts. On the consumer side, almost every one of the nation's 93 million homes now is equipped with a television set.[34]

From the 1960s through the 1980s as competition for viewers grew, local news emerged from a corner office staffed by several announcers who read the newspaper or ripped stories from a clacking wire service teletype to the hub of local stations. News became the largest, most expensive, and most profitable single department.[35] The growth in staff size and equipment sophistication continued into the 1990s. By 1992, the median (the middle station in a list ranked from largest to smallest) newsroom employed 22 full-time and 3 part-time persons—up 26% from just 5 years earlier. Such gains occurred despite staff cutbacks at as many as two of five stations, according to research conducted by Professor Vernon Stone for the Radio-Television News Directors Association.[36] Many of the larger stations owned or leased helicopters and trucks capable of communicating stories between remote locations and the studio by satellite.

Growth in the number of hours of local news broadcast paced staff growth. By 1986, the typical station aired an hour-long newscast in the early evening, a half-hour in the late evening and perhaps a 30-minute newscast at noon. Stations serving larger metropolitan areas often had longer newscasts.[37] A 1992 survey showed that although the recession that ushered in the 1990s closed a handful of newsrooms at independent stations (those not affiliated with networks), many stations added newscast time, particularly in the morning and on weekends.[38] In 1989, a Los Angeles independent station announced that it would launch a 3-hour evening newscast, one of the first to challenge entertainment's hold on prime-time programming. The addition meant that in Los Angeles 14.5 hours of local news was broadcast daily by seven stations. Local news has also spread to cable television, including a 24-hour station on Long Island, NY.[39] Another continuous news cable channel was planned in San Francisco.[40]

MORE POPULAR THAN NETWORK
AND PERHAPS PRINTED NEWS

National samples of American metropolitan areas indicate local news may far outstrip the popularity of network newscasts. The most recent[41] was a 1988 study of 29 representative metropolitan areas. It suggested that national news broadcast by CBS, ABC, and NBC combined reached about 47 million viewers nightly. The combined viewership of local television newscasts reached an estimated 80 million.[42] Although the expansion of cable channels has contributed to a decline of about a third in the audience for news from CBS, NBC, and ABC,[43] local newscast viewership has remained robust, perhaps because cable rarely offers its own local reporting.[44]

Although public consumption of local television news has been growing over the past three decades so that by 1988 about 56% of American households tuned in on weeknights,[45] the percentage of the population buying a newspaper daily has plummeted. Responding to a 1990 national survey conducted by Times Mirror, a newspaper company, only 43% of American adults reported reading a newspaper the day before they were polled. That's down by almost half from 78% in 1970.[46] Some researchers feel the Times Mirror survey understates newspaper readership. Guido H. Stempel III, for example, argued that since 62 million papers are sold daily and the nation has about 100 million households, about 60% of American adults read the paper daily.[47] What is not in dispute are the trend lines, up or stable for local television news watching, down—especially among Americans under 35—for newspapers.

CREDIBLE AND FAIR

Attitudes about the news media change with the flow of events—particularly during times of war and government scandal—and with the wording of questionnaires measuring opinion. Over the past 20 years, however, the majority of polls indicate that most Americans believe what they see on television news, and where it was broken out as a separate category, on local newscasts.[48] In 1984, the Gallup Poll asked a national sample of adults to rate a variety of news media on their credibility and other characteristics. Local television news and network news tied as the media rated most accurate; 81% called them accurate, compared to 73% for local newspapers, 77% for radio, and 78% for "nationally influential" newspapers. Local television news was also rated as fair by 82%—more than any other medium, except radio.[49] A nationwide 1993 *Los Angeles Times* poll found that 83% rated their favorite local TV newscast fair and impartial, compared to 77% for favorite network news program and 68% for favorite newspaper.[50] Not only does televised news appear to be more believable to Americans than newspapers, the gap between them may be widening. In 1959 the Roper Organization began a yearly poll that asked a national sample of adults which version of the same story they would believe if the account differed among newspapers, radio, television and magazines. In 1959, television and newspapers tied. Since then, however, the public has increased its trust in television news and lowered its faith in newspapers. By 1991, 51% named television, more than double the 20% who found newspapers most credible.[51] The 1993 *Los Angeles Times* poll mentioned above found that 50% found television more reliable than newspapers, while only 33% relied more on the newspaper.[52] In a 1993 Harris poll, 45% of a national sample agreed that television news "gives the news most accurately," compared to 28% for newspapers. Respondents with college or graduate degrees, however, trusted newspapers over television.[53]

CONSIDERED INFLUENTIAL AND RESPECTED

Americans consider local TV news to be a powerful influence on public opinion and generally approve of how that power is used. In 1985, a *Los Angeles Times* survey indicated that 86% of a national sample said their local station had "some" or "a great deal" of influence on community opinion. That was substantially more than the number who said then President Ronald Reagan, major corporations, or organized labor had some or a great deal of influence.[54]

Public satisfaction with local TV news also appears quite high. When asked their overall impression, 27% of a national sample of Americans phoned by Times Mirror pollsters in 1989 described local newscasts as "very favorable," another 53% said "mostly favorable." Given the poll's margin of error, respondents were as satisfied with local as network news and slightly more satisfied with televised news than with newspapers.[55] The 1993 *Los Angeles Times* survey recorded similar opinions: 89% rated the local newscast they watch most to be doing a good job overall. The network rating was identical while the local newspaper was rated favorably by 81%. The more recent poll did show a drop-off, however, in those giving each news medium the highest favorable rating.[56]

UNIFORM

Despite its high viewership, credibility, and public esteem, local television news could hardly be considered a powerful social influence on the nation if all 740 stations producing newscasts went their own direction in terms of news selection and quality. However because most commercial stations purchase research on how to select, gather, and report news profitably from a relatively small number of news consulting firms, the similarity of advice given by those firms,[57] and because of similar economic and technological constraints, a surprising orthodoxy has become evident in local television. Both within a particular market and between markets, even across substantial differences of resources due to market size, the organization of news production and the values underlying selection appear remarkably similar.[58]

HIGHLY PROFITABLE

Over the past 30 years, local television broadcasting has amassed enormous profits. Even with the recession that accompanied the beginning of the 1990s, stations in large metropolitan areas were earning average pre-tax profits in the mid-30% range—four times the national manufacturing average. And most smaller stations reported above-average returns as well.[59]

AWARD-WINNING AND UNIQUE

Particularly in times of crisis, local television news has begun to distinguish itself as an informational medium.[60] For example, KGO, a San Francisco station owned and operated by ABC/Capital Cities, was once satirized for its "Penis on the tracks; details at 11" style of journalism. In 1990, KGO won a prestigious Peabody award for its virtually around-the-clock coverage of the Loma Prieta earthquake.

In fact, local television journalists make several unique claims for their medium:

- Television news is the most democratic of news media. By constantly measuring its popularity, local television news has become more responsive to the will of the community's majority than any other medium.

- Local newscasts, more than any other news source, integrate communities. This argument turns upside down the criticism that local television news is aimed at the "lowest common denominator" of viewers. The newscasters say the critics' emphasis on "lowest" is not only overplayed, it obscures the value of "common." In a society where powerful forces are driving apart people with different incomes and interests, local television news is an important and unique counterbalance, bringing together disparate strata to heed a common message. Moreover, television offers access to news to tens of millions of Americans who experience difficulty reading English—recent immigrants and the less educated.

- Because television news is interesting, it attracts the attention of persons who would otherwise be uninformed. The critics derision of local newscasts as "infotainment," misses the value that entertaining techniques add to information.

Both as the model for market journalism and in its own right, local television news deserves analysis.

Notes

1. C. Bernstein, 1992.
2. Walter Cronkite (1989, October 27). Speech given after receiving the Allen H. Neuharth Award for Excellence in Journalism at the University of South Dakota. Copies prepared by the Allen H. Neuharth Center for Excellence in Journalism, University of South Dakota, Vermillion, SD 57069.
3. Bagdikian, 1990.
4. For brevity, I'll use the term *market journalism* in place of *market-driven journalism*.
5. Stepp, 1991, pp. 22-23.
6. Freedom Forum Media Studies Center, 1992.
7. Meyer, 1987; Underwood, 1988, p. 27.

8. Underwood, 1988, p. 27.

9. Schor, 1992.

10. Coen, 1992.

11. But for an excellent journalistic inquiry into market journalism see Doug Underwood's *When MBAs Rule the Newsroom*, New York: Columbia University Press, 1993.

12. Lippmann, 1922.

13. Because no human observer can objectively record what passes before her or his senses, this book substitutes the term *social reality* for *reality*. Our inherent subjectivity prevents us from knowing reality; we call real what we agree on among ourselves. What we define as real is thus a social process, although not one we usually think about.

14. Discussion here follows Main & Baird, 1981.

15. I am expanding here on Meyer, 1987, pp. 38-39.

16. This subsidy, however, may not be as large as some have supposed for newspapers. Studies show that most American newspapers earn between 70% and 90% of their total income from advertisements. But about 70% of their content is also advertising. Ben Bagdikian and Guido H. Stempel III have both pointed out that a newspaper relying on subscriptions for all of its funding would spend far less on paper than one supported by so much advertising. Production and distribution costs for a thinner paper would also be somewhat less as well.

17. Allen, 1992; Hallin, 1992.

18. Stepp, 1991, p. 21.

19. Underwood, 1993.

20. Stepp, 1991, p. 21.

21. Stepp, 1991, p. 21.

22. Bogart, 1982, p. 60.

23. Auletta, 1991.

24. Auletta, 1991; Schoenbrun, 1989.

25. Alter, 1986a, pp. 52-54; Auletta, 1991; Schoenbrun, 1989.

26. Alter, 1986b, p. 53.

27. Hallin, 1992, p. 16.

28. Auletta, 1991.

29. Sanit, 1992, pp. 17-18.

30. Hume, 1991, pp. 23-24.

31. To my knowledge, only three studies of local television news production have been published as books. David L. Altheide's (1976) *Creating Reality*, Ron Powers's (1977) *The Newscasters*, and more recently, Phyllis Kaniss's (1991) *Making Local News*. All are worth reading, but none realizes the breadth of Edward J. Epstein's (1973) analysis of network news, *News From Nowhere*.

32. *Television and Video Almanac 1991*, p. 20A.

33. V. Stone, 1993c, pp. 26-27.

34. Nielsen Media Research, 1991.

35. Barrett, 1978; V. Stone, 1993a, pp. 32-33.

36. V. Stone, 1993c, pp. 26-27.

37. For example, more than 35 affiliate stations in the largest 25 markets aired 90 minutes or more of local news in the early evening according to *Television/Radio Age* ("Major Market News Growth Halts," 1986).

38. Standish, 1993.

39. Lev, 1989.

40. Antonucci, 1993.

41. Though Nielsen and Arbitron measure national audiences for network programming, they don't aggregate viewership for types of local programming such as news because there's

no financial incentive to do so. The draw of a local newscast is of economic importance only to the originating station. As a consequence, the total national viewership of local newscasts must be estimated from periodic studies of samples of stations.

42. The largest and most recent sampling of local television news viewership was conducted by Thomas Baldwin at Michigan State University and his colleagues T. F. Barrett and Benjamin Bates (published in 1992). They tabulated Nielsen Station Index data for the month of November from 1981 to 1988 for 29 television markets. The markets were selected purposively so the sample would have roughly equal numbers of small, middle, and large metropolitan areas. Baldwin's team totalled the percentage of television households watching local news on all of the stations in the market for both early evening and late evening newscasts. Using the network rule of thumb that half the viewers of the late local newscasts have watched the earlier newscast, we can estimate the number of unduplicated viewers local news attracts each weeknight. (Researchers at CBS's affiliates division have found that about half the viewers of late evening local news have also seen the early evening newscast, according to Jack Wakshlag, director of research at CBS, in a personal communication, November, 1991.) Here are Baldwin's figures for November, 1988.

Local Television News Viewership

Market	Percentage Watching		Unduplicated Estimate (%)
	Early News	Late News	
Small Markets:			
Bangor, ME	64	17	73
Beaumont-Port Arthur, TX	59	44	81
Chico-Redding, CA	36	39	56
Columbus-Tupelo-West Point	47	28	61
Harlingen-Welasco-Brownsville	37	34	54
Laredo	25	26	38
Macon	44	26	57
Medford-Klamath Falls	31	13	38
Topeka	38	36	56
Wilmington	37	18	46
Medium Markets:			
Boise	36	39	56
Buffalo	44	36	62
Chattanooga	42	18	51
Corpus Christi	43	47	67
Fort Wayne	40	23	52
Memphis	43	41	64
Rochester	38	24	50
Wilkes Barre-Scranton	42	27	56
Large Markets:			
Atlanta	37	37	55
Chicago	30	52	56
Cleveland	43	41	63

Local Television News Viewership

Market	Percentage Watching Early News	Late News	Unduplicated Estimate (%)
Large Markets: (continued)			
Fresno-Visalia	28	15	36
Indianapolis	30	24	42
Los Angeles	20	30	35
Miami-Ft. Lauderdale	30	37	49
Oklahoma City	38	43	60
Orlando-Daytona	40	29	65
St. Louis	39	49	64
Washington, DC	31	36	49

Attention to local newscasts varies in the sample from an estimated 35% of television households to 81% watching on a given weeknight, but many markets cluster around the median of 56%. Baldwin's sample gives only an approximate picture of local news viewership. But it does suggest that local television news has become enormously popular. If national viewership were in the vicinity of 56% of television households, with 1.6 persons viewing in the evening (Broadcasting Publications, 1991) in the average household, there would be approximately 80 million viewers. Consider that in 1988, the combined viewership of ABC, NBC, and CBS evening news was only 32.2% of American television households, about 47 million viewers. Daily newspaper readership has stabilized at about 62 million (Bogart, 1989).

43. Auletta, 1991.
44. Allen, 1993.
45. Baldwin, Barrett, & Bates, unpublished data from their 1988 survey.
46. Times Mirror Center for The People and The Press, 1990a.
47. Stempel, personal communication, February 26, 1993.
48. Whitney, 1985.
49. Dennis, 1986, p. 13.
50. Shaw, 1993.
51. The Roper Organization, 1991.
52. Shaw, 1993.
53. Louis Harris & Associates, 1993.
54. Dennis, 1986, p. 12.
55. Times Mirror Center for The People and The Press, 1989.
56. Shaw, 1993; on a less optimistic note, the 1993 survey showed considerable erosion in the number rating local television news "very good." Between 1985 and 1993, the percentage who rated local TV newscast very good fell from 51% to 29%. Newspapers fell even further, from 65% to 22%, while network news fell least, from 43% to 30% "very good." Even though Americans remain positive about media performance, they seem to be moderating their earlier enthusiasm for media coverage.
57. Renick, 1982.
58. This conclusion arises from examining Anderson, 1972; Atwater, 1984, 1986; Davie, 1992; Dozier & Hofstetter, 1985; Harmon, 1989; Powers, 1977; and Stone, Hartung, & Jensen, 1987.
59. Helregal, 1991.
60. Lichty & Gomery, 1992.

2

The Nature of News Reconsidered

In 1949, Wilbur Schramm, the godfather of the academic field of communication, published an article called "The Nature of News." He defined news commonsensically as "an attempt to reconstruct the essential framework of the event."[1] His definition seems entirely inadequate to describe what goes on in the modern newsroom. Consider this case study of news production at a television station in a large western city.

Case Study:
An Attempt to Reconstruct the
Essential Framework of the Event?

At first it seemed very strange: Reporters for a local station traveling to Central America?

The *network* usually covers foreign news. But there it was. The station with the most popular newscasts in the metro area had sent reporters and photographers to Nicaragua and El Salvador. At the station I was studying, the second most popular, news managers reluctantly decided that to be competitive they must follow suit. The decision to produce a different kind of news revealed the machinery of news-gathering—its theories and assumptions—that is normally obscured by routines in local reporting. Going outside the country for news was to cause a great deal of tension in the brick and glass newsroom of the station, which I'll call KLRG to keep my promise of confidentiality.

KLRG planned two series of stories based on reports from abroad for the next "sweeps" month—one of the four times yearly that ratings services like Nielsen estimate the number of households tuned to each program for the purpose of setting advertising rates. The first series had three parts. The writer explained that she would show how Salvadorans were recovering from a devastating earthquake 3 months before, then go into the increasing political and military strife in the small nation:[2]

> We start with people working brick by brick digging out after the earthquake. It's a strong emotional hook. Then go into the conflict between the people and the [President José Napoleon] Duarte government. We'll show how Duarte and his government are U.S. puppets, so it's skeptical of U.S. involvement. It's from the people's point of view and different from the official line. It shows the contrasts between Duarte's promises and reality, how three quarters of U.S. money goes to the military.
>
> The third part will show that how the earthquake has been handled provides further fuel for the war between the government and the guerrillas. It will show how Duarte is using Vietnam-type tactics of massive relocations of the peasants. There'll be interviews with both sides.

That was the original story. It was based on 24 videotapes, each 20 minutes long, shot by the producer of the station's minority affairs program. The producer, a Chicano, was trained as a journalist and fluent in Spanish, but was not a newsroom staffer. He had spent 3 weeks in Nicaragua on an earlier documentary, he said, and 5 days in El Salvador gathering the current series. His air fare was paid by a U.S. peace group he said he abandoned after his plane touched down. The producer based his videotapes on interviews with Duarte, government military commanders, and people he met in villages. The U.S. Embassy refused to comment, and after half a day of trying to contact the FMLN guerrillas, he gave up.

When he first saw the El Salvador series the news director was exasperated. He was inflamed by the pictures and peasants' complaints about the government's policy of burning down villages and crops to deny recruits and supplies to the guerrillas. The writer, an experienced reporter, was politicizing events, he said. "She should not use sources saying the burn and relocate strategy is either cruel or brilliant."

The news director criticized the writer. She was arrogant, he said, to include sources critical of U.S. policy when she had not been to the country and the tapes were based on only 5 days of reporting by someone from outside the newsroom. But at lunch with me, the news director expressed a different sentiment that had little to do with arrogance or journalistic objectivity. He said his impression was that local viewers were "polarized"— about half strongly supporting U.S. intervention in Central America and the other half just as committed to opposing it. This created a "lose-lose" situation for the station, he explained. Were the station's coverage to be seen as pro-United States, one half the viewership might switch channels. Were reportage seen as anti-United States, the other half might tune out.

I asked if journalism should do its best to tell the truth and not worry about how it is received by the public. He replied: "The issue is so remote. I doubt if very many of our viewers really care about the issues. For something so marginal, it's not worth it."

At the news director's insistence, the writer changed the series. She focused more on the earthquake's devastation and deleted all but one criticism of Duarte for not meeting the people's needs. She was perturbed about the ethics of changing the political angle of the story, but unwilling to protest. She explained:

> [The news director] said we are not here to make a political statement. [The producer] is Hispanic and he's been there before. His focus is with the left side. So I had to swing right. That was [the news director's] ultimatum.
>
> If this was a story I had done from the very beginning, then I probably would have gone to bat for some of my ideas. But since I'm essentially picking up the pieces for somebody else . . . I don't have the emotional involvement.
>
> This is a foreign country that no one around here knows much about . . . or cares about.

The second Central American series produced even greater friction because the person sent to Nicaragua was not so timid. He was a staff reporter, one of the best in the news director's estimation. And this time the reporter covered the story himself at the station's expense, spending 8 days in Nicaragua.[3]

The news director and reporter had carefully planned the coverage. Each of five parts was to focus on an individual from the station's signal area who was trying in some way, such as providing medical care or building windmills to generate electricity, to aid the Nicaraguan people. The reporting, it was agreed, would stay clear of whether U.S. support of the "Contra" rebels was helping or hurting the country.

Again on the flight down the reporter accompanied a group of Americans, most of whom were sympathetic to the Marxist Sandinista government. But again, once in the country the reporter said he broke free both of the group and of the government tour.

Nicaragua turned out to be different than the reporter and photographer imagined. It was a place, they said, where citizens were open and friendly and the government permitted them to go unescorted where they wished. But Nicaragua was also a place of terrible suffering that every source they encountered, except U.S. embassy spokespersons, attributed to the Contra rebels. Still the reporter tried to edit out blame:

We were told the Contras had blown up the day-care center and that [the night before we arrived] they burned down a dairy co-op. We just say it was bombed. They say it was the Contras and the [American] lady who runs the re-built day-care center says it was the Contras. Probably they're right. But until there's conclusive evidence I don't want to put my name to it.

Even the edited version upset the news director. At a meeting with the assignment editor he complained:

Profiles [of individuals] were the point of the story. But he found the individuals were pro-Sandinista. They will all profess that they're all nonpolitical, but I just don't believe them. We could take the whole trip and throw it in the trash can!

At this point the assignment editor suggested having a spokesman from the U.S. government answer each criticism. But the news director said the U.S. position was already in the story. The news director continued:

Who the hell are we to blow into some foreign country and pretend we can intelligently tell the great global issues? What we can do is show you some of your neighbors who have gone down there and what they're doing, hopefully without saying they're morally right or wrong.

[The reporter] went down there for a simple fact-finding story and what he came back with was a Sandinista P.R. [public relations] piece. He went to villages that were safe, therefore pro-government. He doesn't speak Spanish. He was in a group led by the government, so he doesn't know. The question is what was it he didn't get to see.

The problem is, he'll be on target with what he saw. But what didn't he see? I just refuse to do a P.R. job!

The reporter expressed both puzzlement and disappointment with the changes in his series. The editing was more intrusive, he said, than he had ever experienced at KLRG:

I've had a great sense of apprehension by somebody important about this story. I have the feeling that something's happened up here in management, or somebody's raised some major concerns that I haven't been aware of. I'm still trying to find out why this is being so heavily watched.

A Model of Commercial News Production

How can we make sense of such a news production process? Here's a model, or explanation, of news production—in both local television and newspapers.[4]

Although the vast majority of news consumed by Americans of all latitudes, Europeans, and, since the fall of the Soviet Union, many Asians, is produced by profit-making businesses, no comprehensive model of news production has included the concept of markets. And none have used economics to explain what happens in newsrooms. The present model is a first attempt at filling both gaps.

Joseph Turow's analysis of the influences on production in any mass media industry provides a useful starting point for such a model because, unlike much media theorizing, it features a full cast of primary players. There are roles for news sources, revenue sources, consumers, investors, corporate executives, and the news department with its reporters and editors.[5] Turow defined the relationships among these players using a theory called "resource dependence"—the notion that parties seek to avoid depending on other actors while increasing others' reliance upon themselves. In a news context, resource dependence would predict that a news source, say a city councilwoman, would try to make a media firm, such as a local TV station, depend upon her for certain types of information. As supplier of information she would exercise some control over what the public learns, an obvious advantage to a politician. At the same time she might cultivate reporters at other stations so she wouldn't have to depend upon the one station for access to the public via the evening news. For its part, the news department tries to make the councilwoman need the station more than the station needs her.

Rather than resource dependence, I'll use a similar, but broader, theory—exchange. There are three reasons: First, *exchange* better describes the relationships between media firms and outside actors such as consumers, sources, advertisers, and potential investors. Such relationships are more often cooperative than the power struggle resource dependence implies. Second, because so much news is commercially produced, there must be an underlying economic logic to its production. Third, because what constitutes resource dependence is not as well understood as what constitutes exchange. An entire subdivision of social science is devoted to the latter—microeconomics. In Chapter 4 we shall see how economic concepts such as oligopolistic competition—when a few major competitors share a market; market power—when one supplier of a resource controls a significant share of it; and buyers' and sellers' markets—when there are more sellers for a commodity than buyers, and vice versa—help explain the dynamics of relationships between the media firm and news sources, advertisers, and other important players in news production.

Recently economic logic has been applied to behaviors such as religion that would seem (to all but cynics and clergy) to have little to do with economics.[6] Note that economic logic is not restricted to transactions where money changes hands. Money is only a *symbol* of value. The exchange of anything upon which people place value is the real subject of economics.[7]

One caution before we begin: Every model of reality is a simplification. This model uses economic reasoning as an integrating concept: that each independent person and organization in the model attempts with a logic that varies in sophistication to increase its supply of what it sees as valuable by trading with others. This is not to argue that such reasoning is the *only* explanation of news production. In each relationship described, other factors enter. But what is common and central to all the relationships in the model, I contend, is a way of reasoning that is essentially economic. In other words, there is a "bottom line" to each of these relationships, even if the participants choose to operate at a higher level.

Introducing the Players

THE ENVIRONMENT

Interactions among the nine parties in the model (see Figure 2.1) are powerfully shaped by the enduring values of the culture in which they take place, by laws such as those on libel and privacy, and by regulations such as those covering a station's license renewal, and by the available technology. This relationship is reciprocal. The norms of culture, laws and regulations, even the direction of technology are all influenced by what does and doesn't become news. This interrelationship between environmental forces and those represented in the model will be considered in detail in Chapters 3 and 10.

INVESTORS

These are the owners of the media firm or its parent corporation. Because most U.S. news media belong to "chains" or to larger conglomerate corporations, and most of those are publicly traded on Wall Street, most investors are stockholders.[8] Stockholders exercise their will through election of, or participation on, the corporation's board of directors. The election differs from the democratic model of one person one vote. Since a stockholder's vote is weighted by the number of shares held, the greater the proportion of a company owned by a stockholder, the more influence that person has over the board of directors.

PARENT CORPORATION

The parent corporation owns and oversees several media firms and perhaps non-media businesses as well. The Gannett Company, for example,

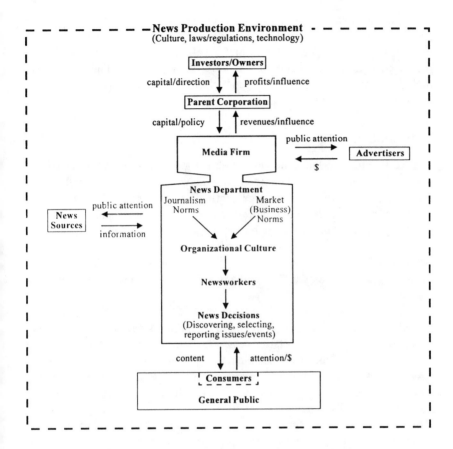

Figure 2.1. A Model of Commercial News Production

owns *USA Today,* nearly 90 local daily newspapers, several broadcasting stations and a national billboard company.[9] Through the stock market, the parent corporation sells shares in the company to investors. One or more top executives of the parent corporation are usually non-elected members of the board of directors, by virtue of their position. The parent corporation's top managers serve at the pleasure of the board but often nominate board candidates who are voted upon by shareholders. Parent corporation executives may also become substantial stockholders through options and performance clauses. These executives direct the operation of subsidiary companies by formulating policy and selecting their top managers.

MEDIA FIRM

The media firm is the local branch of the parent corporation, a single station or newspaper. It is directed by a general manager in television and a publisher in newspapers. These chief local executives are responsible to parent corporation managers and serve at their pleasure. The media firm includes a variety of departments: production, syndication, advertising sales, news, distribution, public relations, and so forth.

NEWS DEPARTMENT

This division produces the news within a given media firm and depends upon it for resources. I have chosen to use the word "department" rather than the more common terms "news organization" or "news firm," because I think it's more accurate. In contemporary commercial journalism, the news is produced by a subunit of a media firm; not an independent company that generates its own income and reports back to the parent corporation or investors. The news director in a TV station works at the pleasure of the station's general manager. The managing editor of a newspaper works for the publisher.

In addition to being a subordinate unit of the media firm, the news department is not large enough in employee numbers nor in content production to represent the whole station or newspaper. About 90% of the broadcast day for a local station is entertainment programming. Calling the station a *news* organization because of the remaining 10% is misleading. Although newspaper people may consider their product to be news-centered, most of its content also is not news. About 70% of the average newspaper is advertising and some of its editorial sections are explicitly designed to entertain. At most newspapers the proportion of the budget that goes into reporting is well below 20%.[10] Calling television stations and newspapers *news* organizations exaggerates the importance of that function and distracts analysis from the media firm's other functions.

Within the news department a culture exists, a common set of understandings about how things are done. Although this culture differs with the department, in most newsrooms there are two sets of "oughts," those of journalism—representing the interests of citizens; and those of business—representing the interests of investors. These govern the exchanges with parties outside the news department.[11]

The principal *norm of journalism*—whether broadcast or print—is public enlightenment: the most learning about consequential current issues and events for the largest number of persons. The Code of Broadcast News Ethics of the Radio-Television News Directors Association states: "The responsibility of radio and television journalists is to gather and report information of importance and interest to the public accurately, honestly and impartially." Broadcast journalists "will evaluate information solely on its merits as news, rejecting sensationalism or misleading emphasis in any form."[12] This norm is repeated in the code of ethics of the Society of Professional Journalists, which uses language similar to the American Society of Newspaper Editors: "The primary purpose of gathering and distributing news and opinion is to serve the general welfare by informing the people and enabling them to make judgments on the issues of the time."[13, 14]

The principal *norm of business* is to maximize profits over an indefinite period.[15] Pushed by investors who seek maximum short-term returns and by pressures from mergers and buyouts, American corporations, including those in the news business, appear to be shortening the "indefinite period" over which profits are to be maximized.[16]

Newsworkers includes all employees with a direct hand in creating news content, for example, news directors, managing editors, reporters, videographers, writers, copy editors, producers, directors, and so on.

News decisions are rarely made by consciously thinking through the components of business and journalism standards, but by reference to the organizational culture that integrates the two into practices that are rewarded, tolerated, or punished within a particular newsroom.[17] Key decisions occur at each of three stages of production.[18] The first stage of production—discovery—requires a series of decisions about how a news department shall deploy its resources to learn what is going on in the community that might be newsworthy. The second stage—selection—requires choices of which events and issues discovered in Phase 1 ought to be reported. The third stage—reporting—requires decisions about how to cover the events and issues selected in the previous step, for example, where to point the camera and whom to interview and which quotes and background to use to create a narrative account.

In this model, newsmakers operate within constraints set by others.[19] Newsworkers are *employees* with few of the characteristics of semi-independent professionals such as doctors, engineers, lawyers, or tenured university professors. Newsworkers are not self-employed nor employed in professional partnerships. Nor are they certified or disciplined by organizations of professional peers. Nor do they elect top editors nor make policy by consensus. Nevertheless, newsworkers do have an influence over story production. Print journalists usually have more latitude than broadcast journalists because in most newspapers, reporters may originate ideas for stories, subject to approval by editors. At most stations, reporters are assigned stories by the assignment editor. Newsworkers also influence news production unconsciously because, like all humans, the "lenses" of their personal histories and self-interest shape news. But both conscious and unwitting orientations must conform to the selection biases of the news department. There is little evidence that journalists who are out of step with the news selection orientation of their employers are tolerated.[20]

Note that reporters and editors may *feel* free to report the news as they see fit. But their freedom may seem larger than it is for two reasons. First, those who hire on with a particular news department often know—and perhaps agree with—its orientation beforehand; they expect to conform.[21] Second, the boundaries of the news department's organizational culture are nearly invisible until crossed. Until such a story is proposed, a reporter may not know that she cannot initiate consumer reporting or other coverage critical of major advertisers such as car dealers, realtors, or grocery chains. Organizational culture normally steers reporters away from sensitive topics before a confrontation point by defining response to certain public information needs as beyond the resources the firm is willing to commit to news, or outside the proper purview of news.[22] The news department, following policy set by the media firm, defines the acceptable scope of reporting, not the journalist.

News Sources. News sources are the providers of the raw material of news. They include anyone reporters turn to for information—government and business officials, bureaucrats, witnesses of events, parties to issues, persons on the street.

Advertisers. Advertisers are the providers of the income that fuels the enterprise. Local and national advertisers supply nearly 100% of broadcast income,[23] and 70%-90% of newspaper revenues.[24]

News Consumers. News consumers are individual viewers, and for newspapers, readers.

The General Public. These are all those individuals in a society who do not consume news from the media firm under study.

Primary Relationships

Given the nature of American culture and its market-based economy, commercial media firms must compete for necessary resources in four markets—one each for investors, sources of news, advertisers, and news consumers.

1. BETWEEN INVESTORS AND PARENT CORPORATION

Turow defined this relationship as one where investors contribute capital to establish or upgrade the corporation and set general operating conditions. In return, investors expect profits. Because news creates the images of reality upon which people act, investors may also expect influence or prestige. Such influence could be broad—perhaps improving society by producing useful goods or services—or more specific—perhaps gaining political or business advantage. The parent corporation sells its stock to investors for whatever the market will bear. If the profitability of the stock falls below the competition, so does its price and thus the amount of capital available to the corporation for expansion or improvement. Any fall in stock price, of course, also diminishes the wealth of current stockholders, including managers. Public trading also makes the corporation vulnerable to buyout by investors who believe they can generate larger profits than current management. Thus pressure on the firm to maximize profits is exerted from above not only by current investors, but also by prospective ones. The exchange between investors and the parent firm differs from all of the others in the production of commercial news in that investors gain explicit influence within the corporation.[25] The other three trading partners—news sources, advertisers, and consumers—exercise their influence from outside the corporate structure. In the investor-parent corporation relationship, ownership subordinates the purposes of management of the parent company to those of investors. In fact, management has a legal responsibility to serve the economic interest of owners.

2. BETWEEN PARENT CORPORATION AND MEDIA FIRM

Parent corporation management allocates capital and sets company policy under the broader dictates of the board of directors, and it chooses media firm executives. In return for direction and capital, the parent corporation collects revenues from the firm for disbursement either in profits to shareholders or to allocate to other business properties. The parent corporation also channels influence upward from the news department. As corporate executives act as subordinates to investors, local managers of firms are responsible to corporate headquarters and serve at its pleasure. The parent corporation can serve as a leveling agent for its corporate "children." One firm's profits can be siphoned off to aid a struggling sibling station or newspaper or company in a non-media business, or to pay off debts from mergers or expansions.[26]

3. BETWEEN MEDIA FIRM AND THE NEWS DEPARTMENT

Besides hiring and firing the chief newsroom manager, the media firm's executive—in television the general manager and in newspapers the publisher—sets the news department's budget and audience goals. General news policy is also established.

In newspapers, the proportion of the media firm's revenues spent on the news department apparently has been falling over the past decade.[27] In television, however, news departments have become more important. Local newscasts affect the station's bottom line more than you might expect given the approximately 10% of air time and 15% of station revenues[28] they consume. For stations affiliated with networks, local news is one of the few programming slots over which local management exercises much control. The content of network programming is decided in New York. For such programming, the station receives a clearance fee—a part of the advertising revenues the network collects for the show, and a limited number of open "spots"—30-second periods that a station can sell to advertisers directly. The spots are usually more valuable than the clearance fees because the fees are shared with hundreds of other stations airing the network program. For locally originated programs such as news, however, all commercial time—usually about 16 minutes per hour (or 32 "spots") are sold by the station. Nothing has to be shared. An inexpensive and popular newscast, therefore, profits the station more than a similar amount of program time turned over to the network.

A second reason why local newscasts disproportionately affect stations' profits is what broadcasters call the "halo effect." Viewers tend to identify the station with its news personalities, particularly its anchor men and women. Parasocial "friendships" or trust relationships built with the news team appear to create an allegiance that carries over to the station's other programs. As a result, the station whose newscasts attract the largest audiences may improve its ratings for the rest of the broadcast day as well.[29] Part of this "halo" is explained by the position of news at noon and in the early evening. A popular newscast provides audience flow (viewers who watch a program primarily because they were already tuned to that channel) to later entertainment programming on the same station.

A third reason for the economic importance of local news to a station is the growing competition for viewers described in Chapter 1. This rising competition has not affected local news and other—largely entertainment—programming equally. The addition of independent televisions stations, cable stations, and rental of videotapes has vastly expanded viewer choice everywhere but in local news. The Cable News Network and C-Span, for example, greatly expand choice for national and international news among cable subscribers. Sports lovers can now watch athletes compete day and night on ESPN and there are channels for pornography connoisseurs, for cartoon aficionados, rock music lovers, and many other segments of the viewership. By contrast, the competition in local news has increased only slightly. The variety of entertainment now available has reduced the audience share for the typical station's news programs. But the spectrum of choice has drained a greater proportion of the viewership for entertainment programming because little local news comes through the cable and none from the VCR.[30]

Although many stations with unpopular newscasts still earn substantial profits,[31] local news has become the station's most important commodity.

4. BETWEEN NEWS SOURCES AND NEWS DEPARTMENT

Turow argued that in a mass society, sources depend on news media to reach the public. Conversely, news departments rely on sources for the raw material of news. The concept of exchange—access for information—is also implicit in descriptions of source-news department relationships described by a wide variety of news researchers.[32]

From the exchange perspective, sources cooperate with reporters to the extent that sources believe they and/or their ideas will gain favorable public access. Sources can judge such access in three ways: character and quantity of audience, character and quantity of content, and prestige of editorial environment. First, audience. Not only do sources usually want to reach as many people as possible, certain qualities of those persons are important. The most valuable are those readers or viewers in a position to help sources achieve their goals—people such as political constituents, potential supporters, customers, investors, and so on.[33] Second, content. Positively framed coverage beats neutral or critical reporting. A frame is the tone or spin or slant the story adopts—whether the sources quoted and the material supplied by the reporter without attribution is more supportive or critical. Quantity also counts; extended favorable or neutral quotes are likely to have more impact on the audience than a quick quote, or "sound bite." Third, editorial environment. Coverage in a prestige news product, such as *The New York Times,* may influence consumer attitudes toward a source more authoritatively than reportage in a less respected one. Coverage by prestige news departments also conveys a secondary audience when that department sets the agenda of other news departments. The tone adopted in the prestige coverage is also likely to be duplicated.[34]

Note that incentives for sources to enter a transaction with a news department include limiting the harm of bad publicity as well as gaining favorable attention. It can be just as valuable for a source to respond to negative allegations, putting his or her interpretation of an event before the public, as to gain favorable notice.

More sophisticated sources are likely to be more realistic about what kind of exposure they will receive in return for their information. But even naive sources are unlikely to respond if they think participation will result in more harm than good. For official sources, particularly those who must win elections or who depend on the public to buy their company's products, the "payment" of favorable access to the public eye and ear is a valuable return for information provided. In fact, politicians now refer to such news coverage in explicitly economic terms as "free" time.[35] (In contrast to "paid" time in political advertisements.) For private individuals, fame is usually an adequate return.

Some sources, however, prefer cash. The rise of "checkbook journalism," in which news departments buy material from sources, makes the exchange between sources and journalists explicit. For example, George Holliday, the Los Angeles plumber who turned the police beating of African American motorist Rodney King into a public event, knew his videotape was hot property. He sold it to a local television station and later sought to bill every other local station that aired his video.[36] Buying information from famous or notorious sources is commonplace not just in "tabloid" television shows such as *A Current Affair,* but at the major networks.[37]

News departments, for their part, seek information that will interest and/or inform consumers at the least cost. The greater the volume and quality of such information a source controls at a given cost, the greater the motivation of reporters to use that source.[38]

5. BETWEEN ADVERTISERS AND MEDIA FIRM

Robert Picard, a media economist, described this relationship as an explicit exchange.[39] Advertisers pay for the public attention the media firm delivers based on independently gathered statistical estimates of the size, wealth, and stage in life of the consuming group. In general, the larger the audience, the greater their wealth, the greater the proportion in the highest consuming age bracket (those establishing or expanding homes), the more valuable the advertising space is to retailers and the higher the fees stations or newspapers may charge. Here again there is an environmental dimension. Advertisers value news environments that create what Bagdikian calls "a buying mood,"—a curiosity about and a desire to possess goods and services that is generated by purported news content.[40] Examples of such content are stories—or whole sections of newspapers—extolling the virtues of new automobiles, computers, the joys of home ownership, of gardening, of fashion, and so forth. As a corollary, a supportive environment would also exclude or downplay news that denigrated advertised products, services, or companies. Advertisers also value a second aspect of the news environment: Advertisements surrounded by news content that consumers find believable may gain credibility for their claims by association.[41]

6. BETWEEN NEWS CONSUMERS AND NEWS DEPARTMENT

This relationship is also based on an exchange. The consumer's attention is traded for information. Consider the advice a prominent news executive gave fellow local broadcasters:

> A marketing approach demands that we treat a newscast as a consumer durable good, a commodity that a viewer "purchases" by spending time watching it. We must understand that when a viewer watches a specific television program, the viewer really is spending a precious resource: time. And time for many people is spent as carefully as money.[42]

Researchers have argued not only that viewers "invest" their time in news, but that many apply a rudimentary cost-benefit analysis. The likelihood of a consumer choosing a particular news product is proportional to the amount or intensity of some expected reward—being informed and/or entertained—relative to the effort or cost thought to be required to gain the reward.[43] For its part, the news department seeks the attention of various audiences both for journalistic purposes and to sell to advertisers.[44] Newspapers differ from broadcast media in this exchange. In addition to their attention, subscribers must pay a direct charge for the newspaper, but almost always somewhat less than the actual cost because of the advertisers' subsidy.

7. BETWEEN NEWS CONSUMERS AND THE GENERAL PUBLIC

Not all members of the public watch or read the news from a particular media firm. So differences can arise between the consumers of one news department's products and those who consume another's or don't keep up with news. If the informational differences are significant, cultural and economic divisions can follow. The dotted line separating consumers from the rest of the public indicates that while the two groups differ in access to information, interpersonal news-telling creates a permeable boundary.

Who Has the Most Power?

If you look back at the model introduced as Figure 2.1, it may look a bit like a Rube Goldberg contraption: no pulleys, but lots of boxes and arrows.

Where does one drop the pinball to get it all started? Is there one player that sets the conditions for all of the others? Scholars disagree. Robert Entman and Philip Meyer pointed to the consumers as the key players.[45] Herbert Gans said news media are caught in a tug-of-war between powerful sources and consumers.[46] J. Herbert Altschull argued that "whoever pays the piper calls the tune." In this case that would be the advertisers.[47] Joseph Turow also nominated the advertisers or "patrons,"[48] but later settled on the owners.[49] Ben Bagdikian and news critic Robert Squiers fingered the owners and large investors.[50] Conservatives such as Robert Lichter, Stanley Rothman, and Linda Lichter argued that liberal reporters are in charge.[51] Critics from the left, such as Edward Herman and Noam Chomsky, pointed to the rich and powerful within society.[52]

Within the environmental framework of current U.S. laws, culture, and technology, I would argue that the primary role is played by major investors[53] and owners. Of course commercial news departments must pay attention to consumer tastes. And to the degree that they are supported by advertisers, media firms must provide them competitive vehicles for their messages if they are to stay in business themselves. And news departments must maintain access to news sources. The degree of control exercised by these outside forces, however, rarely matches the influence investors/owners wield through top management. Of the four trading partners—consumers, advertisers, sources, and investors—only the last is also a boss.

Applying the Model

Obviously, there's much more to say about how this model of commercial news production works. But rather than piling on details now, it may be better to apply the model in crude form to a real case. Let's use it to make sense of the Central American reporting that began the chapter.

ENVIRONMENTAL FORCES

First, we need to look at the external environment—laws and regulation, the cultural climate and technology.

Laws and Regulations. With only 5 years separating reapplications for its license to broadcast, stations such as KLRG must keep Federal Communication Commission regulations constantly in mind. Although license renewals are routinely granted, prominent politicians sometimes have threatened purveyors of unwelcome news. Most of these threats—which peaked during the late 1960s with Vice President Spiro Agnew's accusations of liberal news bias—were aimed at network rather than local newscasts. Such warnings were taken seriously by local stations, however, because their licenses were at jeopardy for carrying "biased" news regardless of its origination.[54] The concern about bias among local newscasters at the time was boosted by a regulation (which the FCC stopped enforcing only months later) called the "Fairness Doctrine." It required stations to cover controversial issues and give relatively equal time to all sides, even if that meant providing free air time to spokespersons for unpopular factions.[55]

The Cultural Climate. As the news director suggested, in early 1987 when I visited KLRG, the United States involvement in El Salvador and Nicaragua was highly controversial. Critics of U.S. Latin American policy were casting the issue as one of rich against poor, playing to the American cultural values of fair play and support for the underdog. The issue was framed by the Reagan Administration as part of a global crusade of America against communism. So it appealed to such basic cultural norms as nationalism and individual freedom. Public opinion was about evenly divided at the time as to whether the United States should help crush socialism in the two nations or let each nation settle its own fate. The station may have possessed more localized poll results. The news director, for example, had expressed fear of offending rural residents. People living on farms and in small towns, he said, considered support of the national government the only patriotic option.

Technology. Videotape technology made television news-gathering much less cumbersome and expensive than in the days of film. Sending a crew into rough terrain without access to electrical outlets or generators was technically more feasible than before. Although KLRG did not have a satellite "up link"—the means of transmitting a report from the jungle to a satellite (where it would be sent back down to the studio in the United States)—the spread of such technologies meant that other large stations were expanding into areas of coverage previously left to the networks.

FORCES WITHIN THE MODEL

Next we examine the various forces within the model: investors, parent corporation, media firm, advertisers, news sources, consumers, and the news department itself. Although our model distinguishes between investors and parent corporation, their influence in this case appears to be congruent. For parsimony, let's begin with the parent corporation.

Corporate Influence. Profit demand at KLRG was very strong according to the news director. The parent corporation was based in Texas, which at the time was undergoing a recession induced by the fall of oil prices. There was speculation in the newsroom that the corporation was putting extra profit pressure on its stations outside that region to compensate. Actual profit figures for KLRG were not made public. But stations of KLRG's size were reporting annual median returns at that time of $9 million on revenues of $30 million, a pre-tax profit of 30%, more than three times the national manufacturing average.[56]

Media Firm Influence. The general manager of the station appears to have been passing along pressure from above, but my field notes are not detailed enough to be sure. In any case, the news director was adamant about controlling coverage to avoid criticism of government policy.

Advertiser Influence. According to the research literature, advertisers may exert two kinds of pressures on news decisions: The first is to select and package news to attract the largest audience likely to buy the products advertised; the second is to create a favorable, or "buying," environment for those ads within news content.[57] The first kind of pressure may conflict with journalism norms when the desire to please the audience overtakes the desire to inform viewers. The second type of pressure can collide with journalistic standards when news unfavorable to an advertiser or product is censored, or when non-newsworthy information favorable to the advertiser or product is included. Note that advertiser pressure can also reinforce journalism norms. Gathering large audiences serves public enlightenment as well as advertising.

The first type of pressure—to maximize audience, in this case by avoiding antagonizing and driving away viewers on either side of the Central American conflict—was evident in the news director's comments. Although it is possible that one or more major advertisers may have exerted pressure for a presumably conservative slant, I heard no mention of such influence in the newsroom. Nor was there any obvious connection between products advertised on KLRG and coverage of the two Central American conflicts.[58]

Source Influence. Not only sources, but potential sources who refused to talk, shaped the Central American coverage. Both reporters said that the peace groups with whom they traveled to Central America attempted to supply a one-sided framework for understanding what was occurring. In fact, a peace group even paid the airfare of the producer who traveled to El Salvador, introducing a conflict of interest forbidden by journalism norms. The Sandinista government had arranged a tour for the KLRG reporter, although it permitted him to leave it. The reporter believed the tour would have misled him into a pro-government story. The U.S. Embassy in El Salvador refused to comment to the KLRG producer. Such a refusal might seem to be avoidance of influence. But a "no comment" is itself a statement, particularly when it comes from an official source paid by taxpayers and presumably accountable to the public. In this case, the producer interpreted the embassy's behavior as a powerful influence attempt: U.S. officials sought to scuttle the story by opening it to a charge of one-sidedness. Apparently, sources representing the FMLN guerrillas were also uncooperative. The producer reported spending half a day attempting contact before giving up. Whether they were directly quoted or only relied upon for background, the collection of sources interviewed contributed the substance of the report. Those who were excluded or refused to cooperate, or who could not be reached, shaped the resulting coverage by their absence.

Consumer Influence. As far as I could tell, no local consumers were polled or otherwise consulted for either series. But their interests, their loyalties, their politics, their tastes, and their need to know what their government was doing in their name were considered by all parties to the construction of the two reports. Competition for the consumers' attention was the primary reason for initiating the foreign reports. The dominant station in KLRG's market had begun to do reports from abroad. Further, this station was promoting its foreign reporting as a reason to watch its newscast. To the extent that covering Central America attracted viewers away from KLRG, there were both compelling journalistic and business reasons for competing with its reports from abroad.

Organizational Culture Within the Newsroom. Journalistic standards call for independent, fair, and complete coverage that will maximize public understanding of important events. Were these norms to dictate coverage, we would expect reporting to center on the most important public question for local viewers: What is the effect of U.S. involvement in the nation? Reporters would have been expected to spend whatever time was needed to gather the most representative opinions of the various sides and then sift the evidence for those positions in as nonpartisan a manner as possible. The resulting coverage would give each side a chance to answer the central question, but would also report the preponderance of evidence.

Market norms call for maximizing return to investors. Were purely economic norms to prevail, coverage would center on the least expensively gathered information likely to generate the largest audience advertisers would pay to reach.

The model predicts that both sets of norms will figure in deciding what's news. But their influence is not necessarily equal. Where investor direction is for maximum profit, market norms will dominate journalism norms when the two conflict.

The decision to cover American involvement in Central America generated both journalistic and economic benefits. Citizens needed to understand the substantial U.S. intervention in both countries; the topic was clearly important. From the station's economic standpoint, coverage denied the competing station an exclusive story, and thus what economists call a comparative advantage. Also, the series promised a large audience because the stories were likely to be highly visual, conflictual, topical (in 1987), and emotional.

Decisions about how to do the stories, however, presented conflicts between journalism and business ideals. The Salvadoran series risked compromise from the start when the station cut its costs by accepting a subsidy from a local peace group. Despite the flawed beginning, both the producer and the reporter assigned to write and edit the series said they had produced a balanced report that helped viewers understand what the U.S. investment was yielding. The news director, however, censored the material most likely to serve that journalistic function. Left intact was the emotion and tragedy useful for maximizing audience. The approach avoided the risk of regulatory intervention and conflict with societal cultural values, such as nationalism and anticommunism.

From its inception, the Nicaraguan series was designed to *avoid* the central journalistic question of the effect of U.S. intervention. It was aimed at the peripheral issue of what local residents were doing to alleviate suffering in Nicaragua. When the reporter found he could not avoid the impact of U.S. intervention, he moved into conflict with the news director. After censorship, the human interest material remained, while the information needed to understand the nature of the conflict was excised.

The reasons the news director gave reporters for his decisions were journalistic: What right had they to barge into a foreign country and in a few days attempt to understand the central issue? The news director's warning about the difficulty of attempting to understand a complex situation in a short period of time is very responsible from a journalistic standpoint. However, KLRG routinely sent unprepared reporters to complex events, and broadcast their hurried reports without so much as editing a complete transcript of their stories. During my visit, the Central American stories were the only ones in which either the video or comments of sources were reviewed before broadcast.[59]

Secondly, if the reporter's visit was too short to address the most important issues, why not increase his stay? If he didn't speak Spanish, why not hire an interpreter? Although such extended reporting might have cost several thousand dollars, the station only mounted a handful of such ambitious projects in a year, and the median pretax profit of stations like KLRG was $9 million annually. A third, less expensive alternative that might violate the journalistic norm of independence, but not of pursuing the consequential, would be to patch together network or trusted third-party reports about the impact of U.S. involvement. A fourth would be to cooperate in a consortium of news departments supplying reporters to cover the issue.

Privately, in our conversation away from the newsroom, the news director acknowledged that the series sacrificed journalism norms to business goals. With a polarized audience, he explained, coverage that evaluated U.S. intervention was likely to lead some viewers on one side or the other to switch channels. He justified the compromise with the argument that the countries and issues were so remote, viewers didn't care what was happening there. But the justification contradicts itself. If viewers didn't care, why would they switch channels at the hint of partisanship?

Conclusion

Although the cases described above were more involved than most, we shall see in following chapters that even the most basic reporting is far more complex than an "attempt to reconstruct the essential framework of the event." The present model suggests that primary news decisions—about how to learn what's going on outside the newsroom, about selecting from among those events and issues a subset to cover, about what to report in each story—are quite complex. In light of instructions from owners/investors and profit demand from the market for investors—which are channeled through corporate headquarters and media firm management—and guided by an organizational culture combining business and journalistic standards, the media firm competes in markets for investors, sources, advertisers, and consumers. Thus news, rather than the "reflection of reality" that its producers have sometimes claimed it to be,[60] becomes a commodity to fit the market demands of a collection of special interests. As such, it is an elaborate compromise. We'll explore the environment framing this compromise in Chapter 3.

Notes

1. Schramm, 1949, p. 288.
2. At the time, the United States was spending about $2 million per day, mostly in military aid, to help the Salvadoran Army fight guerrillas of the Farabundo Marti National Liberation Front, according to *Newsweek*, March 2, 1987, p. 35.
3. At the time, the U.S. Central Intelligence Agency was secretly supplying military aid, estimated at tens of millions of dollars, to the "Contra" rebels, according to a *Frontline* report on the Public Broadcasting Service produced by Bill Moyers (1990) entitled "High Crimes and Misdemeanors."

4. Network news follows similar logic, but has several additional players.

5. Turow, 1984, 1992.

6. Iannaccone, 1992.

7. Becker, 1976.

8. Bagdikian, 1990.

9. Bagdikian, 1990.

10. Squiers, 1993.

11. Epstein, 1973.

12. *The Communicator,* January, 1990, p. 10.

13. American Society of Newspaper Editors Board of Directors [October 1975], cited in Day, 1991, p. 351.

14. Note that these are the *norms* of journalism, the ideals. Actual practice in newsrooms is modified by economic and sometimes other norms. Critics, such as sociologist Gaye Tuchman (1978), who hold that a norm like journalistic objectivity is a "strategic ritual" for avoiding conflict with the powerful in society and a means not to inform the public, may accurately describe the reality of journalistic practice in some news departments, but they are not describing norms. Likewise critics of professionalism in journalism, like James Carey, are warning against the self-serving practices of professionals rather than the ideals of journalism (Carey, 1978).

15. Main & Baird, 1981.

16. Auletta, 1991; Bagdikian, 1990; Lambeth, 1991; Shoemaker & Reese, 1991; Squiers, 1993.

17. Bantz, 1985.

18. This is an expansion of Dimmick, 1974.

19. Entman, 1989, chap. 2.; Reese, 1990; Soloski, 1989; Weaver & Wilhoit, 1986.

20. Breed, 1955; Reese, 1990; Sigalman, 1973; Soloski, 1989.

21. Breed, 1955.

22. Reese, 1990; Soloski, 1989.

23. Local TV revenues come primarily from advertisements the station sells directly to local and national advertisers. Some national advertising revenues collected by the networks are also passed along to stations through "clearance" fees—what the network pays for a local station to "clear," or broadcast, network programs. See Owen, Beebe, & Manning, 1974.

24. Udell, 1978.

25. A few media firms, most notably The New York Times Company, have created two tiers of stock, voting and nonvoting, in an effort to maintain family control over company policy. Although offering some protection from hostile takeover, stock issued without voting rights has less value than that with such rights because it deprives the shareholder from exercising influence to maximize return.

26. Auletta, 1991; Squiers, 1993.

27. Squiers, 1993.

28. Helregal, 1991.

29. Sabreen, 1985, p. 24.

30. Baldwin, Barrett, & Bates, 1993.

31. Helregal, 1991.

32. See, for example, Crouse, 1973; Fishman, 1980; Gans, 1979; Molotch & Lester, 1974; Tuchman, 1978; and especially Entman, 1989; and Reese, 1991.

33. Jamieson, 1992.

34. Reese, 1991.

35. Jamieson, 1992.

36. "Plumber Shocked Over Instant Fame in Taped Beating," 1991.

37. Meeske & Fedler, 1993.

38. Gans, 1979.

39. Picard, 1989.

40. Bagdikian, 1990.

41. Meyer, 1987.

42. Sabreen, 1985, p. 24.

43. Rivers, Schramm, & Christians, 1980.

44. Picard, 1989.

45. Entman, 1989; Meyer, 1987.

46. Gans, 1979.

47. Altschull, 1984.

48. Turow, 1984.

49. Turow, 1992.

50. Bagdikian, 1990; Squiers, 1993.

51. Lichter, Rothman, & Lichter, 1986. See also Bozell & Baker, 1990.

52. Herman & Chomsky, 1988.

53. Major investors are defined by the federal Securities and Exchange Commission as "insiders." They hold 5% or more of the corporation's outstanding shares of stock. Because of their powerful position, they and top executives are required to report their trading of the stock.

54. Barnouw, 1990.

55. Patricia Aufderheide (1990) cited evidence that in the wake of the FCC's August 1987 decision to suspend enforcement of the Fairness Doctrine, controversial news programming has diminished.

56. Stanley, 1986.

57. See, for example, Bagdikian, 1990, or Turow, 1992.

58. But were an advertiser to have made such a threat and management to have censored itself in response, such an abridgement of journalism norms might well have been hidden from the staff to avoid harming morale and productivity.

59. It's possible that the reason these two series received more editing than others during the month of my visit at KLRG is that they were not being hurried into that day's newscast; there was simply more time. My data are simply not detailed enough to discount this explanation. However two pieces of evidence suggest that it was the political volatility of the Central American stories rather than their preparation ahead of deadline that caused such unusual pre-broadcast review. I followed one other series in preparation for the sweeps month—on steroid use—and it escaped the scrutiny of the Central American reporting. Secondly, the reporter who produced the Nicaraguan series had prepared many other special reports for later broadcast during a ratings period. And he could not recall such intense editing before.

60. Epstein, 1973, quoting the congressional testimony of CBS News president Frank Stanton, Ph.D.

3

Environmental Influences
on News Production:
How Culture, Technology,
and Laws and Regulation Shape News

A s powerful as media firms, their parent corporations, their advertisers, sources, and mass audience are, all operate within a broader set of conditions largely beyond their ability to change except incrementally over a period of years. Among the most important of these environmental constraints are culture, technology, and the laws and regulations governing reporting and broadcasting. Because these influences are constantly in the background of news decision making, they are often taken for granted. To make these forces more visible, let's try an experiment in imagination.

An Experiment in Imagination

Close your eyes and relax the "But what about . . . ?" response for a few paragraphs:

Suppose that community replaced individualism as an enduring *cultural value* in the United States. Stories about how an individual beat the odds against nature or the competition to achieve "success" might be far less common if such victories were seen as oddities rather than models to be followed. "Rugged individualists" might be portrayed as quirky or perhaps uncooperative, rather than as admirable. Compromise might lose its negative connotation. What might happen to the self-esteem of the poor, or the rich for that matter, if the portrayal of success and failure as due primarily to an individual's innate goodness or badness, talent or incompetence, were to give way to a different—and more realistic—common understanding of behavior? Would the rich be as arrogant and isolated or the poor as despondent and self-loathing if media descriptions were based on the reality that the material success or failure of Americans can be predicted with great accuracy from the wealth and education of their parents?

Suppose *technology* were slightly more advanced and phone companies connected each household to a network of fiber optic cables carrying hundreds of channels including capability for two-way communication. Consumers might tailor their own newscast from a list of available stories. They might also order their news by asking questions reporters could answer. With their own camcorders, consumers might even feed stories into the network, creating a news cooperative.

Such a system might change even the nature of news. Because mass advertising has come to support so much of news production, both in broadcast and print (and now even in public broadcasting), events and issues have often been selected for their wide appeal. On an interactive videotext system, viewers might begin to pay for the stories they ordered and eliminate unwanted advertising messages. News providers could earn as much money creating high-quality stories for smaller audiences willing to pay for them, as producing "lowest common denominator" reports to attract the large audiences mass advertisers seek. Further, if news dissemination no longer depends on corporations that can afford multimillion dollar presses or that have claimed scarce broadcast licenses, reporters might be able to deliver their stories to the public directly—without formally joining a newspaper or station's employ and thus having to conform to corporate control.

Suppose broadcasting *regulation* were quite different. Now advertisers pay stations directly for the number of consumers whose attention the news attracts. What if all the advertising dollars spent on all newscasts in a metropolitan area were collected by a semi-independent federal agency? Rather than paying on numbers, the agency would poll the public at regular intervals to discover how much they know about public affairs. Each station's income from news would be determined by how much was learned by how many. Premiums might be paid for closing knowledge gaps between more and less educated segments of society. The current incentive for popularity would be replaced with a reward for effective public service.

From Imagination to Reality

These three environmental factors are not fixed, but changing and interacting. To understand their influence on news production, we shall very briefly examine current U.S. culture, technology, and laws/regulations. Only this time we'll begin not with imagination, but with an actual case study from a television newsroom.

Influences That Are Predominately Cultural

CASE STUDY: CULTURAL INFLUENCE

The public relations firm hired by the hospital probably knew it could gain media attention by appealing to a prominent American cultural value—progress through science and technology. The press release sent to the medical reporter at KLRG, a station in a large western metropolis, promised to demonstrate a "new technology" for treating kidney stones that destroyed them with sound waves, eliminating the need for surgery.

The story seemed a natural to the medical reporter. She chose it without apparent hesitation from among a host of press releases advertising other story ideas. But she was not certain why. The metropolitan area had two other such machines, she said, and she'd done stories in the past on this treatment for kidney stones. "I have no idea what I'm going to do to make this any different," she explained. Although 12% of viewers were affected by kidney stones—according to the press release—the story would have consequence for them only if the new machine was superior to its competitors, perhaps more convenient or less expensive. This angle was not pursued, however. The demonstration was visual, but other news values such as emotion, timeliness, celebrity, conflict, unusualness, and humor were missing. The selection appeared to hinge on the attraction of the theme of technology conquering an age-old human problem. In fact, the reporter referred to the new machine as a "marvel." It struck a cultural chord.

PRIMARY CULTURAL NORMS

News is often described as "objective," free of cultural bias. Television news executives once testified before Congress that a newscast is simply a "mirror" held up to society, a neutral reflection.[1] But no human activity, particularly a corporate activity, is value free. Every act has a value dimension, a bias, because it represents a choice of one use of time over alternatives. There are theories and assumptions underlying all conscious activity, including the production of news.[2] When pressed, journalists acknowledge some of these values, and label them as what makes events and issues newsworthy. But there are other values so broadly accepted in U.S. culture that most journalists are blind to them.[3] They are so much taken for granted that these values are considered "natural," or "common sense." There have been a variety of efforts to catalogue these commonly held American values. Robin Williams compiled one of the more comprehensive:[4]

1. Activity and work—are seen as inherently worthwhile, particularly if the work is seen as socially useful. Idleness is a vice.
2. Achievement and success—performance in competition with others is seen as valuable to the extent that that performance meets some standard of excellence, or better, exceeds the performance of competitors.
3. Moral orientation and humanitarianism—there is an obligation to certain moral rules regarding the treatment of others that cannot be set aside for expedient reasons.
4. Science and rationality—empirical observation coupled with logic betters the human condition.
5. Efficiency and practicality—quick, easy solutions are favored so long as they appear to work.
6. Material comfort and hedonic enjoyment—material well-being and pleasure are good in themselves.
7. Progress—the quality of life is generally improving.
8. Aesthetic values—creative and performing arts are goods in themselves.
9. Equality—equal opportunities for all are desirable, even if equal outcomes are not.
10. Freedom—there should be as little constraint as possible on the behavior of individuals.
11. Democracy—leaders should be elected, representatives of people should make laws, and people have basic rights that cannot be voted away.
12. Conformity—particularly in smaller communities, there is an inclination to go along with the majority.
13. Nationalism—America is the greatest country in the world and it generally acts for the benefit of other nations.
14. Individual personality—every human has unique worth and dignity and the potential for controlling his or her own destiny.
15. Racism and group superiority—a diminishing value, but one still held to some degree by many; it may be based on racial, ethnic, religious, or class distinctions.

Not all Americans share these 15 values. But these or similar values are expressed by a majority in a variety of surveys conducted over the past 30 years.[5] Nor do Americans believe in them equally. For example, when Gallup surveyors recently asked whether personal freedom or equality was more important, Americans preferred freedom over equality, 72% to 20%.[6] Local cultural values will also shape news decisions. Such local values might be a strong sympathy for a regional industry such as tourism in a beach community, logging in a forested area, or petroleum in the oil patch. Local culture may also be marked by antiunion sentiments, advocacy for environmental issues, a Christian fundamentalist orientation, a climate supportive of women's abortion decisions, and so forth.

Do the values of journalists differ from those of mainstream America? Most surveys of reporters and editors suggest that journalists are centrist or moderately liberal while managers of news departments and media firms are more conservative.[7] David Weaver and Cleve Wilhoit, for example, found in a 1992 survey of American journalists that 44% call themselves Democrats, 34% say they are independents, and 16% identify as Republican. Compared to the overall U.S. population, journalists are 5 to 10 percentage points more likely to identify as Democrats and 10 to 15 percentage points less likely to say they are Republicans, depending on which poll you use as a baseline.[8]

But even were working journalists significantly more liberal than the average American, they face pressures to conform to centrist positions in the newsroom.[9]

Influences That Are Predominately Technological

CASE STUDY: TECHNOLOGICAL INFLUENCE

The story was conceived as a "doughnut," but not a simple one. To make a doughnut the reporter begins the story "live," usually from a site in the field, then introduces a videotaped section prepared earlier in the day, then returns live to add late developments or answer questions from the anchor; the live parts of the story surround the videotape. The live shots often feature action in the background—people passing, or planes landing, or a fire burning. They create a sense of urgency and break up the routine of the show, the KLRG producer who made the assignment explained. He aimed for two per newscast. What made this doughnut difficult was logistics. The site was in front of a military base at the outskirts of the metro region. So after gathering information from the base, the reporter would return to the newsroom near downtown to produce the videotaped sections of the story, then race back in the middle of the afternoon commute in a specially equipped truck to be in position for the live part.

Technology helped shape this story long before a photographer warmed up the "remote" truck with its hydraulic microwave tower, however. The assignment was to advance a report from Washington received the night before that the Pentagon was considering closing a nearby Air Force base to save money. After reading an account in the morning newspaper, the reporter—one of the most trusted at KLRG—hit the phones. None of the calls were to gather information, however, only to schedule on-camera interviews. "If I were working in print," he explained, "I wouldn't have to move. But in TV I go out for every interview." On-camera interviews, he conceded, "are logistically more difficult and people are much more guarded in the glare of TV lights [with] a microphone in their face," but "it's much more powerful if you have someone talking on videotape."

The key interview was with the base commander, but he wasn't available for a face-to-face until 3 p.m. Even if the interview only lasted 5-10 minutes, with a half-hour drive in light traffic and the need to be headed back out to the base by 4:15 (to be in position for the opening segment of the 5 p.m. newscast), there would be only about 30 minutes to write the script, edit the videotape, and record the reporter's narrative over the visuals.

The reporter was concerned about having so little time to tell a complicated story. "It's a great newspaper story," he complained. "It's complex. Too much complexity can't be handled on TV because the story can't be repeated or re-read."

Because of the substantial economic contribution the base made to the region, the most newsworthy questions in this story were estimating the likelihood of closure and learning what, if anything, might be done to prevent it. Secondary questions might probe the official reasons given or explore how and when the closure would take place, or what its impact on the community might be. The primary reason for shutting the base down, according to an Air Force spokesman in Washington, was a diminished need for navigators in new high-tech planes. The local base was a primary navigator training facility. A minor reason had been a point of local controversy: The Air Force and the county planning board had been at odds for years over how close housing could be permitted to the runways because of noise.

Were he working for a newspaper, the reporter might have called a number of sources in Washington, trying to answer the primary question of likelihood of closure. After all, the story began in Washington with the Pentagon decision and local news media were alerted to it by a long-distance call from their congressman, who opposed the closure. But gathering news by telephone to work into a reporter's narrative or to audiotape sources for broadcast violated the technological orthodoxy of television journalism. The KLRG reporter felt compelled to pursue an angle he could capture on camera, even if that meant missing the most important aspects of the story. Perhaps without conscious thought, he substituted the minor controversy between the Air Force and local planners for the primary cause for closure.

In a morning interview taped for the noon newscast, a local planning commissioner said the Pentagon was playing its "ace" in a metaphorical poker game with the commission. The planning commission was to vote soon on a comprehensive plan including the area surrounding the base. She charged that the Pentagon was attempting to pressure the commission with the announcement. Without checking this line of reasoning with base spokespersons, the reporter characterized the issue as a "high-stakes card game" between the Pentagon and local planners in his report for the noon news. The reporter did not feel his one-sided noon report violated journalistic fairness standards (getting both sides of a controversy) because the base commander could not go before the cameras until that afternoon. Telephoning the base for a response or perhaps an audiotaped comment from the commander or a spokesperson was simply out of the question. Even if it were good journalism, it would not be "good television." Calling officials in Washington, even the local congressman, was not discussed for the same reason.

With the phone off limits as a news-gathering device, the reporter could not pursue the central questions about the threatened closure. So he spent the early afternoon cruising a neighborhood near the base looking for people to ask if runway noise bothered them. He didn't intend to poll a representative sample of the neighbors. Nor did he seek out community leaders who might know the neighborhood's opinion. Neither approach would have provided the visuals of everyday people he wanted. The intent, he explained, was to "people-ize" the story. By adding human interest, he would save the story from becoming "government soup," a bureaucratic wrangle that might not interest many viewers. The effort yielded only two interviews, one from a woman so camera-shy that she answered most questions with only a word or a phrase. One man refused to respond. And one woman said jet noise interrupted her child's naps.

At 3:09 the base commander met with the reporter. The colonel said housing "encroachment" around the base was a minor reason for closure. He denied any effort to pressure the local planning board. The commander expressed surprise that the reporter could believe that Pentagon brass thousands of miles away would form national policy to bluff a county planning board. If anything, the commander pointed out, the timing of the government announcement would make planners *less* likely to restrict development. With the Air Force likely to move out, why limit housing? Not having scouted the Air Force's position by phone, the reporter was unprepared to pursue other story angles. Questions about the likelihood of closure, how it might be prevented, and what it might mean for base employees went unasked. At 3:25 the interview was over. And it was now too late to schedule and execute further on-camera interviews for the 5 o'clock newscast.

Returning to the station at 4, the reporter conferred with the producer and began selecting quotes, called "sound bites," from the videotape of the commander. The story was ready only 35 minutes later. But that didn't leave enough time to return to the base during rush hour. So the producer let the reporter go "live" from the newsroom. By airtime, the doughnut was ready. All the interviews combined consumed less than an hour. Writing the story and marrying the words and visuals took another 35 minutes. But the sum of the time spent gathering and presenting information totaled less than half the time spent driving.[10] The resulting story stuck with the angle that the Air Force was "playing a trump card" in its "card game" with the local planning commission. Despite the base commander's plausible denial, the reporter said the Air Force's "big fear . . . is that more housing will be allowed."

"I wasn't real pleased with the story," the reporter said afterward. "Most of that was based on the time constraints. Had the interview been at two instead of three, it would have made a world of difference. Because of the time crunch, I didn't even look at the total tape of the colonel. This is the way it came to me first and I didn't have time to diddle around with it. You only have one time to make it."

Obviously, technology alone didn't determine the course of this story. The economic self-interest of the station played a shaping role. The logic of going for visuals over information gathered by phone suggests that making the account interesting was more important than making it either newsworthy or accurate.

PRIMARY TECHNOLOGICAL INFLUENCES

Think of a news department as a kind of factory.[11] As in any factory, technology plays a part in securing raw materials, processing those materials into saleable products, distributing those products, and managing demand for them through advertising. The raw material of news, regardless of technology, is information supplied by various sources. Because television requires both visual and verbal information if it is to maximize its comparative advantage over radio and print, securing input is technically more complex and therefore more expensive than in other media. A newspaper reporter may carry only a pen and pad, at most perhaps a pocket tape recorder and laptop computer. A radio reporter would carry a tape recorder. Most television reporters, however, are accompanied by a photographer belted with battery packs and carrying a camera costing many thousands of dollars. There are two salaries to pay, plus substantial equipment costs. The same complexity increases processing costs. Television editing consoles and sound-insulated facilities for recording the reporter's voice "track" over the video action are quite expensive. Using them adds time and money to preparing a story.

The output of broadcast and print news "factories" also differs markedly. A newspaper is a physical product, paper, while television and radio news are energy patterns, a progression of electromagnetic waves. Paper, ink, and distribution costs—trucks, fuel, drivers and paper carriers—consume much more of the typical newspaper's budget than all expenses of news-gathering combined.[12] But electricity bills for television transmitters are only a small fraction of station expenses. Finally, because the news products are so different, the means of consuming them are quite different as well.

Differences in technological properties between television and print are worth listing because they profoundly influence newsroom decisions:

- Volume in print is measured in column inches of paper; in broadcast media it's measured in time. Given the current state of licensing and technology, broadcast time is more limited than printed space. There is a fixed number of hours in a day, but no limit on pages of news that can be produced. Although the volume of all television content is growing rapidly with the expansion of cable systems boasting scores of channels, a particular newspaper has more volume than a particular station. The greater space in newspapers permits them to carry both more news and more advertising. The size of the "news hole" has important implications for news selection. The amount of advertising a medium can carry directly affects the amount of resources that can be devoted to news production.

- Sensory impact in print is visual, but static. And it's tactile. For some the tangibility of a newspaper is an attraction, for others it's a recycling burden. Television ignores the fingers but reaches both eyes and ears. And its pictures move. Television is closer to real life than print or radio. When the visuals and spoken words match, learning is enhanced over either modality by itself.[13]

- Watching and listening to television is less effortful than training your eyes to follow abstract printed symbols across rows of print. Brain wave patterns are less active for viewers processing television content than for readers processing print.[14]

- Televised messages reach a much broader audience than printed ones. Reading skills are necessary to decode language symbols. Television is accessible to preliterate children and adults who can't read English. The reinforcing combination of pictures and words on TV encourages comprehension even among those with a marginal grasp of the spoken language. But print represents a more formidable barrier than once thought. A startling proportion of Americans are functionally illiterate in English. A 1993 survey in which a cross-section of 26,000 adults was tested by the federal Department of Education showed nearly half had a great deal of difficulty with tasks as simple as reading a newspaper. The department concluded that in the face of poverty and massive immigration of non-English speakers, literacy in the United States is falling.[15]

- Transmission pace in print is controlled by the consumer. In television the pace is set by the sender. A reader can slow down on the difficult parts, or stop to think, or re-read. A viewer has to rely on the producer to anticipate where the going gets difficult.

- Sequencing, and to some degree, choice of stories in print is controlled by the consumer; in television, by the sender. Newspaper readers can select a subset of stories in the paper and read them in any sequence while consumers of electronic media must follow a sequence programmed by someone else. You aren't free to skip to the sports or weather when the 6 o'clock news comes on. In computer talk, print is a "random access medium."

- While a physical product like a newspaper can be zoned—different content for different communities within a circulation area—an electromagnetic signal is uniform across the region.

- A televised message can be viewed only once, and then at a specific time, unless the consumer owns a videocassette recorder. By contrast, after delivery a newspaper is ready when the reader is, and can be stored in a file drawer with scissors-level technology.

- Because its route across public airwaves must be protected from interference, television signals are regulated by the Federal Communications Commission. All outlets are licensed. Printed news is protected from such restrictions by the First Amendment to the Constitution. Licensing also erects a barrier to you starting your own TV station: But no one will stop you if you begin printing a neighborhood newspaper.

- Televised news can be delivered "live," that is, at almost the speed of light; printed news is delayed hours or days by the necessity of printing and distributing paper products.

- Scale economies exist in both print and electronic media, but are more important for the latter. All editorial costs are incurred in creating the first copy of the newspaper. Each additional paper sold contributes revenue but adds only the cost of the paper, ink, a spin through the press, and delivery. Up to a point, the more papers produced, the greater the profit. At some point, however, it costs more to produce and, particularly, deliver, the next paper than is collected in revenues. Television is different. The station's cost to produce and distribute an additional "use" of the signal is zero. There is no point of diminishing returns within the signal area.

- Partly because of the technological barriers to charging per program, broadcast news is almost exclusively funded by advertisers. The consumer pays no direct costs for a newscast after buying the TV set. Printed news often costs a subscription or per-copy fee.

Influences That Are Predominately Legal or Regulatory

CASE STUDY: LEGAL/REGULATORY INFLUENCE

The rumor had been circulating for weeks that the local newspaper was investigating charges that the mayor had mishandled public money and frequented a prostitute. At KMID, a station in a mid-sized western metropolitan area, two reporters occasionally worked on the story. Finally, the newspaper broke the story. Sources claimed the mayor was guilty of an extramarital affair and selling influence. That evening, on its 11 o'clock newscast, KMID became the first TV station to air the charges. But rather than provide the results of its own investigation, the KMID reporter, broadcasting live from in front of the newspaper building and waving a copy of the paper in his hand, was careful to attribute every charge to the newspaper. In effect, he read the story to viewers.

The incident embarrassed some KMID reporters because it seemed so timid. "Our peer group just laughed at us," said one reporter. KMID management is "just afraid of being sued," said another. "We had to wait till the paper came out for fear of libel. [The reporter] actually held the paper in front of the camera. We weren't saying it, the [newspaper] was saying it." Although the news director said the newspaper "had little more than we had," he defended the station's caution. "We have a license to protect. Print media don't." Reminded that libel laws don't apply differently to televised and printed news, the news director responded that the mere fact of licensure, "makes us very determined that before we break anything on the air, we have all our bases covered. We didn't have signed affidavits of witnesses saying, 'we saw it.' "[16]

Some months later a reporter at KMID learned that a rival station was about to air its investigation of another rumor: that a federal office complex employing about 5,000 persons was rife with drug use. Working over the weekend before the rival broadcast was to air, the reporter went door-to-door in an apartment complex near the federal agency's office buildings. He found one woman who said she was an employee of the agency and had witnessed drug use. The woman said 20 of the 30 employees in her unit drank alcohol and used illegal drugs in the parking lot, returning to work high. The reporter did not know the woman's name or position, nor did he confirm her employment, nor learn which unit employed her. She signed no affidavit saying she saw these activities. Although she was the only source and supervisors for the agency categorically denied the charges and the parking lot where the drug use was reported was fenced and patrolled by guards, KMID ran the story the day after it was gathered, getting a jump on the competing station, whose series on drug use in the agency was to air later that same evening.

Why would a station refrain from original reporting of charges that a mayor had acted improperly and several months later rush out an unconfirmed report saying, in the words of the source, "if the [agency] screened all of their workers for drugs . . . they wouldn't have any workers?" One answer might be that the management decided on a harder investigative edge sometime after the first story ran. But there had been no other investigations, and according to reporters and producers, no change in policy. Further, a more investigative orientation would presumably have resulted in further sleuthing to confirm the allegations of the drug story's single unnamed—and virtually unknown—source. Laws and regulations governing broadcast journalism did not change between the two stories. The newsroom was not left unsupervised when the second story aired. Nor did an investigative reporter join the staff. In fact, the reporter who broke the drug story also was one of those investigating the mayor.

It is difficult to know why the two stories were handled in such opposite fashion. Both contained substantive information about the integrity of persons performing important public functions. A key difference between the two stories, however, is that the potential for a libel suit exists when an individual, such as the mayor, is named and defamed. Because libel requires that *individuals* be identified in some way, the drug story was safe. Saying that "some" unnamed members of a large group are acting illegally may not sufficiently identify them, under state law, for a libel claim to succeed.[17]

PRIMARY LEGAL/REGULATORY INFLUENCES

Although the First Amendment forbids Congress from making any law abridging the freedom of printers to publish whatever they wish, the Supreme Court has never interpreted those words as a grant of absolute freedom. Journalists can still get into trouble with the law when they spread falsehoods that damage an individual's reputation, for example, or harm the nation's security by giving away government secrets. Although there are a variety of laws affecting the gathering and content of news, broadcasters are most affected by two. The first is libel, a set of laws designed to balance protection for a person's good name with the journalist's freedom to report critically on society. Despite the news director's comments above, libel laws bind both print and broadcast news similarly.[18] The second law applies to broadcasters only. It's the Federal Communications Act and it includes a set of regulations several of which influence content either directly or indirectly.

Libel. The most common reason for a media firm to be called before a court is to defend against a charge of libel.[19] Laws vary by state, but generally speaking media firms, print or broadcast, may be found at fault and punished for disseminating false information that hurts a living, identi-fiable individual's or corporation's good name.[20] The key words are "at fault." A news department may be found at fault if it cannot prove that whatever defamatory information it reports about someone is true, or that the damaging information came from a protected arena, such as a court room, certain public documents, or legislative meeting of a body such as a city council or state assembly. There is one exception. If the individual identified is a *public figure*—any politician, or government official, or a private person who seeks public attention—a news department may be wrong as long as it cannot be proved to have been reckless in its reporting (failed to follow accepted standards of care with facts) or to have known it was spreading lies. Because the mayor was a public figure, KMID was in little danger of libel if its reporting on the mayor followed journalistic standards of care.

The law attempts to balance the competing rights of individual reputation and free press. By most accounts it has led news departments to be more accurate when an individual's good name is at stake. But because legal advice has become so expensive, there is a disincentive for a news depart-ment to entertain even the possibility of a suit. An investigative report that alleges individual wrong-doing requires at minimum that a lawyer be re-tained to review the story before broadcast. And it may require a court defense that would be costly even if the station won. As a result, cost-conscious newsrooms may become not careful but timid, surrendering the important journalistic role of keeping watch on government, the very role the First Amendment was designed to protect.[21]

Federal Communications Commission. In addition to libel laws, television stations—newsrooms included—must conform to regulations adopted by the Federal Communications Commission, from which print media are exempt. The justification for regulating broadcast news despite the First Amend-ment's ban is based on a technological difference. Although any number of printers can publish without interfering with each other, there are a limited number of broadcast frequencies that can be clearly received with inexpen-sive tuners. The scarcity of airwave channels prompted government to allocate this common resource "in the public interest, necessity and conven-ience."[22] The sharpest teeth in FCC regulations lie in the Commission's power to refuse a license to a nonconforming broadcaster. This enforcement power has seldom been used because the guaranteed right to a clear channel is so valuable that stations are reluctant to risk even a semblance of noncom-pliance.[23]

If broadcasters must act in *the public interest* to gain or renew a license, how is it defined? In his classic analysis of network news, Epstein found three basic assumptions underlying this concept in FCC and court decisions from 1934-1970:

1. In the words of the FCC, the "basic purpose" of broadcasting is "the development of an informed public opinion through the public dissemination of news and ideas concerning the vital public issues of the day." The Commission elaborated: "The foundation stone of the American system of broadcasting . . . is the right of the public to be informed, rather than any right on the part of the government, any broadcast licensees or any individual members of the public to broadcast his [or her] own particular views on any matter."[24]

2. It is absolutely "essential to the welfare of the public" for news and ideas to come from "diverse and antagonistic sources."[25] The Commission embraced the Libertarian notion advanced by Thomas Jefferson and John Stuart Mill of a "marketplace of ideas" from which truth would emerge. A corollary of this reasoning was that there should be competition among stations as well as competition among sources broadcast from a particular station.

3. On the assumption that local needs require local solutions, the Commission has consistently attempted to impart a local nature to broadcasting. The FCC's precursor, the Federal Radio Commission, said in 1928, "a broadcasting station may be regarded as a sort of mouthpiece on the air for the community it serves, over which its public events of general interest, its political campaigns, its election results, its athletic contests, its orchestras and artists, and discussion of public issues may be broadcast." Therefore, stations must undertake "a diligent, positive and continuing effort . . . to discover and fulfill the tastes, needs and desires" of the locality served.[26]

Broadcasters, including many newscasters, chafed at some of the regulations put in place to realize these fundamental goals. They argued for the same freedoms of their colleagues in print.[27] Industry lobbying of Congress began to bear fruit when Richard Nixon was in the White House. According to attorney Victor Ferrall:

> A process of regulatory pruning, variously styled "reregulation," "unregulation," and "deregulation," was begun by the FCC during the Nixon years and continued under Presidents Ford and Carter. The essential underpinnings of regulation, however—that free broadcasting, particularly local broadcasting, is vital to the public interest, that station licensees are public trustees of the publicly-owned airwaves, and that continued realization of a broadcasting service responsive to public needs requires continuing federal government scrutiny—were not challenged.[28]

This underlying assumption was to change beginning in 1981 with President Ronald Reagan's appointment of Mark Fowler as FCC chairman. Fowler's solution to critics of television was simple: Businessmen operating in an open market can serve the public better than government regulators. Midway through his tenure, Fowler explained:

> If we let the industries operate with fidelity to the markets they want to serve, the public is better off. And even if the improvements aren't all that great, the old system of heavy-handed FCC regulation hadn't led to a sense of public satisfaction. If complex regulations still had begot the vast wasteland, maybe a new approach was needed to make the desert bloom.[29]

Under Fowler, the Commission:

- Eliminated the practical limit of 16 minutes per hour of advertising.
- Eliminated the working requirement that 5% of a station's broadcast week be devoted to news and public affairs programs, and at least 10% to news and other nonentertaining programming.
- Dropped the requirement to "ascertain" the most important issues and problems by periodically surveying the community.[30]

In 1987, shortly after Fowler's departure, the Commission suspended application of the Fairness Doctrine to news. The Doctrine, established in 1949, required broadcasters to cover controversial issues and present contrasting viewpoints.[31]

With the abolition of requirements for set amounts of news and public affairs programming, and the repeal of the Fairness Doctrine in news programming, broadcast newsrooms found themselves closer to the First Amendment freedoms of newspapers than they had ever been.[32] Implicit in government licensing, however, remained the threat of government control.[33]

Changes in government regulation of one industry can also impact news production in another. A 1991 federal court interpretation of FCC regulations permitted entry of regional Bell telephone companies into the business of originating content.[34] As high-capacity fiber optic cable begins to replace the low bandwidth copper wires of conventional phones and data compression techniques squeeze more information through existing wires, video and text on screen news and ads may be produced by telephone companies or their business partners. Increased competition for advertising and attention to news could have profound impacts on local television news and perhaps even more on newspapers.[35]

How this competition among media firms for necessary resources impacts news production is the subject of the next chapter.

Notes

1. Epstein, 1973.

2. For an excellent review of such influences and the limitation of the notion of objectivity for journalists, see Hackett, 1984.

3. All but one study of the values of U.S. journalists have concluded that journalists are not very different from the mainstream of American thought. The exception is the survey conducted by S. Robert Lichter, Stanley Rothman, and Linda Lichter in the early 1980s and published, among other places, in *The Media Elite* (Lichter et al., 1986). It examined the views of 140 journalists and news executives at CBS, NBC, and ABC only. The survey, which alleged that elite journalists were dangerously liberal, has been refuted as misleading by Herbert Gans (1985). Other surveys, both of network and local journalists, have shown a center-liberal political orientation as typical. See for example Epstein, 1973; Gans, 1979; Robinson & Sheehan, 1983; Sigal, 1973; Roshcoe, 1975; Tuchman, 1978; Weaver & Wilhoit, 1986, 1992. In many of these surveys, journalists also report that the more conservative views of news executives and other forces on news production make their personal views largely irrelevant.

4. Williams, 1963.

5. See, for example, Niemi, Mueller, & Smith, 1989.

6. McClosky & Zaller, 1984.

7. Epstein, 1973; Gans, 1979, 1985; Lichter, Rothman, & Lichter, 1982; Weaver & Wilhoit, 1986, 1992.

8. Weaver & Wilhoit, 1992, pp. 6-7.

9. Gans, 1985; Reese, 1990.

10. You might think part of the driving time was spent discussing, outlining, or conceptualizing the story, so some part of the hours in the KLRG truck were productive. This wasn't the case, however. In fact, during the entire study, on only one occasion did I observe a reporter working on a story during travel. At KMID, a reporter on deadline wrote a story script in the car. Perhaps because of the constant presence of photographers, who rarely seemed interested in the stories covered, reporters routinely turned on the radio, talked shop with the cameraperson, or asked me questions. Only one reporter I interviewed among the scores of TV journalists contributing to the study said she routinely used travel time to build stories.

11. The logic here follows Bantz, McCorkle, & Baade, 1980.

12. Compaine, 1980.

13. Gunter, 1987.

14. Krugman, 1965.

15. "Nearly Half in U.S. Can't Read Well," 1993.

16. It's not uncommon for news directors to have an exaggerated sense of FCC oversight, according to one study, Busby, 1979.

17. Pickerell, 1988.

18. Shapiro, 1988.

19. Franklin, 1982.

20. Shapiro, 1988.

21. Massing, 1985.

22. Pool, 1984.

23. Ferrall, 1989.

24. FCC, "Editorializing by Broadcast Licensees," Docket No. 8516, June 1, 1949, p. 4., cited in Epstein, 1973, p. 48.

25. *Associated Press v. U.S.*, 326 US1, p. 20, cited in Epstein, 1973, p. 48.

26. *Network Broadcasting,* p. 124; FCC, "Report and Statement of Policy re Commission En Banc Programming Requirements," FCC 60-970, Mimeo., 91874 (July 29, 1960), Exhibit 7, p. 13, in Epstein, 1973, p. 49.

27. Epstein, 1973.

28. Ferrall, 1989, p. 15.

29. Fowler, cited in Ferrall, 1989, p. 19.

30. Ferrall, 1989.

31. Epstein, 1973, p. 63.

32. But contrary to their argument that the Fairness Doctrine inhibited coverage of controversial issues, broadcasters aired no more controversy after the Doctrine was suspended than they did before. In fact, they may have aired less (Aufderheide, 1990).

33. Pool, 1983.

34. Andrews, 1991.

35. See, for example, *Media at the Millennium,* a report of the First Fellows Symposium on the Future of Media and Media Studies, New York: The Freedom Forum Media Studies Center.

4

Finding the Logic of Commercial
News Production

This chapter examines how competition within the four markets surrounding the media firm shapes the news.

Case Study: What's Going On Here?

The story originated with the assistant news director at KVLG, which boasts one of the nation's largest local television news staffs, asking his Washington, D.C., bureau for a story about how the Reagan Administration planned to educate the public about AIDS. For weeks, the Washington correspondents were promised that federal officials were completing such a plan. The administration had released a set of general guidelines the day before that were reported in the morning newspapers. The assistant news director told the assignment editor to have the station's health reporter compare federal and local guidelines.

The health reporter, a prize-winning veteran who specialized in AIDS reporting, rolled her eyes at the assignment. "I'm confused over what I'm supposed to do," she told the assignment editor. Even if the story were confined to what schools would teach about AIDS and ignore what health departments might do to inform the general public, the proposed comparison would require phone calls to a score or more of school districts just to poll the largest school systems in the metropolitan area. "I'm going to get so much information, there's no way I can tell it in a minute-thirty [seconds]."

She proposed an alternate story. She knew that the department of public health in the signal area's central city was meeting that day to approve new AIDS education guidelines for public schools. So she offered to match those regulations with the federal ones. The assignment editor quickly agreed and promised to forward whatever details the Washington bureau might learn about the new guidelines.

Before the board of health meeting the reporter asked the board's public information officer about the new guidelines. He encouraged the story, telling her the new guidelines "could be controversial." "This is pretty interesting," she agreed, leafing through the regulations. "I can see parents getting upset."

Rather than attend the meeting, she set up brief interviews with two officials and "to illustrate the story" arranged to visit the classroom of a high school teacher who had previously gained media attention for his frank sex education classes. She conceded that meetings turn up valuable information and establish rapport with officials. But meetings aren't visual, she explained, and they provide too much information for a 90-second story. "It's so boring to go to a meeting," she said. "All I need from a meeting is the results." The reporter and photographer spent much of the afternoon at the high school, returning to the meeting only for an image, a slow camera pan of the board members.

Meanwhile back at the station, the assignment editor had little luck getting elaboration from federal officials about their new regulations. The Washington bureau had obtained only generalities: The new regulations bowed to local standards and insisted that any program "should encourage responsible sexual behavior—based on fidelity, commitment, and maturity, placing sexuality within the context of marriage." The feds were so vague and unforthcoming, the comparison of local and national standards was dropped.

The resulting story began with this lead-in from the anchor: "[City] public health officials today released their guidelines on how to handle AIDS among teenagers." The reporter, however, listed but one guideline, the one she found most provocative: "start sex education early." To illustrate, the story jumped to video from the high school classroom. The class had nothing to do with the new guidelines, however. Filled with 10th graders, it came late, not early, in public education, and it was not specifically about sex education or AIDS, but "family life," and it conformed not to new guidelines, but to the old.

The camera caught humorous video of students wrapping diapers around sacks of sugar and "feeding" the sacks with baby bottles. The reporter interrupted the class as students were coloring birth certificates and asked the teacher how he could attempt to instill morality while urging students to use condoms. She included video of part of his explanation: "I tell them not to have intercourse without a condom. Even if it's embarrassing . . . especially for girls to carry condoms."

The story jumped to a shot of the health commission meeting as a transition back to the new AIDS guidelines. Her script then implied that

AIDS education would begin in kindergarten. An official quoted in the ensuing sound bite, however, said only that kindergartners would be taught about hand-washing and germ theory. (Her story omitted the fact that discussion of sexually transmitted diseases would begin in the sixth grade, just where it began under the old guidelines.) The story concluded with the reporter delivering an apparent non sequitur: Teenagers' fear of AIDS makes it hard to teach them to avoid it.

If the central purpose of journalism is to help the public understand its environment, it's fair to ask what the public may have learned from this story. On the plus side, the topic, fighting AIDS with early education, commands enormous significance. And the story was told in a lively way, illustrated throughout with interesting video. More specifically, viewers were alerted to the presence of new guidelines about AIDS education and the content of one: As early as kindergarten, students would be taught about hand-washing and germs. On the down side, beyond that single guideline—which had no direct connection to AIDS—nothing else in the story pertained to the apparent topic. The content aroused more than it informed. Viewers saw amusing video of sugar sack "babies"; were confronted with the shocking—and false—idea of kindergartners learning to avoid AIDS; and with the disturbing prospect that teens' fear of AIDS might impede sex education.

To find the logic of such newsmaking, look again at the middle part of the model of commercial news production developed in Chapter 2 (see Figure 4.1).

The model shows that most modern commercial media firms must simultaneously compete in four different markets.[1] Each market has its unique set of exchange partners. And in no two are the same things traded. Because the media firm must compete successfully in every one of the four markets, each has some influence over the news product. Before analyzing the example, let's explore the theory embedded in our model. It should help us assess the influence of these trading partners on the interplay of journalism and market (business) norms within the newsroom.

Market Logic and the Public Good

Journalists, both print and broadcast, don't like to talk about news as a commodity subject to market forces. From reporters to executives, they prefer the language of public service. As the assignment editor at one of the stations participating in the study explained: "The rules of journalism are the rules of public service." But at least since the days of the "Penny Press," about 150 years ago, most news production in the United States has been a business and news therefore a commodity—something bought and sold. To say this doesn't mean that commodities are bad or that news is only a

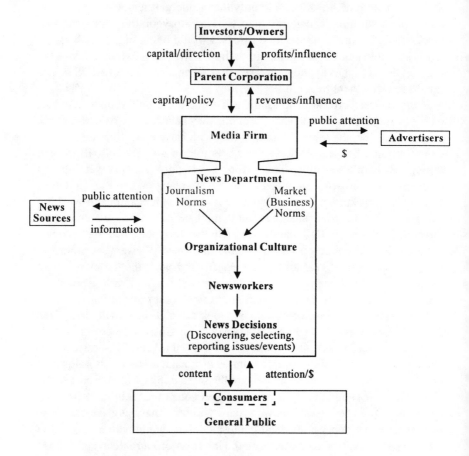

Figure 4.1. News as a Four-Way Commodity

commodity. By definition, commodities are what economists call "goods," products or services people are willing to give up something to have.

HOW NEWS IS BOUGHT AND SOLD

The first step in understanding the logic of news production is learning just what kind of commodity news is. Most commodities are simpler. If you buy a car, house, or shoes, you fork over the money directly. For news production it's more complicated. Advertisers contribute 70%-90% of the gross revenues of newspapers and almost all income networks or stations derive from news programming.[2] As Figure 4.1 indicates, news consumers trade their attention—and in most newspapers, a small per-copy fee—to media firms for information. The firms then sell that attention to advertisers.[3] Though intangible, consumer attention is extremely valuable. Advertisers spend well in excess of $100 billion per year in the United States to capture it.[4]

The complexity of how news is bought and sold has implications for journalism. Let's take the case of televised news first. Broadcast news is what economists call a "public good."[5] One person's consumption of the product doesn't diminish the supply available for others. So it costs no more to reach all the viewers in a station's signal area than to reach some. Adding viewers who possess the characteristics advertisers value increases the station's revenues. The result is an economic pressure to attract as many as possible.

Newspapers don't differ greatly. Although they are not public goods like television, they do enjoy substantial economies of scale.[6] After the publisher has paid for the reporting and photography in the first paper off the press, printing additional copies generates the same revenue per paper but costs are limited to paper, ink, and distribution. Such economies also generate pressures for mass audiences.

For both newspapers and television, having advertising rather than consumers as the primary source of income means that the way to increase profits is to produce a product that has a minimal threshold appeal to the maximum number of demographically desirable consumers in the signal or circulation area. Because consumers pay little or nothing directly for the news, it would be inefficient to produce content that attracted a smaller number of more interested consumers. The economics of newspapers and television favor breadth of appeal over depth.

An illustration may help. Suppose a television station committed the money to hire a large staff of excellent journalists and produced a premium quality product—a "Mercedes" of a newscast that met the highest standards of journalism. Because the station can't charge each viewer for the premium product, it must turn to advertisers. But as former newspaper advertising executive Leo Bogart pointed out: "Advertisers have no functional concern with the meaning or consequences of mass communication except insofar as it provides a mechanism for the delivery of their messages to prospective customers."[7] If the premium newscast drew no more prospective customers to its ads than a run-of-the-mill newscast, the station would not earn as great a profit as it might have with a less expensive production. Further, if the premium newcast were like the journalistically acclaimed *The MacNeil/Lehrer News Hour*, it might attract a smaller audience than competitors.[8] The loyalty of that small viewership and the esteem with which journalists held the station might be admirable, but not bankable.

Contrast the above scenario with a commodity, say a real Mercedes, that is purchased directly. In the case of commodities unsubsidized by third parties, those who value a premium product pay a premium price. Building a Mercedes may cost the factory more than producing a Ford, but the extra cost is recouped in the sale price. In television, and only to a slightly lesser degree in newspapers, advertising's "subsidy" makes a definition of quality based on popularity more profitable than one based on less widely shared professional or craft standards.

CONDITIONS FOR SOCIALLY BENEFICIAL EXCHANGE

There are other news-shaping elements of the exchanges media firms conduct with consumers, sources, advertisers, and investors. To see them clearly, it's useful to review the concept of exchange in microeconomic theory. The idea of free enterprise as developed by Adam Smith and generations of his followers is that society gains wealth not by persons or businesses working for the common good, but by each working for its own self-interest.[9] If certain conditions are met, the resulting competition should raise the quality of goods and services while it lowers costs to consumers. So both parties should benefit. Indeed the whole society should benefit unless the exchange harms third parties. If the underlying conditions are not met, however, self-interest may lead to conflict, with one side taking advantage of the other. This is because every exchange has an adversarial, as well as cooperative, side. *Caveat Emptor*, economists say. "Let the buyer beware," because each side is trying to get the maximum return for the minimum investment.[10]

Four conditions must be met to set the "invisible hand" of social benefit in motion:[11]

1. that both parties to the transaction act rationally to pursue their self-interest;
2. that both parties are knowledgeable about both the product's quality and the market;
3. that the market offers competition; and
4. that negative externalities—costs to society that are generated by the transaction—are absent.

The more numerous and serious the deviations from these four conditions, the greater the likelihood that one party will victimize the other or harm society as a whole.

THE TRANSACTION BETWEEN
THE NEWS DEPARTMENT AND CONSUMERS

How well are these conditions met in the transaction between consumer and news department? Let's examine them one at a time.

Rational Pursuit of Self-Interest

Classical economists simply assume that individuals—be they persons or corporations—are self-interested rational agents.[12] Although the failure of individuals and corporations to make wise choices calls this assumption into question generally, rationality seems somewhat more reachable for organizations than individuals. As organizational sociologist Richard Scott noted: "It is impossible for the behavior of a single, isolated individual to reach any high degree of rationality. The number of alternatives he [or she] must explore is too great."[13] The best that individuals can hope for, according to sociologists James March and Herbert Simon, is "bounded rationality"— logically intended selection among a number of choices constrained by the individual's limited experience and resources.[14] But even "bounded rationality" now seems an overly optimistic estimate of the ability of a consumer to pursue his or her self-interest. If individuals are rational, they ought to be logical. But Amos Tversky and Daniel Kahneman have demonstrated that most individuals are only quasi-logical. They habitually commit reasoning errors, such as generalizing from a small, unrepresentative sample to an entire population.[15]

Among the scarcest resources for individual news consumers is time. For most, scouting out prices and quality of a good or service is restricted to their leisure time. For corporations, on the other hand, analyzing consumer preferences and market conditions is somebody's job, or the task of an entire department. At a minimum, media firms possess greater potential for rationally pursuing self-interest: They command greater resources for learning about consumers than individual consumers possess for learning about them or their news products.

The idea that consumers act rationally in their self-interest also implies that they assign *their own* values to goods and services rather than uncritically accepting the values of others. Professors Robert Entman and Steven Wildman argue that for most consumers this simply isn't realistic:

> The market school too often fails to recognize that the desires individuals bring to the market may be the products of choices the market already offers, and of the impacts of communities of taste, peer groups, and other external forces—that is, it ignores the impact of culture and socialization on preference formation.[16]

The first of these "other forces" is likely to be the industry's advertisements for itself. Networks, television stations, and newspapers continually promote the quality of their news products.

In sum, the assumption that media firms and consumers are rational agents seeking their own self-interest is problematic for both parties, but more so for the individual than for the corporation. There is a fundamental inequality in the available resources for recognizing and analyzing self-interest that firms bring to the exchange with the individual.

In fairness, the assumption of the classical economists originated in the late 18th century, long before mass advertising and market research and corporate giantism, even before brand names.[17] While appropriate for a time of farmers and peddlers selling their wares from wagons in the village square, the assumption today is faulty and promotes the corporate interest at the expense of the consumer. But this imbalance of power, while important, is probably no greater for news than for any other commodity an individual buys from a corporation without consumer assistance. The larger difference between consuming news and other market commodities is determining its quality, the next condition to be examined.

Evaluating the Market and the Quality of the Commodity

Consumers are likely to have adequate knowledge of the presence of news providers in their community; most media firms advertise themselves. Consumer knowledge of the quality of news products, however, is a very different matter. If news departments follow journalistic codes of ethics, they pledge themselves to deliver accurate, fair accounts of significant current issues and events in a context that gives them meaning. The condition of informed purchase, therefore, requires assessment of at least three qualities of a newspaper or newscast: (1) that the accounts presented be accurate and fair to all sides; (2) that those events and issues the community ought to know about are chronicled; and (3) that enough context be reported to permit widespread comprehension.[18]

Consumers may be able to evaluate whether a news account has sufficient context to render it meaningful. But they are unlikely to be able to satisfy either Criterion 1 or 2.

Are news stories accurate and fair? By definition, news is what the public *doesn't yet know*. Consumers are rarely in a position to compare even a single news account with their own experience or the experience of a trusted third party. So consumers rarely can determine the fairness or accuracy of that account, much less the contents of an entire newspaper or newscast. This remains true even though many consumers are familiar with recurring themes of news,[19] familiar with narrative strategies of telling news, and can supply background knowledge necessary to understand allusions and processes on their own.[20] You may expect news of city council actions, anticipate how the story will be reported, understand the process of municipal legislative action, and still have to accept on faith the media's coverage of what the council did last night.

The second criterion—assessing whether a newspaper or newscast has reported most of the day's pressing issues and events—lies just as far beyond the reach of the individual reader or viewer as the first. No master list of consequential events and issues occurring in a community exists against which one can measure the performance of local news departments. Even with great resources, such a list would be very difficult to compile because powerful actors might fail to report or actively hide actions likely to damage the public welfare.[21] You could monitor all of a metro area's news departments. But not only would this be extremely burdensome—and require videotaping simultaneous newscasts—you would still fail to learn of those events beyond the reach of the routines of local news departments.

Economists recognize three categories into which commodities may fall:[22]

1. *Search* or *inspection goods* are those whose quality is evident merely from examining them. You might, for example, kick the tires of a car and check the compression of the engine's cylinders;

2. *Experience goods* are those whose quality can be assessed only after using them for a period of time. For example, you might not be able to judge the quality of food at a restaurant by looking at the menu, but eating there once or twice would provide evidence for an opinion.

3. *Credence goods* are products that must be consumed on faith. In such cases it is difficult for the consumer to assess the quality of the product even after having experienced it. Economists Michael Darby and Edi Karni place medical treatment, and auto and other appliance repairs as examples of credence goods. If the consumer brings in an improperly functioning television set and receives back a working set with an expensive new picture tube, how is she or he to know whether a less expensive part or adjustment might have corrected the problem? The cost of discovering the quality of the repair or treatment is prohibitive for the consumer.[23]

These three distinctions are useful to economists because the adversarial nature of exchange suggests sellers may take advantage of buyers when buyers are unable to distinguish high- from low-quality goods.

So what kind of good is news? Unless you or someone you trust witnessed the news event, or one that should have been publicized but wasn't, news is not an inspection good. Some news is an experience good. If there is a prediction of rain, or an agenda of a meeting, or notice of a road closing, consumers can check the report against their experience.

Consumers also can compare one news department's story against another's.[24] But consider what would be required to gain some evidence for accuracy. First, two or more news departments would have to cover the story. Second, the consumer would have to monitor all local news departments to record the multiple accounts. Third, those accounts would have to agree in essential details. As Professors Kurt and Gladys Lang demonstrated almost 40 years ago, independent accounts of the same event—in this case a parade—may show considerable variance even if observers strive to be accurate and impartial.[25]

But even if several accounts of the same event were similar, consumers could still be misled. Often multiple news media uncritically report the same false or misleading description of an event from a self-interested source. Public relations firms, such as Hill and Knowlton, for example, have netted whole schools of reporters in deceptions such as the fabricated descriptions of Iraqi atrocities in a Kuwaiti hospital staged to influence the congressional debate about whether the United States should launch the Persian Gulf War of 1991.[26] More recently conservative activist Clint Bolick of the Institute for Justice wrote an op-ed article for the *Wall Street Journal*. In it he claimed to find evidence of "pro-quota," left-wing extremism in the writings of Lani Guinier, President Clinton's choice for head of the Civil Rights Division of the Justice Department. Although Bolick grossly distorted Guinier's scholarship, national media including *The Washington Post, Newsweek, Los Angeles Times, U.S. News and World Report,* and others relied more on Bolick than on digging through the legal research articles for themselves. Partly as a consequence, Guinier's nomination was withdrawn in a firestorm of public indignation.[27]

Much, if not most, of the news is neither an inspection nor an experience good. It's a credence good. Either we never learn whether the newspaper or newscast was accurate, fair, and complete, or we must wait, perhaps until historians can document what really happened.

At the national level, instances of important news that was misrepresented or went unreported until after key decision points had passed are numerous: Senator Joseph McCarthy's charges of communist infiltration of the government in the 1950s; President John Kennedy's description of U.S. non-involvement in the 1961 invasion of Cuba; Richard Nixon's denial of a Watergate coverup during the 1972 presidential campaign; Ronald Reagan's repeated assertions that the United States had not traded arms to Iran for hostages;[28] the nature of U.S. involvement in El Salvador, in Nicaragua, in Chile, in Iran, in Guatemala, and in other countries was unknown to most of the public until after decisions affecting millions of lives and billions of dollars were made.[29] And these are just cases where deception has come to light. Many more may remain concealed.

News at the local level may be even more suspect. Compared to the national press corps, there are normally fewer and less accomplished journalists covering a particular "beat," or topic area, in a given metropolitan area. The accuracy and fairness of much of local reporting—and the existence of what's missed or hidden—may be even less likely to be established.

When the quality of a commodity is particularly difficult to determine, consumers can sometimes rely on brand names, that is, the reputation of commodity providers.[30] But what evidence might there be for the reputation of a particular media firm? Consumer groups rate cars, computers, stereos, and toasters, but not news. Journalism prizes? Most are given for individual stories or perhaps a series, rather than for consistent quality. Further, prizes are awarded by groups of widely varying journalistic expertise, and with the exception of Pulitzers (which are only awarded to newspapers), they are not prominently reported. Journalism schools? News researchers rarely name the firms they study and their object is usually theory development rather than consumer reporting. In fact, a rigorous operational definition of *news quality* has yet to be developed. Academics, such as those on the Hutchins Commission, have gone no further than a broad definition of quality journalism.[31]

Even though all news products are difficult for consumers to judge for quality, broadcast news is particularly difficult. A first reason is obvious. On most stations news stories are quite brief, averaging fewer than 90 seconds, and followed quickly by other stories or advertisements.[32] Unless recorded, the pace makes evaluation extraordinarily taxing. A second reason is more complex. It has to do with the nature of truth claims made with images rather than words.

Images carry the appearance of reality. Yet, as anyone who has ever shot home video or edited videotape knows, the camera is a malleable witness. What viewers see is only that small part of the action immediately in front of the camera, and then only that part of all the videotape recorded that the editor selects to include in the finished product. In the case of news, the 5 to 20 minutes of videotape rolled on a typical story is compressed to fewer than 90 seconds. Camera angles and distance from the subjects can also change the appearance of the "reality" photographed.

An example may help illustrate. At KVLG, the station in the very large metropolitan area, an experienced reporter and photographer were covering the collision of an automobile and a school minivan carrying handicapped (autistic) children. When the pair arrived on the scene, the images were dramatic. The badly frightened and mostly nonverbal children were being placed on stretchers for medical examination. There was much screaming and the bewildered and wild-eyed children were squirming enough that some

had to be taped down to the gurneys. The photographer made his way among
the youngsters, panning slowly over their faces and bodies, as if the camera
were a geiger counter. Amid flashing ambulance lights and piercing sirens,
the children were whisked to a local hospital. The children had been wearing
safety belts, however, and none was seriously hurt.

After visiting the hospital, the reporter sighed: "It's your basic minor bus
accident." The photographer immediately rejoined, "Until we show the kids
on the gurneys screaming." During the drive back to the station the reporter
and photographer discussed the ethics of making a story of a "minor bus
accident." They agreed that the ethical decision would be to kill the story.
The images, the reporter said, overstated the seriousness of what happened.

Despite his qualms, the reporter began the story with video and sound of
the wailing children on stretchers. Over their cries, he launched his narrative:

"They lay on stretchers.

"Or taped to gurneys.

"Or stared blankly into space.

"Thirteen children on a school bus that never finished its morning pick-up."

Viewers learned that none of the children were seriously injured only near
the end of the story. The producer found the account so compelling she
placed it near the top of the opening segment of the newscast. Nothing in the
story was untrue, but the suggestion of reality created by the emotionally
charged images the reporter selected distorted the event to the point where
even the reporter and photographer conceded that it was unethical journalism. What viewers saw looked like news, but it was a hollow manipulation
of sound and images that the reporter and photographer both realized was
not newsworthy. The technique of manipulating images to make false claims
about reality takes advantage of public faith that "seeing is believing." While
such faith may be well founded when the viewers are at the scene, it leaves
television viewers open to exploitation.[33]

Sociologist Neil Postman has argued that TV has changed the nature of
truth-telling. We are accustomed to refuting illogical arguments made ver-
bally or in print, he contended. But most of us don't even recognize arguments made with images. The example he provided is specifically directed
toward advertising, but it could also be applied to news:

Today, on television commercials, propositions are as scarce as unattractive
people. The truth or falsity of an advertiser's claim is simply not an issue. A
McDonald's commercial, for example, is not a series of testable, logically
ordered assertions. It is a drama—a mythology, if you will—of handsome
people selling, buying and eating hamburgers, and being driven to near ecstasy
by their good fortune. No claims are made, except those the viewer projects
onto or infers from the drama. One can like or dislike a television commercial,
of course. But one cannot refute it.[34]

About the best an individual consumer can manage in terms of news evaluation is to monitor several local media; develop alternative information sources through membership in community or trade organizations that report/discuss current events; attend government meetings such as school boards, planning commissions, and city and county councils; correspond with state legislators and agencies; and maintain a healthy skepticism. Unfortunately, only a small proportion of consumers have jobs or resources—principally time—that permit such community surveillance.

The Presence of Competition

At first glance, this condition of cooperative exchange appears to be met. If consumers are willing to use several media, they enjoy a choice among news providers. Due to the expansion over the past 30 years of local television news, every major metropolitan area boasts competing newsrooms.[35] Where local daily newspapers once competed, now a single daily, three or more television stations, and one or more weekly papers vie for consumers' attention.[36] At the national level, news consumers enjoy unprecedented choice. They can now subscribe to national newspapers such as *USA Today* and national editions of *The New York Times* and the *Wall Street Journal,* or a weekly edition of *The Washington Post.* Cable subscribers can now access CNN and C-SPAN. An increasing number of public radio stations broadcast National Public Radio newscasts such as *All Things Considered,* and *Morning Edition.*

But a closer look indicates that as you go from the national to the level with the greatest impact on consumers' daily lives—the local municipality, school district, police, and planning jurisdictions—competition declines precipitously. Ben Bagdikian asserted:

> In 1920 there were 2,722 urban places and 2,400 daily papers [in the U.S.]. By 1980 there were 8,765 urban places and only 1,745 dailies. Today more than 7,000 American cities have no daily paper of their own.[37]

Bagdikian's analysis downplays locally zoned reporting in metropolitan newspapers, ignores local television news, and predates the expansion of weekly papers. But the media firms he neglects are still not numerous enough to provide head-to-head competition in many localities. Another reason why community-level competition may be scarce is something called an "umbrella" pattern of competition: Metropolitan newspapers and television stations may cover regional issues or the city at the center of their circulation or signal, but rarely compete with smaller dailies and weeklies for news of the smaller political jurisdictions.[38] Recently, researchers Clarice Olien, Phillip Tichenor, and George Donohue documented a trend away from covering nonmetropolitan areas at all.[39]

When there are a few major competitors operating in a market and the costs of entering the competition—opening or buying a newspaper or television station, or perhaps establishing a news department within a station—are high, economists classify the competition as an oligopoly.

In order to maximize profits, oligopolistic competitors tend to act cooperatively—monitoring and following each other's pricing and product standards.[40] A firm that greatly changes its product takes serious risks in this type of competition, often with little reward. If unpopular with buyers, the change hazards the substantial share of the market the firm now holds with its few competitors. And if the change gains market share, it is likely to be copied by competing firms, providing only temporary advantage. Competition pushes oligopolistic firms to copy each other as they seek to please the majority of the customers in the market. This central tendency seems especially strong in mass media with their inherent economies of scale and advertiser-based funding.[41]

Particularly in local television newsrooms—where competition is the most direct and thus fierce—what other news departments are doing strongly influences news production. Above all, departments seek not to get "beaten" or "scooped"—when a competing news department airs or publishes a major story first. Newsroom ethnographer Matthew Ehrlich wrote: "TV newsworkers and organizations love to get 'scoops' or 'exclusives,' but an even more important goal is to make sure they get the major stories that their opposition gets."[42] The result is a "pack" mentality among reporters.

Ehrlich and others[43] found that this competitive mentality leads to careful monitoring of each other's newscasts and an assessment of quality coverage based not on the standards of journalism—which would require an independent assessment of what the community needed to know—but on an attempt first to remove any reason to watch another newscast and second provide some "exclusive" reason for watching one station. Winning or losing this competition is measured by audience ratings. Measures of journalistic quality are secondary.

Oligopolistic competition may have two other related effects: First, as news products become more similar, consumers lose the differences that are the basis of distinguishing high from low quality. Second, consumers may have choices, but not clear alternatives. To the extent that products mimic each other, consumers can't make the market work to their advantage by patronizing the better product.

The Absence of Negative Externalities

Economists recognize that the results of a particular transaction may have effects on more people than the two trading partners. The purchase of a car built in Japan, for example, affects not only the buyer and the dealer, but the jobs of American car-builders, the balance of trade between the United States and Japan; the purchasing power of the dollar and yen, and so forth. These results affecting other parties are called "externalities."[44] Externalities draw their name from the fact that they are outside the transaction. They have little immediate or direct influence on the trading partners, and thus on the market. But they can have major impact on the public.

Because externalities are results of market forces, we need first to ask what kinds of decisions are likely to result from the market between providers and consumers of news. I have argued that this is a market in which: (1) media firms are likely to be more rational in defining and pursuing their self-interest than consumers, if only because organizations have greater resources than individuals; (2) consumers have difficulty evaluating the quality of a commodity like news that is unknown before consumption and not clearly defined; and (3) competition is oligopolistic, further complicating evaluation by reducing product variation.

Microeconomics suggests that media firms will seek to produce a mix of news content that attracts the largest possible audience at the least cost. Under the conditions described above, firms need not be very concerned about the journalistic quality of news. That should free them from at least some of the cost of normative journalism with its emphasis on digging for information, getting all sides to stories, its high standards of care with facts, and its commitment to revealing unpopular truths. The primary determinant of story selection should be the breadth of appeal—how many find the content interesting, attention-getting. In effect, the market redefines quality as what sells best (a distinction I'll pursue below and in Chapter 5).

Further, because news quality is both difficult for consumers to ascertain and ill defined, media firms have an incentive to model and promote a definition of newsworthiness that helps them achieve profit goals. Finally, the competition among a few news departments for consumers should encourage similarity of news products and penalize diversity. The absence of alternatives may give the commercial standard of news the appearance of normality, even propriety. In such a market, a media firm departing from the pack, even to pursue higher journalistic standards of quality, risks some of its audience.

Microeconomics also predicts consumer behavior. Under the given conditions consumers are likely to seek news content that they perceive best satisfies their wants at the least cost—in terms of effort and—for most newspapers—money. In the absence of a clear definition of news quality, with little ability to assess that quality, and with limited alternatives in the local market, consumers may accept an uncontested commercial definition of news as inexpensively produced, appealing accounts of current issues and events.

Even highly educated consumers—whom we might expect to be most able to resist such a commercial definition—are still likely to consider the costs

and benefits of consuming news that is not inherently pleasurable. What is
the payoff for forcing themselves each day to read or view important but
boring stories, or those that challenge their biases in ways that make them
uncomfortable, or those whose complexity demands serious mental effort?
If such stories are available, their content may inform the public-spirited
consumer's civic choices. But those choices, the most direct of which is the
opportunity to vote, are almost insignificant at the individual level. Even in
a tiny political jurisdiction one person's vote represents only perhaps one
say in 1,000 about who should hold office or which referenda should become
law. At the state level it's one vote among hundreds of thousands or millions.
At the national level it's one voice among 100 million. And that small say
may have already been limited by a nominating process that screened out
candidates and propositions representing real political change.

Of course those taking the trouble to stay informed can influence others.
But unless they devoted considerable time and money to the effort, they
would likely only raise the statistical impact of their opinions marginally.
And representatives of the status quo might easily swamp their personal
effort with persuasive campaigns of their own backed by the deep pockets
of industry or wealthy individuals. Within the current political system, an
individual doing the daily work of keeping informed—where serious local
news is available—is acting more out of civic obligation—community-
mindedness—than the self-interested logic of economics.[45]

If both news departments and news consumers follow the logic of the
marketplace with a commodity like news, however, the externality is likely
to be negative. Only news that meets commercial standards would be
produced and consumed. As the remainder of this chapter and Chapter 5 will
argue, the overlap of market and journalistic norms is too small to generate
a sufficient volume of the quality of news healthy self-government requires.

Other Transactions in News Production

The three other transactions in the model that influence news production
fit the first three exchange conditions better. But if both parties act rationally
in response to the market alone, again negative externalities loom.

THE TRANSACTION BETWEEN SOURCES
AND THE NEWS DEPARTMENT

Rationality: Recall from Chapter 2 that media firms trade access to public
attention for publishable information. We have already established that the
first condition of cooperative exchange, rational pursuit of self-interest, is

likely to be met to some degree in most media firms. Most reporters are trained in news-gathering and purposively carry out the firm's self-interest. Further, what they report receives at least partial examination by editors. News sources, however, may be divided into those speaking for organizations and those speaking on their own. Many government, political, and business sources have organizational resources equal or superior to the reporter's. In fact, spokespersons for officials and organizations often have specific training in public relations—a field defined by rational pursuit of the source's self-interest.[46] Sources without organizational support, however, must rely on their own experience and shrewdness, which vary widely.

Knowledge of Market and Products: Both organizationally backed sources and well-trained reporters are likely to know the market well. Public relations agents are paid to know which media are most likely to use an item. Experienced reporters may have expanded their information market by developing a network of unofficial sources.

Both organizational sources and news departments are also quite able to evaluate the products exchanged. In Chapter 2 I argued that news sources value three kinds of characteristics of the public attention they seek: First, the size and relevance to their purpose of the audience; second, the slant and volume of the coverage; and third, the prestige of the news department. The first and third characteristics are inspection goods. Sources can estimate viewership from station audience ratings and readership from audited circulation figures. The news department's prestige is likely to be common knowledge. The second characteristic—how the story is framed—is an experience good. News sources can readily compare their actions and statements with media reports of them.

For the news department, the quality of a source's information is often an inspection good. It can be compared against the accounts of other sources before use.

Presence of Competition: The number of competing news departments among which sources may choose approximates the consumers' situation. In metropolitan areas, there may be several. In smaller areas, the choices diminish. But even where there is choice, if the competitors are few and news products similar, sources espousing viewpoints the commercial media don't value may be systematically excluded from the market.

For the news department, the number of competing sources depends upon the information sought. The more witnesses to the event or issue, the greater the number of potential sources.

The concepts of market power and buyers' or sellers' markets help predict behaviors of both sources and news departments.

First, market power. If either sources or news departments dominate the market, they may be able to dictate the conditions of exchange—forcing the weaker party to sweeten the transaction if they wish to make a deal. Parties with great market power can also refuse to enter exchanges at little cost to themselves and thus powerfully affect the public's knowledge of issues and events. Some views may be promoted and others marginalized or censored.

The source with the greatest market power is the Pentagon during war time, particularly since the 1983 Grenada invasion and the imposition of policies forbidding reporters to gather news independently.[47] In the Persian Gulf War only reporters who agreed to military escorts and censorship were permitted into the field. News departments depended primarily on military briefers whose accounts were later discovered to have contained many self-serving errors.[48]

Other sources who have used their market power to favorably influence news reports include top national, state, and municipal officials such as presidents, governors, and mayors, although each of these control access to information through civilian bureaucracies that are generally more open to reporters than military organizations.[49] At the local level, paramilitary organizations such as police departments also exercise great market power. For their part, news departments that dominate a market also may manipulate sources, giving access to the favored on the news department's terms and denying it to those they oppose.[50]

Buyers' or sellers' markets occur when there is an imbalance in numbers between the exchange partners. When many competing sources seek public access from a few news departments, they may have to court news departments. This is usually accomplished by subsidizing the cost of discovering and reporting news.[51] Such subsidies may be as small as notifying the news department of events so it doesn't have to find them on its own. More elaborate subsidies include staging ready-to-report events, what historian Daniel Boorstin called "pseudoevents," with built-in elements of action, celebrity, emotion, or visuals that play to the media's wish to maximize audience.[52]

More recently, sources with deep pockets have financed entire reports on videotape that stations can plug into newscasts as if the news department reported it. Some of these source-canned stories, called video news releases, even include opportunities for fake question and answer segments with local anchors. The tape includes delays for the local anchor to read a pre-scripted question, which the source's "reporter" then answers.[53] Such an arrangement gives the appearance of a live report with the station's own staff. In this exchange the source is permitted to frame "news" to its advantage yet hide its partisanship under the news department's reputation for independent reporting. For its part, the news department receives a nearly cost-free story.

When reporters outnumber sources for a particular story, the opposite may occur. Sources may demand a favorable slant, or a cash payment, or the opportunity to review before publication, or anonymity.

Absence of Negative Externalities: Suppose that the first three conditions for beneficial exchange between sources and news departments are met. Would the resulting externalities be positive? Not if the two parties rationally follow market logic. As long as consumers have difficulty distinguishing the quality of news, exchange between sources and news departments might advance both of their interests at the public's expense. This is because most public officials and businesses require the favorable regard of the voting or consuming public. The most efficient route to such regard may be to build a positive image: offering the media information and events selected, or perhaps staged, to show themselves in a positive light *and* serve the media firm's desire to attract a large audience at minimum cost. To the extent that such image construction misleads or diverts attention from more significant news, the public interest may be harmed, while the media firm and source do well.[54]

THE TRANSACTION BETWEEN
ADVERTISERS AND THE MEDIA FIRM

Here advertisers trade money for access to public attention. Of all the transactions shaping news, the one between advertisers and the media firm is the most equal.

Rationality: Here both parties are usually organized businesses. Although there may be differences in size between the trading partners, both presumably are seeking their self-interest in more or less logical fashion. Further, small "mom and pop" advertisers often use agencies with specialized expertise to place their ads.

Knowledge of Market and Product: The interaction between media firms and advertisers is remarkable for the precision with which both the market and the products can be known before contracts are signed.[55] Through their professional organizations, as well as their own ad departments, media firms can accurately estimate what advertisers are paying to place their messages with competitors. For their part, advertisers can purchase statistical estimates of the number of potential customers their message reaches. In addition, they can readily evaluate the commercial supportiveness of the news environment— the extent to which stories encourage consumption by emphasizing advantages of products or companies and downplaying or censoring disadvantages—by examining past news products; or perhaps by negotiating a customized environment in a specialized section of a newspaper or newscast.

Presence of Competition: Most American communities host a variety of advertisers, both local and national, wishing to buy time or space for commercial messages. The rise of chain merchandising—one regional or national corporation owning multiple stores—and the emergence of advertising agencies acting on behalf of smaller retailers, are both increasing concentration in the advertising market, however.[56] This means media firms face fewer and larger ad buyers with increased market power.

Advertisers, on the other hand, enjoy an increasing choice of vehicles, both news-carrying and otherwise. Not only has the spread of cable access to more than half of U.S. households multiplied available commercial spots, but direct mail and "shoppers"—printed advertisements circulated weekly with little or no news content—have begun to saturate the advertising marketplace. The result? A buyer's market for advertising that contrasts sharply with the seller's market of the last few decades when monopoly newspapers and the few local stations on the air could raise advertising rates with near impunity. In a buyers' market media firms have to sweeten their deals to compete.

Absence of Negative Externalities: The notion of news departments providing a "supportive" environment for advertisements conflicts with the central journalistic standard of objectivity. This would seem to contravene the market journalists' argument in the first chapter about the value of objective news content to advertisers. Because that argument is one of the principal pillars of the belief that the American system of funding news-gathering through advertising is symbiotic, it deserves analysis here.

Journalist-turned-academic Philip Meyer argued that the ideal climate for advertising is objective journalism both because it attracts a larger audience than biased reporting, and because it lends ads an air of credibility. His argument is worth quoting:

> There is no reason for the advertiser to exercise any control or influence over the editorial [news] content. Indeed, to do so would be counter-productive, because it would undermine the independence that creates the trustworthy editorial environment that, in turn, gives the paper [or other news provider] its influence.[57]

But, the literature of news research, as Meyer concedes, recounts many instances in which advertisers have balked at having their products associated with honest news reports when such reports were either unsupportive of what was being advertised or of the values of advertisers—primarily a culture of material acquisitiveness.[58]

Why the gap between the real and ideal? If consumers believe a news report is accurate and fair, the product of a high-minded news department, Meyer is probably right to suggest that ads placed in such a context gain credibility. But his assumption that consumers can evaluate qualities of accuracy and fairness is questionable in light of the preceding discussion. If consumers can't detect subtle bias toward advertisers, then the door is open for the type of manipulation of news content that has been documented. In fact, the ideal editorial climate for advertisers is likely to be one that appears objective to consumers, but permits some covert influence from advertisers.

Note that if bias toward advertisers became obvious, the news department might lose both its air of integrity and the attention of intelligent consumers. Such losses would make the station or newspaper much less valuable as an advertising vehicle. So news departments could not ignore events or issues unfavorable to advertisers that became widely known, such as a train wreck or an airline crash, without risking their credibility. Less noticeable events, however, could be downplayed or ignored and news departments could avoid uncovering negative information themselves by directing reporting resources elsewhere.

If both advertisers and media firms follow market logic, advertisers should be more important customers of the media firm than consumers. This is partly because advertisers pay with money and consumers pay primarily with attention. But this cannot be the whole explanation. If media firms lose their audience, they will have nothing to sell. The more fundamental reason for the inequality is because advertisers are more equal trading partners with the media firm than are consumers. Advertisers possess organizational resources, can evaluate product quality with precision, and enjoy a variety of alternate vehicles for carrying their messages to potential customers. Those who consume news cannot claim the first two attributes, and may not be able to select among competitors at the local level.

A simple analogy may help illustrate. Suppose you manage a store that sells cloth to apparel makers. The owners you report to expect healthy profits because that's what past managers have provided. Let's say you have two types of customers: buyers for large factories, and individuals who make clothes for themselves and their families.

The buyers are experts, armed with computer printouts from their marketing departments indicating which textures and blends are in style. Because of their training, they can evaluate the quality of cloth to perfection. They also know what others are charging for the same material. The buyers also can go to a variety of other retailers if you don't offer a superior deal. To capture their business, you must offer a price close to your own cost.

The customers shopping for themselves, on the other hand, are not experts. They buy what they like or what strikes them. They have no special training and no sheaves of data. They are only moderate judges of quality and price.

They rarely travel across town to look over the wares of competing cloth merchants. As a result, to some degree they can be fooled.

Because you're a fair person, you want to treat both groups equally. You certainly don't want to cheat anyone. But the market dictates that you offer low prices and high quality to the expert buyers. If you don't, the market will put you out of business. The market will permit, however, higher prices and lower quality for the customers buying for themselves. In fact, if you are to make up for the diminished profits from sales to the experts, you must earn more from the individual customers, or risk being fired. Between the requirements of the owner and those of the market, you must place the interests of the more savvy buyers ahead of those of the less able individual shoppers.

Let's return to the exchanges media firms conduct with their two classes of customers, advertisers and individual consumers. To the extent that news consumers have difficulty rationally pursuing their self-interest, evaluating news quality, and finding competing news sources, media firms following market logic should subordinate the interests of consumers to advertisers. Further, media firms seeking to maximize profit should sweeten deals with advertisers first where it costs least—making the news supportive of commercial messages. Media firms that resist such logic in a market where their competitors accede, are likely to pay a price in profitability.

When news departments follow market logic, their primary purpose is selling consumer attention rather than informing the public. Society may be harmed when news routines designed for selling conflict with those required for informing:

First, because advertisers seek public attention rather than public education, news programmers and newspapers are not competing in a *news market*, but in a *public attention market*. Such a market may contain many persons with little interest in understanding the significant events and issues of the day. If the attention of such consumers is to be captured, narratives of current happenings must be made entertaining, perhaps by injecting drama, emotion, and confrontation in the style of CBS's *60 Minutes*. Perhaps non-news content that is purely entertaining should be added.

The market for serious news that demands reader or viewer concentration because of its complexity or depth, except in times of crisis, is a subset of the broader public attention market. Indeed the market for serious news may be a small subset if audience ratings for news documentaries and dense newscasts such as *MacNeil/Lehrer* are indicative.[59]

Second, because advertisers seek a supportive environment for their messages, news departments should avoid turning up negative information about advertisers and ignore or downplay reporting of such information made public by others. Positive information about advertisers, their industries, and the value of consumption should be developed and reported. However, neither suppression of negative news nor promotion of positive news should become obvious enough to damage the news department's credibility with consumers.

Third, because advertisers primarily seek potential *customers,* news of interest to undesirable income and age groups should receive low selection priority, except as it affects the interests of potential customers.

A Final Note About Advertising

This discussion of negative externalities arising from market journalism should not be read as an attack on advertisers. It merely applies market logic to a complex transaction. There is nothing wrong, for example, with the singleness of purpose of H. Thomas Wilson III, an executive of a major New York advertising agency, in advising clients against buying news spots during the Persian Gulf crisis:

> I'm taking a cue from direct marketers who see declines in response rates during times of crisis. While attention to news will be very high, and it seems that's where you should advertise, it will probably be neutralized by the fact that minds will be diverted to very serious things.[60]

The simple fact is that the interests of advertisers and those of journalists diverge as much or more than they overlap.

THE TRANSACTION BETWEEN INVESTORS AND THE MEDIA FIRM

In many respects the transaction between investors and the media firm is similar to the one between the media firm and advertisers. The primary difference, however, is that of all the transactions described, this one gives the buyer a formal role inside the media firm as a stockholder. Investors who own a significant portion of a corporation are in a powerful position to affect news policy because they appoint the members of the parent corporation's board of directors, whose decisions ripple downward through the entire corporation.

Rationality: Investors, particularly large investors, normally buy expert advice from stock brokers. Institutional investors, such as pension funds, may have organizational resources to analyze the market and firms whose shares are bought.

Knowledge of the Market and Product: The investor's broker provides expert knowledge of both market and product. Further, the federal government's Securities and Exchange Commission regulates the stock market and demands under penalty of law that companies offering shares reveal a great deal of accurate information about their economic standing. The soundness of a company is normally an inspection good. Its future performance is an experience good.

Presence of Competition. Competition is present here more than in any other transaction involving media firms. Investors have their choice among thousands of corporations offering stock. In addition the investment market includes non-stock alternatives such as bonds issued both by governments and corporations, and savings accounts with banks and other monetary institutions. Because an investor can receive interest in bank accounts and government bonds, where the principal—and in the latter case the interest as well—are guaranteed by the federal government, private corporations offering stock must generally exceed interest rates in earnings potential to justify the risk of investment. Stock prices—and thus the capital a media corporation can amass from sale of shares—correspond to investors' assessment of the stock's return both in dividends paid each quarter and its appreciation over time.

Absence of Negative Externalities: As long as they can credibly promise profits, news entrepreneurs can raise cash on the stock market with other people's money. The market can help build media firms much more quickly than might happen if a fledgling firm could expand only with operating profits. But there are dangers as well. Although the owners of media firms that are *not* publicly traded can, if they wish, protect the news department from demands for profits that are competitive with Wall Street, publicly traded companies must compete with other investment opportunities of similar level of risk if they wish to attract investment. Although some investment houses have inaugurated "responsible investment" portfolios that investigate the way firms do business, most investors still restrict their inquiries to risk and the expected profit performance of a company before purchasing shares. In the stock market, the best quality journalism is the most profitable journalism.[61] If a corporation's board of directors seeks to maximize profits in order to boost its stock's value, management may place pressures on their news departments to take advantage of the gullibility of consumers. Because of their relative advantage over consumers in the transactions shaping news, major investors may also use their news departments' influence over the public to benefit themselves at the public's expense.

Forces Outside the Market

When a good or service is poorly suited to market conditions because consumers find it difficult to evaluate—or for lack of competition, or because the results of market decisions may harm society—government agencies, professional associations, or both may be called in to regulate the market. By virtue of the First Amendment, however, news quality is largely exempt from government regulation. Stations are federally licensed to operate in the public "interest, necessity and convenience," but there is little inquiry into the quality of journalism, particularly since the Federal Communications Commission dismantled the Fairness Doctrine.[62] Nor is the quality of news subject to professional peer review as is the case with the practice of law, medicine, and other professions. News departments can't lose professional accreditation as can universities or hospitals. Neither can journalists lose licenses as can physicians, lawyers, and accountants.

The closest U.S. journalism has come to peer review was the National News Council, established in 1973 to review complaints about coverage. The Council had no enforcement power save censure. The Council, however, lasted barely 11 years, dissolving in 1984 for lack of industry or other support.[63]

The quality of contemporary news is subject only to the demands of the marketplace and to whichever, if any, standards of journalism a particular news department upholds. Before exploring how market demand and journalistic standards interact in the next chapter, let's apply our understanding of forces acting on commercial news departments to the case study that began this chapter.

Applying the Model

The topic for a story on AIDS education suited both journalism and business ideals. The AIDS epidemic had killed hundreds of people in the station's signal area and threatened thousands more. At the time of the broadcast, public fear rivaled public ignorance of how AIDS was transmitted as peaks on the pollsters' charts. That fear alone could draw the wide viewership the station sought to sell to advertisers.

Executing the story, however, brought market and journalism norms into conflict. According to the station's general manager, the family-held corporation that owned the station expected continuation of pre-tax profits in the range of 40%-50% return on gross revenues—that's between five and six times the national average for such profits. The owners had gotten used to such returns and were reluctant to accept less if they could help it. To generate such enormous return the station had to attract a large audience of potential customers for the advertised products. Long bureaucratic stories, even about life and death topics, were thought certain to drive away some viewers.

The reporter demonstrated the market logic demanded by the owners when she balked at spending much of the day on the phone comparing the federal AIDS education guidelines with those of local school districts and health departments. First, there would be simply too much information to fit into the standard 90-second slot allocated to reporter "packages"—locally originated stories in which the reporter appears. Second, such an information-rich story had no visual component. "Talking heads" may bore marginally interested viewers, causing them to select a more interesting competing station (or other use of time). As proposed, the story so flagrantly violated market logic that the assignment editor didn't consult with the assistant news director before reducing the scope of reporting. He merely assumed his superior couldn't have intended such a dull comparison. In a discussion later in the day, the assistant news director approved the change.

The simpler comparison of federal and city AIDS education guidelines still followed journalistic norms. It was important, although primarily for residents of the central city. But maximizing viewership requires more than the variety and quick pace of short stories. To gain the largest possible audience, every narrative must attract even the viewer whose interest is primarily to be entertained. In the reporter's own words, the meeting of the board of health was "boring." Her attempt to enliven the story with talk of condom-carrying teenage girls and humorous video substituted emotionally arousing content for relevant information about the story's topic, the new guidelines. Here the compromise favored economics over journalism.

While advertisers might wish an informative over a merely interesting story, they were paying for the qualities of the audience—its size, wealth, the buying potential of its stage of life—not the quality of the reporting. Were the story to have driven away those watching for entertainment with a more serious treatment, advertisers would have reached fewer prospective customers.

How about the transaction with news sources? As we shall explore in greater detail in Chapter 6, high profit expectations favor news sources over newsrooms. The less news departments spend to build a network of sources within important business and government bureaucracies, the more they must rely on official pronouncements both to learn of news and report it. In this case local health officials wanted attention for their new guidelines. Their press agent had baited the story with the promise of controversy. National officials, on the other hand, were keeping a low profile. The Reagan Administration apparently hoped to avoid angering conservative voters who opposed sex education efforts. Faced with limited cooperation in Washington, KVLG eliminated the federal component and concentrated on the local. It was less expensive, principally in reporter time, to go after what was offered than to ferret out what was hidden.

And the transaction with consumers? The final product had the appearance of news—real people and appropriate officials being quoted by a reporter in a timely manner on an important topic—but there was little of consequence to learn. The product was hollow. Its emptiness, however, escaped notice in the newsroom. Considering how typically the story was constructed and KVLG's competitive position in audience ratings, the public also may have accepted the story as competent journalism. It was, however, a product more designed to sell than to inform. Consumers may have gotten what they wanted, but not what they needed.

Notes

1. Most U.S. news departments are located within publicly traded media firms or conglomerates. Privately owned media firms must serve three markets, all but the market for investors.
2. Picard, 1989; Udell, 1978.
3. The present approach differs somewhat from the simpler view of British Marxists that media sell audiences to advertisers. Thinking of audiences as simply raw material to be marketed oversimplifies the exchange occurring between consumers and news providers. It also assumes away journalism's role in serving the public interest.
4. *Statistical Abstract of the United States, 1990.*
5. Picard, 1989.
6. Udell, 1978.
7. Bogart, 1991, p. 6.
8. Nielsen Test Market Reports have shown small shares for *The MacNeil/Lehrer News Hour* in most markets over a period of years. However the difference between the program and commercial network news is exaggerated by the fact that public television stations reach fewer viewers than the commercial networks.
9. Adam Smith, 1909.
10. Main & Baird, 1981.
11. Entman, & Wildman, 1991; Rotzoll & Haefner, with Sandage, 1990.
12. Brennan, 1991.
13. Scott, 1981, p. 60.
14. March & Simon, 1958.
15. Kahneman & Tversky, 1973.
16. Entman & Wildman, 1991, p. 20.
17. Beniger, 1986.
18. Of course, for those watching news solely for entertainment, the definition of quality has little to do with journalistic standards.
19. Rock, 1981.
20. Carey, 1986.
21. Barney, 1987.
22. Darby & Karni, 1973; Main & Baird, 1981.
23. Williamson (1979, 1981) characterizes such expenses as transaction costs. When these costs are high, he argues, markets should not be relied upon to govern transactions.
24. If you think the monitoring of each other's news products that most local news departments conduct provides a measure of quality control, fast forward to Chapter 8.
25. Lang & Lang, 1968.

26. Mundy, 1992. For other examples of public relations scams on the press, see Sibbison, 1988.

27. Leff, 1993.

28. Barnouw, 1990.

29. See, for example, Herman & Chomsky, 1988.

30. Main & Baird, 1981.

31. The Commission on Freedom of the Press, 1947.

32. Harmon, 1989.

33. Such manipulation of images was the norm rather than the exception in my study.

34. Postman, 1985, p. 128.

35. V. Stone, 1993c.

36. Gale Research, 1990.

37. Bagdikian, 1990, p. 177.

38. Lacy & Dalmia, 1991.

39. Olien, Tichenor, & Donohue, 1991.

40. Picard, 1989.

41. Dominick & Pearce, 1976; Fowler & Showalter, 1974.

42. Ehrlich, 1991, p. 6.

43. Ehrlich, 1991, 1993; Kaniss, 1991. My own dissertation field notes also show similar effects of competition at each of the three stations visited, and at a fourth station that served as a pilot site.

44. Picard, 1989.

45. A 1993 survey conducted by the Times Mirror Center for the People and the Press (August, 1993) showed little public interest in a variety of serious news events. The debate in Congress over President Clinton's restructuring of tax laws attracted only 30% of the respondents' interest; the Bosnian War, only 19%; the Supreme Court nomination of feminist Ruth Ginsburg, only 18%. Audience ratings for other serious stories, however, contradict the theory of the apathetic public—with 41% of Americans paying close attention to stories about the U.S. economy, and 65% following reports of the Midwest flood.

46. Boorstin, 1961.

47. Hertsgaard, 1988.

48. Small, 1992.

49. Barnouw, 1990.

50. Bagdikian, 1990; Collins, 1992; Underwood, 1993.

51. Gandy, 1982.

52. Boorstin, 1961; Hertsgaard, 1988.

53. Salmon, 1993.

54. Hume, 1991; Jamieson, 1992.

55. Picard, 1989.

56. Bagdikian, 1990.

57. Meyer, 1987, pp. 38-39.

58. Bagdikian, 1990; Barnouw, 1990; Collins, 1992; Lesly, 1991; Singer, 1991; Zachary, 1992.

59. Barnouw, 1990.

60. Rothenberg, R. (1991, January 12). "Crisis Raises TV News Audience," *The New York Times*, p. A46.

61. Squiers, 1993.

62. Ferrall, 1989.

63. Abel, 1984. Minnesota still operates a news council, however, and it does hear cases from outside the state. Recently Oregon and Washington have formed a news council, but its future is uncertain due both to funding and lack of cooperation from major media firms (as reported by Arnold Ismach of the University of Oregon to a panel at the Association for Education in Journalism and Mass Communication, Kansas City, MO, August 13, 1993).

5

Does Serving the Market Conflict With
Serving the Public?

We have seen the news-shaping pressures exerted by market logic outside the newsroom. Now let's look at how it might apply within. Where do market forces reinforce the public service standards of journalism and where do the two conflict?

A Market Theory of News Production

To the extent that the business goal of maximizing profits dominates, the foregoing analysis suggests that rational news departments should compete with each other to offer *the least expensive mix of content that protects the interests of sponsors and investors while garnering the largest audience advertisers will pay to reach.* What becomes news then depends upon a type of cost-benefit analysis at each of the three stages of production.

This is not to suggest that workers in market-driven news departments spend much of their day computing cost-benefit ratios and factoring them into algorithms that determine what becomes news. Even were news production more precise and predictable, expending such time and mental effort would be inefficient. Instead, market logic is the mold for *routines* of discovering newsworthy events, selecting some of them for coverage, and pulling information together into a report. These routines constitute the daily expression of an organizational culture—an accepted way of producing news in a particular media firm.

In any industry, routines are rational means to efficiency. In market-driven newsrooms, routines may also serve to hide the pervasiveness of the economic logic that forms them. Media firms may boast to current and prospective stockholders about how tightly organized they are for profit. But to do so to employees might raise alarm about whose interests the corporation serves.[1] In fact, disguising the economic self-interest of media firms serves management.[2] Newsworkers may be more willing to make sacrifices in salary, work hours, and personal danger (e.g., covering a riot) if they see themselves as serving the public rather than profit. Thus, although talk of making money is likely to be rare in market-driven newsrooms, the logic that drives production routines, nevertheless, is economic.[3]

If news is treated as a commodity like any other, a purely market model of news production should prevail. Such a model would be based upon anticipation within the newsroom of four attributes of any event or issue. It might look something like Table 5.1. A purely journalistic theory, Table 5.2, is simpler.

The next three chapters show how reporters and editors estimate each predictor of coverage in the two models using simple heuristics—rules of thumb—or by reference to the organizational culture. But first let's compare the two models conceptually.

Both models share a concern for audience size. Both journalists and advertisers have legitimate reasons for wanting to reach a wide audience. But, as we saw in the previous section, the audience each seeks may have parts that do not overlap: First among those who need to know about a particular event or issue but are poor potential customers; and second among those who have little interest in the news, but are good potential customers.

Notice two obvious differences in the models: (1) The market approach requires bias in stories affecting the interests of the media firms' advertisers, parent corporation, and investors. In contrast, journalism requires the news be told with as little bias as humans can manage. (2) The journalistic theory contains no element of cost or payment, while the economic theory has the word "cost" or "pay" in three terms and cost is implied in the word "harm" in the fourth. The journalistic model is unconcerned about what it costs to discover what's happening in a community. It's equally silent about how much time or other resources might be needed to cover an issue or event. Such a standard presumes unlimited resources and is thus an ideal. This is why actual commercial news production requires some compromise of journalism ideals with business reality. Journalism that costs more to produce than it generates in revenues cannot be sustained in the marketplace.

Where Market Theory and Journalism Theory Converge

Despite having more differences than similarities, the two theories are not always in conflict. Some events and issues that would be deemed newswor-

TABLE 5.1 A Market Theory of News Production[a]

The probability of an event/issue becoming news is:	Inversely proportional to harm the information might cause investors or sponsors, and . . .	Inversely proportional to the cost of uncovering it, and . . .	Inversely proportional to the cost of reporting it, and . . .	Directly proportional to the expected breadth of appeal of the story to audiences advertisers will pay to reach.

NOTE: a. For more development of these ideas, see McManus, 1988.

thy under journalistic norms would remain so under a market theory. A number of consequential occurrences don't threaten the interests of advertisers and investors, are inexpensive to learn of, are inexpensive to report, and promise wide appeal to a demographically "correct" audience. Examples include tragedies such as train or airliner crashes, a fatal fire in a tenement building, and a mud-slinging debate among political candidates.

There also may be trade-offs among the terms of the business theory. A news department might spend heavily to learn of and report a story that generates unusual consumer interest. For example, the money spent investigating a sex scandal involving an important public official might justify its cost by attracting audience away from competitors. Less arousing or more complex official malfeasance, or the misbehavior of a major advertiser, however, would likely be left for some other social institution to investigate.

Ironically, market-driven news departments are at their best when times are at their worst. Events that profoundly influence the entire community served by a media firm—such as hurricanes, earthquakes, floods, riots, or the outbreak of war between the United States and another nation—raise consumers' personal stake in the news. In such cases, consumers who might routinely use news for diversion or entertainment find themselves in need of significant information—perhaps about how to cope. Crises lend greater commercial viability to informative reporting. Such market pressure for information exits regardless of whether advertisers choose to place their messages amid such coverage.[4]

Finally, note that news departments provide a *mix* of content. Newspapers, with their greater volume and random access capability, and to a lesser extent

TABLE 5.2 A Journalistic Theory of News Production

The probability of an event/issue becoming news is:	Proportional to the expected consequence of the story, and. . .	Proportional to the size of the audience for whom it is important.

local TV newsrooms, may find it profitable to produce some normative journalism for those consumers who are more able to discern such quality and willing to pursue it. Because such consumers are presumably those with more education and higher incomes, they are likely to attract advertiser interest. In general, the larger the metropolitan area, the larger this group of discriminating consumers is, and the more it makes sense for market-driven news departments to practice occasional normative journalism.

Where Market Theory and Journalism Theory Conflict

Principally because so few of the conditions for cooperative exchange are met in the transaction between media firms and the public, journalism and market norms conflict more than converge. If the goal of journalism is *public enlightenment,* there is potential for conflict with the business goal of maximizing benefit for investors at each stage of news production.

THE FIRST STAGE OF NEWS PRODUCTION

At the first stage of news production, uncovering potentially newsworthy issues and events: The most significant news is often the most expensive to discover because powerful interests want it hidden. Independent, particularly investigative, surveillance of a community is expensive. It is less costly to rely on other news providers such as wire services and on press agents to learn of community events and issues than to hire adequate staff to infiltrate the community.[5] Such passive discovery, however, creates potential for manipulation of the public agenda by sources powerful enough to hire press agents and "manufacture" events.[6] In Chapter 6 we shall determine whether business or journalism norms are being followed at the stations in the study by categorizing each story aired by the investment required of the station to learn of it.

THE SECOND STAGE OF NEWS PRODUCTION

At the second stage of news production, choosing among those events and issues uncovered in step one a subset for inclusion in newspapers and newscasts, market and journalism norms may collide when important stories are dull—such as economic trends or political apportionment debates. The demands of journalism and those of the market also collide when stories about issues or events question accepted myths or prejudices, popular national policies (such as U.S. intervention in the Persian Gulf), or popular leaders.[7]

News from a specific locality within a market causes an additional problem for regional media such as local television and metropolitan newspapers.

The consequence of routine events and issues is likely to be restricted to a fraction of the circulation or broadcast signal area of a media firm. For example, news that a particular municipality is adding a sales tax, or a school district is exceeding recommended class sizes to meet a budget crisis, or a county is failing to maintain roads, may bore non-affected consumers. Although newspapers can zone editions to reduce this problem and readers can skip stories that don't pique their interest, television is likely to lose customers if it dwells too long on what's important in just a part of the market. From a market perspective, broadcasters—and to a lesser extent, newspapers[8]—are better off with more generalizable stories such as consumer-oriented features and human interest pieces that arouse emotional response, even if the result is news that fails to help consumers make sense of current events.

Measurement here is more complex. But to preview: Each story can be rated for its level of informational importance and for its emotional appeal. Those two dimensions can be crossed because stories may be both informative and arousing. The result is a two-dimensional figure with four quadrants. Stories may be high in both emotional appeal and in informational consequence—interesting and important stories. Stories may also be just the opposite—neither important nor emotionally arousing. The last two quadrants include important but dull stories and, conversely, emotionally arousing but inconsequential stories. In Chapter 7 we shall weight stories by the air time they consume and place them in these four quadrants to determine whether the news departments studied are more oriented toward public interest, private interest, or some compromise. The selection stage of news production is also an appropriate place to investigate the conflict between journalism's requirement that the public be fully informed and the protection market logic demands for the media firm's investors and sponsors.

THE FINAL STAGE OF NEWS PRODUCTION

At the final stage of news production—reporting the story—journalism norms require selection of the most significant quotes from the most relevant sources. Journalism also requires that all sides to an issue be provided in a disinterested fashion, that dubious fact claims be checked, that conclusions not based on common knowledge be supported with evidence, and that enough context be provided for wide comprehension. Satisfying these requirements is expensive because it consumes reporters' time. If a station seeks to maximize profit, less care may be taken with information. And just as the interesting topic may replace the merely important, the interesting source and quote may replace the informative source and quote. Profit demands may also lead to truncated news reports, particularly on television.

Because viewers can't pick among stories, a station might restrict the length of narratives so that few become bored enough to "zap" the station by changing channels.

Case studies are the units of analysis here. Shadowing a reporter permits discovery of priorities in selecting story elements as well as adherence to journalistic norms of objectivity and care with information. Chapter 8 details this analysis.

Is Compromise Viable?

Both the market and journalism models are defined as extremes. If investors are willing to accept lower levels of profit—perhaps in exchange for an investment with less risk in the long term—compromises are possible. As we shall see, the profit levels of most print and broadcast media firms are high enough to accommodate greater journalistic integrity. It's also important to note that technological differences, such as those mentioned in the preceding section, make such compromises more costly for television than for newspapers.

Conclusion

In an ideal news market, where consumers act rationally in their selfinterest, enjoy a variety of news outlets, can discern the quality of reportage, and include within their self-interest society's well-being, the same strategy that yields maximum return to investors would maximize public enlightenment. But given the actual news market, and the peculiar nature of news as a commodity, the logic of maximizing return often conflicts with the logic of maximizing public understanding.

Notes

1. The public also may be alarmed by how media firms speak to investors. News is likely to sell better if described as a good produced, not to yield the highest return, but solely in the public interest; something that ought to be consumed if not because one wants to, then because one needs to out of obligation to the community.

2. Bagdikian, 1990; Underwood, 1993.

3. Matthew Ehrlich (1993, p. 3), for example, argues that while competition for viewers has an economic basis, the notion of competition in local television newsrooms has become ritualized—becoming not a profit strategy, but an almost sacred end in itself, "a daily race

to see who's best." Chapter 9 of this book explores in more detail how economic logic was disguised in the routines and heuristics of the newsrooms studied.

4. McManus, 1988.

5. McManus, 1990.

6. Boorstin, 1961.

7. See, for example, Cohen, 1989; Massing, 1991.

8. This is because it's cheaper to produce one story for the entire press run, than multiple stories, one for each zone.

6

The First Stage of News Production:
Learning What's Happening

This chapter is the first of three to measure the interplay between market and journalistic logic in local television news production. Here we examine how the stations learn what might be newsworthy in their communities.

Case Study: Discovering the News

The first reporter, a young woman with brown and copper hair framing a model's face, arrived at 6 a.m. to begin KMID's news day. The sun had yet to illuminate this mid-sized city sprawling into a rich agricultural valley on a cool, clear October morning. Her task was to excerpt the most interesting stories from yesterday's 11 p.m. newscast and insert them into short breaks in CBS's morning programming. She also made the first check of local police and fire agencies, updating the report with what the agencies were willing to reveal of the night and early morning's emergencies.

A few minutes after 7 a.m., the assignment editor arrived, a man seasoned by 25 years of journalism, both print and broadcast. I'll call him Frank. An assignment editor, he quipped, is "one part father-confessor, one part all around good guy, and one part Ayatollah." At KMID, as at the other three stations visited, the assignment editor's role sometimes included mentor, friend, and dictator. But a better metaphor might be quarterback. The news director was more like a coach. His office was on the sidelines, at the edge of the newsroom, often glassed off from the hurly-burly of news production. The assignment editor's desk lay in the thick of the action, the nerve center of the newsroom. Every idea for a local story had to stop there, at least for approval. And, as we shall see, most also began at the assignment desk.

By 7:09 Frank's black felt pen squeaked as he wrote reporting assignments on the large white marker board behind his desk. Above its columns, the board sported a permanent set of labels: length of story in minutes and seconds; "slug," news talk for the one- or two-word label stories are given in almost every American newsroom—print or broadcast; the time the "crew," reporter and photographer, were to meet the source; and the names of the crew members. If you think of an instantaneous medium like television as being up to the minute in its coverage, you might be surprised to discover that all but three assignments were filled in by 7:30 a.m. Most of this evening's newscast was at least tentatively penciled in the day before. Now, shortly after 7 a.m., Frank added three more assignments. The ideas for two of them originated in the morning newspaper. The third was left by the night assignment editor, a police action learned from the scanner radio.

Even though KMID lies within the largest third of U.S. markets in size, generated the second largest audience for local news in the market, and offered 2 hours of local news per weekday, the reporting staff numbered only eight. Most worked to fill the early evening newscast, but several had responsibilities to the half-hour noon and 11 p.m. newscasts as well.

To produce an hour-long early evening newscast, Frank explained, "we're looking for 26 to 30 minutes to fill with local news and that includes the canned stuff [mailed-in videotapes of Paul Harvey editorials and medical/health features from syndicators]. About 23 minutes of locally originated news." (The plurality of the newscast airtime consisted of commercials—about 16 minutes—two segments each of sports and weather, and, even though Dan Rather's network news program followed immediately, 3 to 5 minutes of national news from the CBS "feed," as the satellite transmission is called.) With eight reporters, each was assigned an average of three stories per day. So advanced planning was necessary. Frank liked his reporters to gather their first two stories before noon.

On the assignment desk rested four telephones, including a radio-telephone connecting him to reporters and photographers as they travel between stories. Two scanner-radios monitored emergency broadcasts from local police, fire, and ambulance services. The radios were programmed to move from one frequency to another stopping only when there was a transmission. A small black and white television set had been installed above the desk to show what other stations were broadcasting.

Frank's morning ritual included reading the metropolitan newspaper at home and listening to the news-talk radio station on his way to work. The early reporter kept her eye on stories coming in on the Associated Press Radio Wire Service printer, the only wire service KMID received. Most of the local AP stories, however, are condensed re-writes of the morning paper.

Throughout the morning Frank listened to the scanner radios. Periodically he called the city's police and fire departments for morning emergencies. He also checked in with the state police for traffic accidents. The reporter called outlying county police and fire departments. "They don't really do us too much good," he said. "If they've had a murder or fire, unless it's very visual, we won't go down to shoot it. But it gives us a chance to call the cops and keep our relations good. Hopefully, they'll call us if something's happening."

Frank said KMID gets lots of phoned in story tips, but most came from public relations agents promoting their clients rather than whistle-blowers. Frank also scanned weekly newspapers from outlying counties. These arrived by mail a day after publication, but sometimes revealed a local story worth covering.

At 8 a.m. the other reporters began to arrive. There were about half as many desks as reporters, so when most of the staff was present, one reporter sat on the desk and the other got the chair. Frank distributed a list of the day's assignments. Each slug was followed by the crew and times from the marker board and a sentence or two of explanation. At 8:20, the news director, a tall slender young man who had been both a reporter and anchor, gave the staff some instructions about the elections coming up the following month. "I've noticed the paper has stepped up its coverage of local races," he said. "So it's a good time to start clipping and saving. Read the [paper] every day."

"Welcome to plagiarism news," a photographer whispered to me. "We rely a lot on the newspaper. I guess all the local stations do. And we don't check the stories, just incorporate them into video. And we do the same with outlying papers. We build our stories using their reports."

Around 9 a.m., the assignment desk staff arrived, two young women. The junior woman held a fresh B.A. in journalism and hoped someday to be a reporter. The senior assignment staffer had a high school diploma. She "fell into" the job and yearned to give it up for something better paying. "We call them the paper dolls," the photographer said, "because all they do is clip through papers that come in a day or two late." The photographer was partly correct, but the two women also scanned press releases, made calls to emergency service dispatchers, and organized mailed-in promotional material for Frank to review for inclusion into future newscasts.

Although newspapers typically rely on reporters to bring in leads for stories, television, said Frank, is more centrally organized. "In this station, we don't have specific reporters in beats. We have general beats by county. [Maria] is our court's reporter. But everybody else is general assignment." He estimated that reporters originate "about 10% of the stories, but that may be high." Despite their assignment to cover counties, however, reporters said they devote little or no time to discovering news. In fact, a common complaint among KMID reporters was that the desk rarely assigned the same reporter to the same topic twice in a row.

Frank acknowledged that reporters had insufficient time to survey the counties they were assigned. "If you've got three stories," he explained, "you don't have time to go down and have a cup of coffee with the D.A. [District Attorney]. We dig up our own news occasionally. [But] when reporters have ideas we usually put them off until the next day because by 8 a.m. the day is set."

Frank said reporters are not routinely assigned to cover county boards of supervisors or city councils even in the larger cities of the six-county market. He acknowledged that such meetings are wellheads of information, but said selection priorities had moved away from government coverage because it was "too boring." His staff did collect "packets"—agenda and supporting materials for government meetings—for the central city in the signal area and the most densely populated county's board of supervisors. But other bodies were merely asked to mail their packets. Asked if such packets routinely omitted or disguised controversial items of public business, he replied, "Yup. That's a problem." KMID relied on the newspaper, he explained, to dig below the surface.

The First Stage of News Production: Discovery

The discovery phase of news selection, in which journalists learn of events and issues that might be covered, is extremely important because it predicates all other decisions within the newsroom. No matter how artistic the photographers, how brilliant or tough-minded the reporters, or how careful the editors, their talents have no effect on issues and events of which the newsroom isn't aware. If unreported elsewhere, such events may fail to exist in the public mind. Their exclusion may lead at a minimum to uninformed public decision making. More threatening are cases in which critical information hidden from the public encouraged serious social and governmental blunders.[1]

Active scrutiny of society, particularly government, is a fundamental obligation of journalism, as Ralph Barney noted:

A first reason for journalists to exist is the gathering and distributing of information, most particularly information that others are taking pains to keep from being distributed. It is that type of information that . . . would prove most valuable to society.[2]

A MARKET MODEL OF NEWS DISCOVERY

As we saw in Chapter 5, if the news is a commodity only, the production of news narratives should follow market logic. Given scarce resources of time and capital, rational media firms should provide the least expensive mix of content that is hospitable to advertisers and investors and generates the largest audience those advertisers want to reach. It's reasonable to assume that passive discovery of events—when television journalists read about them in local and regional newspapers or wire services or in press releases— is less expensive than more active means, such as hiring and deploying reporters or field producers (personnel who set up stories but do not appear on camera) throughout the signal area to cultivate sources and learn what might be newsworthy. This is because subscriptions to newspapers, wire services, and "feeds" from network sources are substantially less costly than reporter or field producer salaries. So if a station acts rationally, a business model would predict largely passive discovery, or at least as passive as competing stations permit.

A JOURNALISTIC MODEL OF NEWS DISCOVERY

If news has a public service component in addition to being a product sold for profit, journalistic norms should influence the business rationale described above. To maximize public understanding of its environment, the fundamental mission of journalism, news departments must actively and independently scrutinize their environments. Even if more viewers could be attracted by selecting inexpensively discovered emotionally charged stories from wire and network sources than from choosing less arousing stories learned from covering local government and business, the journalistic model would require an orientation toward the latter. A journalistic model would predict largely active discovery, or at least as active a discovery process as the station could afford.

Method

To measure how active news discovery is at a particular station, you can examine how the newsroom is organized. For example, who is tasked with learning of events? How do they go about it, and how much time do they spend? It's also useful to classify the numbers of stories actually broadcast by the circumstances of their origination. If stations act rationally, selection priorities should match discovery priorities; a station deploys its resources where it expects to find what it considers most newsworthy.

To evaluate both the journalistic and cost implications of various means of discovery, three categories were created based on the level of observed and reported effort on the part of newsworkers. Two assumptions underlie these classifications: (1) In general, the more active the means of learning of issues and events outside the newsroom, the more completely journalistic norms of independent and objective surveillance of the environment are met. (2) By and large, the more active the means of such discovery, the greater the cost to the news department, principally in terms of staff size and time.

The categories were conservatively designed. Classification rules were not based on rigorous standards of independent journalism. In fact, they permit a station to be rated "highly active" without ever undertaking investigative reporting—where the station tries to establish evidence of socially significant incompetence or wrong-doing. Stories were classified by asking the person who originated the story how it was discovered. The respondent, most often the assignment editor, checked 1 of 11 boxes on a questionnaire corresponding to categories ranging from "from wire services," to "a question to which I wanted to find the answer."[3]

MINIMALLY ACTIVE DISCOVERY

Minimally active discovery includes events or issues that can be learned from promoters or other media firms without leaving or phoning outside the typical newsroom, other than to contact emergency service dispatchers. Such means include monitoring paper, telephonic, or video press releases; newspapers, radio, and television competitors; wire services; video "feeds" provided by networks[4] or mailed from independent producers of generic news materials; and scanning police and fire emergency radio channels. Discovering events from these sources is largely passive. An outside organization, for its own purposes, has revealed the event.

Stations incur two costs for stories discovered with minimal activity: (1) staff time spent scanning these sources; (2) subscription fees for newspapers, wire services, syndicated materials, and satellite feeds. Compared to more active means, such as deploying journalists to walk the halls of government, these costs are minimal. At all three stations, scanning incoming channels of information was primarily performed by news assistants earning the lowest wages in the newsroom. The annual budget for all subscriptions from outside news services was less than the average reporter's salary at each station.

MODERATELY ACTIVE DISCOVERY

Moderately active discovery includes events or issues that either originate from the news department through enterprise or previous reporting, or are communicated to the newsroom but require outside checking to ascertain newsworthiness. Examples are anonymous tips, follow-up stories, and enterprise reporting. These require greater effort than scanning events and issues already certified as news by an outside organization. Enterprise stories, in which a reporter or editor originates a question the story answers, require keeping up with news events and issues so as to notice what hasn't been addressed or what might tie together a series of events. Story leads based on earlier reporting require reporters to think and gather information more broadly than they might if completing only the assigned story. Listening to a phoned-in tip costs practically nothing, but verifying the information enough to proceed with a story may require a number of phone calls.

HIGHLY ACTIVE DISCOVERY

The third category—highly active discovery—required newsworkers to contact sources outside the newsroom. Issues and events reporters learned of while sitting through government, business, or social meetings belong in this category. Covering the bulk of a meeting requires a substantial time commitment. Only a fraction of the proceeding may be immediately newsworthy. Events discovered by conversing with sources the reporter has cultivated also fit in this category because of the time required to develop trust. Also events or patterns of events discovered in searches of government or business records or documents belong here because of the time they require. All investigations of government or corporate wrong-doing as well as systematic polls conducted or funded by the station were included in this category. Even if an investigation began with an anonymous tip, it was classified here because illegal or unethical behavior is often hidden and therefore requires diligence to uncover. Likewise, even though most polls begin as enterprise stories, they were placed here because framing the study questions and delineating the population to be surveyed may require considerable effort and background knowledge.

To assess whether these categories made sense, three veteran television journalists whose stations were not included in the study were asked to sort means of discovery into the three levels of increasing station effort. There was substantial agreement among the newsmen with the coding scheme.[5]

Although it creates only an ordinal measure—one category is higher than another but not by a set amount—the classification scheme has advantages over more precise methods considered. For example, putting a stopwatch on the discovery process for a particular story can be misleading. Suppose a reporter learned of a story within the first 2 minutes of a chat with a source she or he had spent weeks cultivating. If clocked by story, the discovery cost is 2 minutes. The real cost, however, should reflect all the visits during which the reporter was establishing rapport.[6]

Theoretical Expectations

All else held equal, *if a station seeks to maximize profit,* the newsroom will be organized to allocate greater resources to more passive means of discovery than either of the two more active categories. The proportion of airtime consumed by stories originating from minimally active means of discovery will be greater than the proportion originating from the moderately active, which in turn will be greater than the proportion originating from highly active means.

If a station compromises between market and journalistic norms, the newsroom will be organized to allocate roughly equal resources to active and passive means of discovery. One of two conditions should prevail: (1) Airtime will be relatively equally distributed among categories; or (2) More airtime will be found in the middle effort category than either of the others.

Finally, *if a station follows journalistic norms,* the newsroom will be organized to allocate greater resources to highly active discovery than to moderately or minimally active means. Airtime consumed by stories originating from highly active means of discovery will be greater than that originating from stories moderately actively discovered, which in turn will be greater than airtime consumed by stories classified minimally active.

How the Study Was Conducted

Each of the three stations participating in this part of the research was visited 3 days per week, for a total of 12 days over the course of a month. Visits were concentrated on Tuesdays, Wednesdays, and Thursdays to avoid lower staffing and atypical news availability of Mondays and Fridays. Weekend newscasts were excluded for the same reason.[7] On four of those days, one chosen randomly from each week (except in one case when the newsroom was so exhausted an alternate date was selected), I distributed questionnaires analyzing every story on the premier evening newscast. At all three stations the newscast that commanded the greatest newsroom resources was broadcast in the early evening and lasted one hour. Sports, weather, and commercial segments were outside the scope of the study. A total of 239 questionnaires—one per story—were returned of 274 distributed, a response rate of 87%.

In addition, I conducted a series of case studies shadowing reporters throughout their day. At the mid-sized station my sample included all reporters. At the two larger stations, however, there was not time to accompany all reporters. Those management and peers considered most able were selected in order to give newsrooms a chance to show their highest quality journalism.

Results

AT THE MID-SIZED STATION

Case Studies

The discovery function was almost exclusively the task of the assignment editor and two assistants. The description of their behavior that opened this chapter typified their daily routine during the period of study.

Most reporters at KMID were assigned beats—areas to search for news, such as city government, police or the environment. However, with an average demand of three stories per day, no reporter said he or she could spend more than a few minutes a day looking for newsworthy events. As the reporter assigned to cover the environment put it: "It's like a joke." A poll of all eight KMID news reporters indicated that they originated only 2% of the stories covered.

There was one incident of investigative reporting at KMID during the period of study, the "exposé" of alleged drug use at a large federal office complex that was described in Chapter 2. That report, however, named no officials nor departments of the federal agency. Despite that incident, seven of KMID's eight reporters expressed skepticism that the station would investigate suspected official wrongdoing. The eighth gave a neutral response. Most reporters also mentioned the timidity of the station during the local newspaper's investigation of the core city's mayor, also mentioned in Chapter 2.

Reporters were observed covering 16 stories. Of those, 5 were discovered in the newspaper, 4 were submitted by public relations agents, 3 were reported by the wire service, and 3 were suggested by reporters and editors. Of the 16, only the 3 enterprise stories could be classified as a moderately active means of discovery. None involved such active and time-consuming processes as developing sources or searching documents, or sitting through government meetings. Taken as a whole, the case studies describe a minimal commitment to actively examining the doings of local government and business. The business model of news discovery prevailed.

Quantitative Findings

The data from KMID are summarized in Figure 6.1. Frequencies were computed for each category of effort in two ways: The first was a straight count of stories; the second weighted those stories by the amount of time they consumed in the newscast. The second measure is a fairer representation of reality than the first, because it assigns greater value to the longer, major

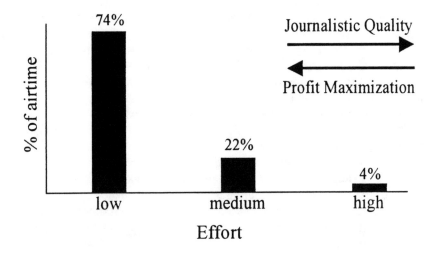

Figure 6.1. Distribution of Airtime at KMID

stories. The bar graph shows airtime for 93 stories. There is little probability that this pattern is due to chance alone.[8]

Regardless of measure, three quarters of the news portion of the broadcast was passively discovered; one-fifth came from moderately active discovery methods and less than 5% from highly active means. The market model overwhelmed the journalistic.

AT THE LARGE STATION

Case Studies

As at KMID, the discovery function was primarily the task of the assignment editor and his assistants. Also like KMID, KLRG learned of news from public relations agents seeking coverage, morning phone calls to police and fire dispatchers, monitoring emergency radio, and from other local media firms—primarily the local and regional newspapers. Network and regional feeds of video and the Associated Press broadcast wire were also received. Like KMID, KLRG also bought generic medical news features. Unlike KMID, KLRG operated a two-reporter bureau in another city within the signal area. News discovery at the bureau, however, also depended largely on secondhand news, particularly the newspaper, and assignments were made from the main newsroom.

Again reporters were assigned beats. Unlike KMID, reporters covered stories within their beats. A poll of 9 of KLRG's 14 news reporters estimated that they originated the ideas for one out of four stories covered, although observation of the assignment desk showed a lower level of reporter initiative. Reporters were supposed to receive one day per week to build rapport with sources and uncover news on their beats, but that day was routinely reclaimed by the assignment editor for a pressing story.

The nine reporters who responded to the survey said they spent one hour per day, on average, looking for newsworthy events and information. During the month of my visit, however, I observed only one reporter searching for future news stories. She relied solely on low and moderately active means of discovery. Charged with covering education in two major cities, several counties, and the state board of education, as well as several state universities within the station's signal area, she expressed frustration. On her desk were a stack of regional newspapers "I haven't had time to read," she said. "It's too much!" Her solution to the overload was to call the public relations officers of the larger school districts and ask, "What's controversial?" The strategy was not particularly effective, she conceded, because public information officers disclose information selectively, usually showing their employers only in a positive light.

Despite its location in a large city, KLRG employed no city hall reporter. "We routinely miss what goes on in city hall, except for the really big things," the assignment editor explained. "And we read newspapers to get that."

Like KMID, KLRG appeared to investigate government and corporations very infrequently. Polled reporters said the station was unwilling to commit resources to investigations. Two stories challenged this perception, however. Both were multipart series prepared for the following month, a "sweeps" month when the station's audience would be measured. The stories both involved week-long trips to Latin American nations, to El Salvador and Nicaragua. The reporting, writing, and editing was described in Chapter 2, so I'll only summarize here. The stories were commissioned immediately after a competing station aired stories from a similar foreign visit. The reporters responsible for writing KLRG's stories both complained of pressure from the news director to depoliticize their reporting—emphasize the suffering but censor references to its causes, particularly criticism of U.S. policy. The news director later explained that both stories were "lose-lose" propositions for the station because in his view the audience was deeply polarized on U.S. involvement in Central America. If the coverage appeared to favor either side, he said, partisans on the other side might switch channels. Such reasoning is the antithesis of investigative reporting—which seeks to reveal the truth regardless of the message's popularity.

I directly observed seven complete stories. Of those: three were suggested by public relations agents, one was taken from the newspaper, and one story's origin was unclear. In the two remaining cases, moderately active modes of discovery were observed; one story originated from checking out a phoned-in tip and another was the idea of a reporter. No observed stories originated from cultivated sources, document searches, or attending government meetings.

Although more attention was paid to news discovery at KLRG than KMID, the station still relied more upon inexpensive outside sources to learn of newsworthy events than on its own staff. More tellingly, when the station did exercise initiative in learning of news, it suppressed reporters' findings when they collided with the economic interest in maximizing audience (and, perhaps, when they might have offended advertisers or the parent corporation and its investors).

Quantitative Findings

The quantitative analysis graphed in Figure 6.2 tells a similar story. Stories discovered with minimal effort consumed about 60% of the news portion of the broadcasts, moderate-activity discovery takes the rest, except for 1% that is highly active. The graph shows airtime for 56 stories. (The count is lower than at KMID or KVLG because I grouped a set of stories about a teacher's strike together into one larger story. Thus, effort that went into any part of the coverage was weighted for the whole. Every benefit of the doubt goes to the station.) Again, the pattern is so distinct there is little probability it can be explained by chance.[9]

AT THE VERY LARGE STATION

Case Studies

Between 7 a.m. and 4 p.m., KVLG employed five persons at its main newsroom to discover newsworthy events within the major metropolitan area the station's signal encompassed. Three editorial assistants listened to emergency scanner radios and an all-news radio station. The assistants also scanned stories sent to the station by the Associated Press and a local news wire service. The assignment editor read the area's four major newspapers and several minor daily papers, monitored the wire services, and kept an ear on the scanners. Lastly, a planner reviewed press releases and clipped stories from newspapers and national news magazines.

The station also maintained a four-person bureau in the area's second largest city, a two-person bureau (since eliminated) in the state capital, and

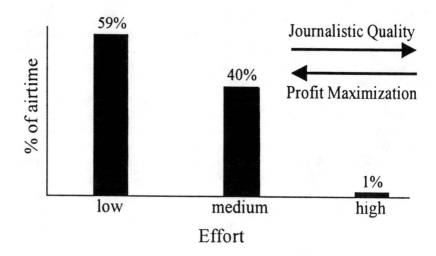

Figure 6.2. Distribution of Airtime at KLRG

a one-person bureau in the third largest city in the area. KVLG also partially sponsored a bureau in Washington, D.C. The bureaus discovered news in the same manner as the home newsroom—relying on the scanner radio and local newspapers, with an occasional story developed by reporters. All assignments were made from the central newsroom.

Only 4—of 19 news reporters and field producers working for the early evening newscast—were assigned to specific beats. The remainder were on general assignment. With 19 journalists to cover an area home to several million persons, a beat system would be a charade, the news director explained. Eleven of the 19 reporters and field producers who responded to questionnaires said they spent an average of 2 hours daily searching for news. The average here is deceptive, however. Several field producers and reporters accounted for most of the discovery time. They belonged to an investigative projects team.

Most reporters interviewed felt discovery was not their responsibility. In a signal area with three large and scores of medium-sized cities, one reporter still managed to complain, "the problem is there's not enough local news sometimes. It produces 'licking the spoon' journalism. There's not much there so you have to lick the spoon." Such a passive attitude suggests an unfamiliarity with enterprise reporting or investigation.

As at the smaller stations, most reporters interviewed and observed tended to rely on public relations officers and top bureaucrats to warn them about news even though they acknowledged that such officials are unlikely to call public attention to controversies that might show their agency in a negative light.

There were several exceptions to the pattern of passive discovery, however. On one occasion, KVLG joined with a local newspaper in sponsoring a comprehensive political poll in the region's major city. Such discovery is expensive. The most impressive exception was investigative reporting. KVLG was one of the few television stations in the nation to have an investigative team and a special projects producer. That producer drew on the 19 newsworkers allotted to the evening newscast. The investigative team comprised 4 field producers who dug up and reported stories but did not appear on camera. The team's efforts, however, were not a daily part of the newscast. Instead, the team concentrated on series of stories that ran periodically. One series ran during the month of observation and the investigative team produced one other story during the observation period and assisted on at least one more. The investigative and special projects work of KVLG reporters accounted for many of the nearly 300 television journalism prizes decorating the newsroom walls.

Because reporters often spent a day on each story, only seven stories could be followed from start to finish within the observation period. Of those seven, three came from minimally active means of discovery—one each from the newspaper, the scanner radio, and the news wire. Three showed moderate activity. They were developed through enterprise—reporters or editors pursuing their own questions. One story—the only Category 3 method observed at all three stations—was generated from a reporter who had developed a relationship with a source.

News discovery at KVLG described a compromise between the market model and the journalistic. It was the only station of those studied to commit significant resources to highly active scrutiny of its environment.

Quantitative Findings

The quantitative analysis of story origination summarized in Figure 6.3 supports the observational study. Although the percentage of time spent in minimally active discovery is nearly twice that spent in highly active, the majority of stories fall in the middle category. The graph shows airtime for 90 stories. Again, the pattern is unlikely to be explained by chance.[10]

Discussion

In all but the sample from the largest station, minimally active—essentially passive—news discovery prevailed. However, station size did make a

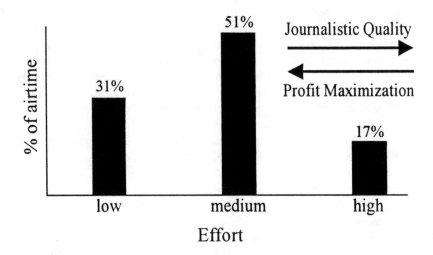

Figure 6.3. Distribution of Airtime at KVLG

difference in discovery effort that cannot be explained by chance. The greater the station's resources, the more active the discovery.[11]

A simple explanation might be that the larger the market, the more the station can afford to discover news actively. But this explanation is too simple, partly because each of the stations visited made enough profit to afford a much more active discovery profile. A fuller explanation arises from the analysis of how markets work, in Chapters 4 and 5.

That analysis suggests that the market model and the normative model of journalism overlap somewhat more in larger than smaller markets. This occurs because as market size increases, the number of consumers who demand informative news reaches a minimum economic threshold—enough people to attract advertisers. If news executives wish to compete for such viewers—many of whom may be middle-class or higher income—they may need to spend more to learn what's going on.

To some extent market reasoning even supports the presence of an investigative team at KVLG: In a market as big and as competitive as the one KVLG served, enough highly educated and motivated consumers live to render the occasional investigative report valuable in differentiating the station somewhat from its competitors. On the other hand, a station maintaining a permanent investigative team pays a high price for a competitive edge. Other strategies for expanding upscale audience may be more cost-effective. At this point in the study, it seems more reasonable to classify KVLG's investigative team as evidence of normative rather than market journalism.

Conclusion

Taken as a whole, these results indicate that when market logic and journalism logic conflicted at the first stage of news production, market logic won most of the time. Even at KVLG with its investigative team, almost twice as much airtime was consumed by stories discovered relatively passively as by highly active means. Across the three stations, the market was served better than the public.

Society enjoys some benefit even when a station merely repeats news reported by other sources—particularly the part of society that doesn't read newspapers. But journalism demands more. At the least, it requires independent scrutiny of the environment in the expectation that the more agencies seeking answers the better for the public's perception of reality. Also, from the time of John Stuart Mill in England and Thomas Jefferson in the United States, a primary social value of news media has arisen from their role as a check on the power of government, and now business as well.[12] In fact, it is the "watchdog" role ascribed to news-gathering that justifies its special protection under the First Amendment.[13] Reliance on passive means of discovering the environment abdicates this role.

Finally, passive discovery tends to surrender control over the public information stream to powerful interests in government, large corporations, and among the wealthy.[14] By reducing the cost of discovery of events and views flattering to themselves, these special interests can take advantage of cost-conscious media to influence what the public learns.[15] The proliferation of public relations efforts suggests that these special interests are eager to assume such influence.[16]

While passive discovery has civic costs, active discovery may have corporate costs. Hiring additional personnel to look for stories might reduce profit margins if larger audiences were not attracted to a more independent newscast. Even were more active news discovery to trim profits, however, there is still room for stations to do well by doing good. Figures compiled by the National Association of Broadcasters for 1985, the year before this study began, showed a median pretax profit on gross revenues of 15.8% for stations of KMID's size and type, 30% for KLRG, and 39% for KVLG. Compare these figures to the national manufacturing average of 9%. Even with some diminishment in network affiliate audiences since this research was conducted, it appears that local television news could afford to do considerably better.

Notes

1. Herman & Chomsky, 1988.
2. Barney, 1987, p. 15.

3. The assignment editor, producer, reporters, and writers were asked the following questions in separate questionnaires. Producers normally selected nonlocal news; assignment editors chose local news. For local stories the responses of reporters, writers, and assignment editors were cross-checked. In the few cases of discrepancies, further questioning led to an assignment of the story to the appropriate category.

I. MINIMALLY ACTIVE DISCOVERY

Did the story idea originate primarily from:
- ☐ A press release/announcement, or phone call from a PIO?
- ☐ Material provided by another news organization—wire service, network or other feed, newspaper, magazine, radio, other television station?
- ☐ Emergency frequency scanner radio?
- ☐ Routine checks with police/emergency dispatchers?

II. MODERATELY ACTIVE DISCOVERY

Did the story idea originate primarily from:
- ☐ A news conference?
- ☐ A phoned-in tip from an unofficial source?
- ☐ A question to which I wanted to find the answer?
- ☐ Reporter/writer enterprise, that is, a story idea suggested by a reporter or writer?
- ☐ A follow-up from a previously reported story?

III. HIGHLY ACTIVE DISCOVERY
Did the story idea originate primarily from:

- ☐ Talking to sources I have developed?
- ☐ Attending a meeting or perusing documents of an institution, either governmental or private?
- ☐ All investigative stories and those relying on systematic polls conducted by the station were also included here, regardless of where the story idea originated. An investigative story was one where a journalist through his/her enterprise uncovered allegations of governmental or business wrongdoing.

4. Because local news programming at each station was immediately followed or preceded by national network news, stories taken from network sources were seen within the three newsrooms as "filler."

5. A coefficient of intercoder reliability, Cronbach's alpha, was .87. The lowest correlation between my placement of sources and those of a coder was .73 (Spearman's rho).

6. The author welcomes suggestions for more precise measures.

7. Because weekend newscasts at each station tended to depend more heavily on wire stories and other nonlocally originated news, this sample makes the stations appear somewhat more active than they were.

8. Chi-square goodness of fit test: chi-square statistic = 73.4, with two degrees of freedom, $p < .001$. Response rate was 94%.

9. Chi-square goodness of fit test. Chi-square statistic = 29.4 with 2 degrees of freedom; $p < .001$. Response rate = 75%.

10. Chi-square goodness of fit test. Chi-square statistic = 16 with 2 degrees of freedom; $p < .001$. Response rate = 90%.

11. A 3×3 chi-square test of association between station size and level of activity shows a significant correlation; chi-square = 40.3, df = 4, $p < .001$.

12. Siebert, Peterson, & Schramm, 1956.

13. Meiklejohn, 1948, cited in Blasi, 1977.

14. Boorstin, 1961.

15. Gandy, 1982.

16. Boorstin, 1961.

7

The Second Stage of News Production:
Selecting Events for Coverage

This chapter examines the interplay of journalistic and market logic in decisions about which of the events and issues learned of at Stage 1 become part of the evening news.

Selection Possibilities

Watching local television news, you might be tempted to think that story selection is essentially random. There's usually a snippet from national news and something from somewhere in the state, perhaps a crop failure, multiple vehicle accident, or natural calamity. Most of the stories are local, but they jump around the signal area. There may be a feature about how one particular class of kindergartners, among the hundreds of kindergarten classes in the area, are celebrating, say, Halloween. And of all the city and county councils and all the planning and utility boards meeting on a particular day in the scores of incorporated cities and towns the station's signal reaches, one is singled out for coverage and the rest ignored. And although numerous incidents of mayhem took place in those cities and towns since the last newscast, only two or three make the evening news.

The list of potentially newsworthy events and issues in the typical television market is virtually unlimited. Factories and offices are opening and closing. Industries are being born and some are dying. The nature of the workforce and the kinds of workers and the education they require are changing. Cities and counties are passing new laws and erasing old ones. Politicians, business leaders, and citizens groups are planning community futures, including who will benefit and who will be burdened. Vital goods and services are dropping or rising in price. Some neighborhoods are becoming safer and the houses repaired, while others decline. The nature of families is changing and both genders are trying to understand themselves and each other. Civic and corporate leaders are rising and falling. Some are dying. Universities and corporate research labs are solving old problems and discovering new ones. Painters, musicians, writers, and artists of every kind are creating. Some schools are closing while others are consolidated and new ones are built. Roads, shopping centers, and new housing tracts are being planned. The traffic is usually getting worse. Air and water quality are changing. Populations are changing; not just growing or declining, but changing in hue, language, and culture. And then there's what occurs in a day by accident, happenstance, or forces of nature.

Despite this wide array of potential news stories, my own research, plus casual monitoring of the competition at each station I visited, suggest that of the minute fraction that are broadcast, many are covered by more than one station. As we saw in the previous chapter, one reason for the similarity is that stations tend to be passive discoverers of their environment. They rely heavily on the same external news departments and public relations officers in government and industry to tell them what's going on. But passive discovery alone cannot explain why competing stations choose the same or similar events for the evening news while ignoring others. Even in the smallest newsroom, so many events and issues are brought to the station's attention and so few make the newscast that a common logic must guide the winnowing process.

At all but one of the stations studied, this logic was so well understood among those choosing the news that little argument or comment arose about what would be included. The theory of selection was evident only from patterns among the choices made. Listening to those selection meetings revealed little of the criteria of newsworthiness. But at one station, the one serving a large market, there was disharmony. And in those discussions, where each side had to justify its selections, the logic was manifest.

At the large station, KLRG, an experiment was under way. The news director had recently hired a young newspaper reporter to the key selection role of assignment editor. He reasoned that it would be easier to teach a local print journalist the rules of television than to give a television journalist hired from outside the market a crash course in what was going on in the region. The word *experiment* implies that there was some risk. Welcoming a print reporter who had never before worked in television news evoked anxiety or, more often, ridicule from the staff. Almost universally it was viewed as a mistake. Although the unusual hire may have had little to do with it, the news director was fired within several months of the decision. And after a year marked by great frustration, the assignment editor returned to newspapers.

But the conflict between the assignment editor, whom I'll call Dave, and the newsroom uniquely illuminated the station's selection logic, a way of thinking only a little different from that in the other newsrooms studied.

Case Study: Journalistic Versus Market Logic

The brick and glass corner office of the news director began to fill a few minutes after 8 a.m. Five persons, four men and one woman, crowded in for the morning news selection meeting. In order of authority they were the news director, his assistant, the executive editor, the producer, and Dave, the assignment editor.

It was a Tuesday morning in January, the day after the station learned of the possible closure of a local Air Force base in proposed Pentagon budget-cutting. Dave seized upon the story as the most significant in weeks. The base payroll contributed many millions of dollars to the local economy. Closure would ripple through the real estate and service industries among hundreds of businesses that served the base and its employees.

As assignment editor, Dave chaired the meeting. He had mapped out four stories related to the closure. He wanted a reporter from the Washington bureau of the group of stations to which KLRG belongs to determine the likelihood of closure. Locally, he wanted one reporter to find out what closure would mean to the local economy. Story three would examine how residential neighborhoods had encroached on areas near the base, violating Air Force recommendations for open areas adjacent to noisy jet runways. The Air Force had mentioned the creeping advance of housing near the base as one reason for closure. Lastly, the assignment editor wanted a story about crowded airspace over the base, another Air Force concern.

In addition to the set of stories about the base closure, four other stories made the "must cover" list for the evening news: (1) the arrival of the "Slice" soft drink blimp on a promotional visit; (2) a humorous "postcard" travel piece by the newsroom's designated feature reporter; (3) an interview with Nazi-hunter Elie Wiesel; and (4) "a cute little VO" (voice over—a story with video and narration in which the reporter doesn't appear) about the "Letterman Club" in an adjacent city. Club members had to resemble humorist David Letterman by having a gap in their teeth large enough to pass a dime through.

These four were approved with little discussion, but the intense coverage Dave planned for the possible closure of the Air Force base stirred a heated debate. The news director was displeased. The newscast taking shape seemed too dull. "I tell you what could be the lead [story]," he said. "Whatever the [professional basketball team in the city] announces today." Dave barely acknowledged the suggestion. The news director tried another tack. Earlier that morning a freak wind storm had shattered several glass windows of downtown skyscrapers in a city just beyond the station's signal area. "The wind is at least interesting, since everyone has to put up with it," he said. "It may be our lead story today. Nothing else I've seen comes close."

The news director also said he'd read or heard that one savings and loan association had recently dropped home mortgage rates to their lowest point in 15 years. The executive editor suggested a story about a power line across state borders that might increase the local availability of electric power.

The news director and his assistant looked again at the base closure stories. They spoke in unison: "Every single thing we have is economic!" Dave defended his choices: "But half of what we do in news could have an economic base. This is not a series of dissertations on economics." He suggested dropping a humorous piece planned on the complexity of new federal W4 forms for withholding payroll taxes.

The news director pushed for a story about an apartment complex where the water had been off for 5 days. How the residents were coping and what the problem was could be "an interesting little story," he said. He was miffed that the story was left out of the previous day's newscast, when he first mentioned it. Dave responded with a hint of exasperation. The landlord had been trying in good faith to fix the problem, he said, was rebating rent during the period, and repairs were expected to be complete today.

The producer lobbied for sending a reporter to a hospital about 3 hours away to cover the story of a local woman who gave birth to triplets after undergoing in vitro (test tube) fertilization. But Dave had already rejected the story, he said, because like the apartments without water, it had little significance. But, the producer argued, "most of our stuff today is institutional. We're in the TV business! This is the kind of story that grabs everyone. A modern miracle. It's interesting." The executive editor agreed: "There's a story that's got everything! It's got modern conflict. . . . It's got cute nurses and it's a damn interesting human story. It's a story that sells tickets."

Ultimately, the evening newscast combined the important with the merely interesting, but not in equal proportions. It answered only one question about the threatened base closure, for example. It addressed the issue of housing encroachment on the runways. The central questions—how likely was the closure and how might it affect the local economy—were left unanswered. The postcard ran. The test tube triplets were covered in a heart-warming way. But neither the science of in vitro fertilization, nor the ethical issues of mixing the ingredients of life in a plastic dish were mentioned. There was an attempt to make fun of the new federal withholding forms. And the winds dissipated, but not before scaring off the Slice blimp.

Selection Logic

The theory of commercial news production developed in earlier chapters predicts that story selections, far from being random, will follow one of three kinds of logic:

1. predominantly journalistic;
2. predominantly market;
3. a compromise between journalism and market.

Which path is chosen depends upon the magnitude of the demand for profit by owners and how managers interpret it.

JOURNALISTIC SELECTION LOGIC

The principal ethical codes of journalism that we examined in Chapter 2 follow what Professor Fred Siebert called the "social responsibility" theory of news.[1] This theory was most clearly propounded by a group that included some of the leading intellectuals and journalists of the day. The group was headed by University of Chicago president Robert M. Hutchins and called the Commission on Freedom of the Press. The Commission listed as the first "requirement" of the news media: "A truthful, comprehensive, and intelligent account of the day's events in a context which gives them meaning."[2] The goal of such information, according to the Commission, was public empowerment through democratic processes, not the private gain of media firms. News should orient people to their environment, thus helping them make informed decisions. At the selection stage, ethical local news departments should choose those current issues and events likely to generate the most learning about the local public's environment for the most people.

MARKET SELECTION LOGIC

Market selection logic is straightforward and similar to that developed in earlier chapters. To maximize return to investors, the newsroom should pick those issues and events that have the greatest ratio of expected appeal for demographically desirable audiences to cost of news-gathering. Further, stories should advance, or at least minimize harm to, the interests of advertisers and investors.

COMPROMISE SELECTION LOGIC

A compromise between these two selection logics can be achieved in two principal ways:

1. Divide broadcast time between stories that follow one logic and stories that follow the other.
2. Concentrate on those issues and events where the two types of logic coincide.

As we saw in Chapter 5, the two logics don't always collide. Some events from which the public is likely to learn a great deal also attract a large audience, including the young and affluent. And sometimes these events can be covered by a single reporter and photographer in only a few hours. News conferences in which government or corporate officials announce major changes in policy may offer examples. An assignment editor might choose to cover events such as a dramatic budget message by a mayor or governor that both educates the public to an important change in the local environment and attracts a large audience. Demonstrations and protests that signal significant issues and changes in the local environment are another example. They are important and they may be widely appealing because of their confrontative nature, which is often highly visual, noisy, and sometimes violent. They are also likely to be inexpensive to cover because they usually occur in a specific, prearranged place and end within several hours. Few of these events are likely to involve the station's advertisers or investors.

Even stories that are expensive to gather, such as investigations of official wrongdoing or stupidity, may generate enough audience to recover the station's investment and a respectable profit. The success of CBS's *60 Minutes*, which has consistently ranked among the most popular programs on television, demonstrates the interest investigative reporting can generate, particularly if it is suffused with emotional, combative interviews. Investigative stories, because they are first reported as "exclusives" and then widely repeated in other media that may credit the originating station, have particular competitive value. A station might seek to be the public's indispensable news source, or at least the first place to seek news.

Investigative reporting can both be profitable and fulfill the highest standards of journalism, but it is a risky strategy for maximizing return to investors. For each investigation that creates a splash in the community, others fail to pan out because the mis- or malfeasance isn't proved, or it excites little public attention. Another danger is the risk of a suit charging libel. Defending in court can cost hundreds of thousands of dollars in legal fees even when the station wins. In fact, legal fees are nearly inevitable in investigative reporting because lawyers must be hired to review stories if stations are to minimize their exposure to libel suits.[3]

Determining Which Selection Logic Prevails

Whichever the news department's selection logic, news content must be appealing. This is because news is produced within the context of a voluntary exchange with consumers. No one is forced to watch. Appeal is a commercial imperative. But appeal is also the necessary means to the end of informing: the news must attract our attention before we can learn from it.

The Two Dimensions of Appeal

What makes news content appealing? A synthesis of research about the "uses and gratifications" of news suggests that people consume news for two basic reasons: The first is primarily intellectual, or cognitive—to orient themselves to their environments. The second is primarily emotional—to be engaged in an entertaining, diverting, or para-social way. In a comprehensive review of uses and gratifications research, Professor Lawrence Wenner argues convincingly for a gratifications "map" with just two dimensions—content and process gratifications. Content gratifications, or rewards, result from primarily cognitive activities: "message uses to gain knowledge, increase or reduce uncertainty in personal and social situations or support existing predispositions."[4] Process gratifications are primarily affective, or emotional: "consumption activities that take place apart from the content per se, and include a myriad of 'escape' uses, stimulation uses that often involve engagement in 'entertainment,' and uses combatting social isolation through connections with mediated culture and its actors."[5] A two-dimensional view is also advanced by Professors Seth Finn and William Christ—"information-seeking and entertainment-seeking,"[6] and developed by Lewis Donohew, Howard Sypher, and Tory Higgins.[7]

In more concrete terms, people watch the evening news for *informational reasons*—to learn who won an election, which parts of their community are safe and which dangerous, what political and business leaders are up to, whether to carry an umbrella tomorrow, and so forth, and for *reasons of entertainment or other emotional reward*—to vicariously experience the fear of someone surviving a fire or traffic accident, to hear the comforting voice or watch the attractive face and physique of a news anchor, to smile at repartee between the news readers and the weather forecaster, to be amazed at the luck of a lottery winner or horrified at the brutality of a killer on trial, and so forth.[8] *Entertainment* will be used hereafter in this broader sense; not just what's amusing, but what contains any of the elements that make media content interesting except those used for orientation.

These two dimensions of news content—orientation and entertainment— suggest a way to analyze which selection logic operates at a news department.

ENTERTAINMENT DRAWS MORE
VIEWERS THAN DOES ORIENTATION

Although public attention may be attracted to news content through either an expectation of orientation or entertainment, or both, the drawing power of these two dimensions is unequal for at least three reasons.

First, on routine news days a particular story containing orientating information is likely to appeal to only a small segment of the public. As Robert Ezra Park observed, "each and all of us live in a world of which we are the center."[9] Although produced for masses, commercial news is consumed by individuals. Their greatest need for orientation is close to home— what's happening to *their* job, *their* neighborhood, *their* child's school. Even if national or state trends may prompt them, decisions about such local matters are usually made by local public and corporate officials and have primarily local effect. A decision to close or build a school or plant, to construct a shopping center or highway, or to raise property or sales taxes is likely to be consequential only for those directly affected. Events and issues with orientation value across the thousands of square miles of the typical signal of a station are not frequent enough to fill daily news programming. Entertainment generalizes far better. A powerful human interest story, a bizarre turn of events, or the doings of celebrities are likely to enjoy wide appeal, whether or not consumers gain understanding of their community from them.

A second reason why orienting information has less commercial value than entertaining information is because orienting information is more likely to be about issues than events. If we are to learn about how our community works, we must enter the world of abstraction and generalization. We give names to trends and patterns in events, linking them together to make sense of them. We speak of crime waves and recessions, of economic booms, of contractions and expansions of school populations, of ecosystems and problems of homelessness. Issues are interpretations of the relationships among events. They are abstractions, and thus invisible. So generally they are more challenging to illustrate than discrete events. Television's technological advantage over newspapers is maximized by selecting visually compelling events, such as a fire with leaping flames or a tearful interview with the survivor of a highway accident. That advantage is not fully exploited by video of "talking heads" discussing how certain types of fires might be prevented by changes in building codes or accidents reduced by redesigning highways. Selecting issues over events for coverage may limit the visual excitement of a newscast.

Last, orienting information may demand more of the viewer's attention than does entertaining content. Reasoned arguments, complexity, detail— these require more concentration than simple descriptions of a single event. The complexity of issues may bore and drive away the marginal news viewer who has tuned in to be entertained. Moreover, serious news may perplex the viewer who is also engaged in a simultaneous activity such as preparing a meal, eating, conversing, and so forth.

ORIENTATION COSTS MORE THAN ENTERTAINMENT

So far we have examined the difference between entertainment and orientation in maximizing audience, the benefit side of the analysis. Orienting content also tends to cost more to produce than entertaining content. Orienting stories normally require background reporting. Because they frequently involve issues, more than one side must be gathered under objectivity norms. And trend reporting, which often links problems faced by one locality to others, is expensive. It requires news-gathering at multiple sites. By contrast, entertaining stories are often about a single incident and the important sources are frequently in one place, at the scene.

The conflict between the news department's interest in maximizing public understanding of current events and its interest in maximizing return to investors originates in these two dimensions of news content. Particularly in television, the orientation dimension has more journalistic value than commercial value. And the entertainment dimension has more commercial value than journalistic. This is not to argue that entertainment values have no place in news. I shall argue that the most effective stories combine entertainment values and orientational ones. And emotion is important for building a sense of community,[10] a shared purpose that motivates learning about local issues and acting upon them. Still, the primary purpose of news should not be to arouse emotion, but to empower by informing.

COMBINING ORIENTATION AND ENTERTAINMENT

Skilled journalists usually can find a way to combine consequential and entertaining content. A creative television journalist can illustrate even the most abstract issue, particularly now that stations have the ability to produce computerized graphs. Secondly, a good reporter can broaden interest in an orienting issue or event by adding elements of entertainment. The reverse is also true.

But these additions usually come at a cost the profit-maximizing corporation may not wish to pay. For instance, a dull school board or city hall story can be enlivened with human interest value by gathering reactions from affected citizens. In printed and radio media, such reactions can be gathered by phone. If television stations seek to maximize their technological advantage over these other media by videotaping interviews, however, television reporters usually must travel to add citizen sources. The travel consumes both reporter and photographer time. Mixing orientational content with reporting of a primarily entertaining event also costs time. Finding a pattern to give an isolated event, such as an accident, fire, or murder, broader meaning may require checking government records or talking to additional sources. Creating bar, pie, or other graphics that give abstractions visual representation also adds cost, primarily in time spent gathering data for meaningful comparisons.

Graphics that run simultaneously with narration may not increase story length. But adding orienting information to a merely entertaining story or adding entertaining touches to a dry orientational piece results in a story that consumes more airtime. For broadcast media, lengthening stories that do justice both to the informational and entertaining sides of stories may drive away viewers uninterested in the subject. In print, uninterested readers can quit or bypass long stories of little personal interest and move on to something they like. Not so in television where the only choice is to wait the story out or invest your attention elsewhere, with a competing station or activity.

Measuring the Two Dimensions

What viewers care enough to watch varies from one individual to the next and can only be estimated from within the newsroom. "News values" are criteria journalists apply to events hoping to make an accurate assessment of what will capture the widest attention and most enlarge public understanding. In general, the more news values that apply and the more intense they are for more viewers, the more newsworthy the event.[11]

A synthesis of research about criteria of newsworthiness yields the following news values:

1. Timeliness—how new, or recent is the issue or event?
2. Proximity—how close to the location of the viewers is the issue or event?
3. Consequence—how important is the issue or event to local viewers?
4. Human interest—how much emotion does the issue or event generate?
5. Prominence—how well known are the people in the issue or event?
6. Unusualness—how unlikely or surprising is the issue or event?
7. Conflict—how much disagreement/destruction is there between persons, organizations, nations, or between humans and nature?

8. Visual quality—how arresting are the visuals that might be gathered about the issue or event?

9. Amusement—how much immediate gratification, such as a smile or laugh, irony, or satisfaction of curiosity does the issue or event have?

10. Topicality—how much audience interest already exists about the issue or event?

Although all 10 news values figure in selecting issues and events for coverage, they are unequal in their contribution. From the viewpoint of social responsibility theory, issues and events that have little or no consequence contribute little to journalism's primary aim—orienting people to their environment by maximizing public understanding. Events that are timely, proximate, topical, visual, amusing, unusual, and involve prominent people in an event of great human interest—say an elaborate and ballyhooed eighth wedding of a local celebrity—still may add little to viewers' understanding of their community. If such issues and events are widely interesting, however, they may enlarge attention to more consequential events in the newscast. Consequence is the primary news value. Given how little space both stations and newspapers provide for news each day, the inclusion of any story with little or no consequence is open to challenge.

To determine whether a station is following journalistic, market, or some compromise set of norms, I asked two pairs of expert journalists to watch videotapes of newscasts, pause after each story, and rate the intensity of various news values incorporated in stories. The journalists were recruited from the highly competitive Knight Fellowship Program, a 10-month sabbatical for mid-career reporters and editors at Stanford University. All were from newspapers;[12] none was affiliated in any way with the stations studied. The pairs rated nearly 300 stories from 12 newscasts, 4 at each of the three participating stations. As in other parts of the study, sports, weather, and commercials were excluded from analysis. All but one of the newscasts were randomly selected. (On one day the staff was too exhausted to undertake a parallel part of the study within the newsroom.) Each member of the journalist pairs rated stories for each news value from 0—the value wasn't represented in the story—to 7—the value was very intense. The judges were instructed to "consider this an account of a routine news day. Set your scales accordingly, that is, accounts of routine news events that are carefully reported should have a chance at high rankings on the values present." The average of the two assessments was used in the analysis. Their agreement on each news value was moderately high; matching the two coders assessments resulted in statistical (Pearson's r) correlations ranging from a low of .5 to a high of .9. (A correlation of 0 would mean no pattern of agreement different from chance while a score of 1.0 indicates perfect agreement.)

The orientation value of stories was based on two consequence values—personal and social. I defined social consequence as "the potential of the event or information to change the social or political environment directly, or indirectly by changing how it is understood, for a least part—say 5%—of those in the viewing area." Personal consequence was defined as "usefulness, potential of the event/information to help at least a part—say 5%—of those in the viewing area improve themselves or their lives in some way."[13] Five other news values—human interest, conflict, unusualness, amusement, and visual quality—constituted the entertainment index. I defined those values as described in the general list of news values. These five tend to build audience.[14] Because the coding journalists had little or no experience of the stations' markets, they weren't asked to assess either topicality or prominence. Two other news values—timeliness and proximity—were interpreted as essential to local news. As other researchers have discovered, these two varied little from story to story in stories the station originated and may be considered inherent in the concept of news.[15] In other words, stories the stations produced themselves usually dealt with issues and events occurring within the market area and almost all had occurred within the past 24-48 hours.

When the entertainment and orientation dimensions are crossed at their midpoints, every story could be placed somewhere in the resulting quadrants. Stories could be orienting and entertaining, neither, or more entertaining than orienting, or more orienting than entertaining (see Figure 7.1).

On the orientation dimension, the higher of the two consequence ratings was used to place the story. Although journalism's codes of ethics clearly elevate social consequence over personal consequence as a news value, both have orientational value. The higher score was taken because there is no reason to expect a story with one kind of consequence necessarily to possess the other.[16]

For the entertainment dimension, each of the five audience-building values present in the story was averaged and stories were again placed above or below the midpoint. Because not every story could be expected to contain each of the five audience-building values, absent news values were not counted in the average. And because editors believed the most salient news values were the most important in selection, the average was weighted with the most intense values counting more than the less intense.[17]

Using this approach, we can count the number of stories in each quadrant and make some inference about which selection path the station had chosen. It would be more accurate, however, to weight the stories by their airtime. If a station spends 6 minutes on a consequential and widely appealing investigation of state government, for example, that selection should count more than a 20-second story that is unimportant and uninteresting. So the quadrants represent airtime rated on its orienting and entertainment values.

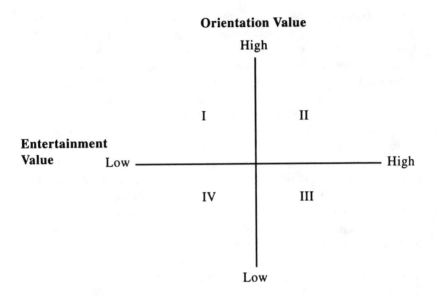

Figure 7.1. The Two Dimensions of News

MAKING SENSE OF THE QUADRANTS

Here's a scorecard by which to judge the results:

Quadrant I. Not a place for the easily bored. Here you'll find issues and events expected to yield content that is high in orientation value, but low in entertainment, that is, important but dull. If the idea is to help as many viewers learn as much as possible, such choices are suboptimal, but defensible given scarce resources. A station with high journalistic integrity but few reporters might concentrate the bulk of its airtime in this quadrant. A station with greater resources, however, would be expected to commit enough reporter time to move some stories from this quadrant into Quadrant II. From the standpoint of the market, Quadrant I is a loser. Such issues and events consume resources to cover, but are likely to drive away many more viewers than they attract. A station organized to maximize profit will generally avoid this quadrant.

Quadrant II. The only place market and journalistic logic agree. Here you'll find events and issues expected to yield content that is high both in orientation and entertainment value, that is, interesting and important stories. Such choices are optimal in terms of journalistic ethics. These choices are also optimal in terms of consumer demand from a market standpoint. They are likely to please both viewers who watch for pleasure and those who watch to be informed. Unless a station has spent heavily to learn about its community, however, selectors will rarely have discovered enough Quadrant II issues and events to fill the newscast. That still leaves open the possibility of converting events/issues that are natural Quadrant Is or IIIs into IIs. Important but dull Quadrant I events can result in Quadrant II stories by adding entertainment values, such as human interest, conflict, unusualness, or compelling visuals, to enliven them. Often, interesting but unimportant events and issues, Quadrant IIIs, can be salvaged by adding personal or social consequence. But either conversion strategy consumes resources. A station with few resources but journalistic integrity would push as many stories as possible into Quadrant II. But such a station might still fall short of placing half its airtime here. On the other hand, Quadrant II should account for the bulk of a large, resource-rich station's airtime.

From a market standpoint, it rarely makes sense to convert Quadrant III events/issues into Quadrant II stories. As we discussed earlier, adding consequence may add affected serious news viewers, but may cost those watching primarily for the entertainment values because the consequential information must either lengthen the story or displace entertaining elements. Unless the added information is very widely appealing, the cost—in terms of additional reporting and risked entertainment audience— may exceed the benefit. Converting dull Quadrant I stories to more appealing Quadrant IIs runs similar risks.

Quadrant III. The cotton candy quadrant. Here you'll find events and issues expected to yield content high in entertainment but low in orientation value, that is, interesting but unimportant stories. Such choices serve the goals of journalism in two ways. A sprinkling of such stories may attract wider attention to Quadrant I and II content. And Quadrant III stories rich in human interest may help form a common identity between viewer and story subjects, thus building community. Community-building is more likely, however, when such human interest is joined by consequence, perhaps showing how the story's subjects fit into—or are excluded from—the community as a group. Because of the orientational limitations of Quadrant III, stations following journalistic selection standards should place only a small proportion of scarce airtime there.

From a market standpoint, audiences for Quadrant III stories are likely to rival those of Quadrant II. As we discussed, stories high in entertainment values generalize well across the market. And as news historian Mitchell Stephens pointed out, even highbrow news consumers enjoy the juicy but inconsequential story.[18] Finally, many viewers may experience difficulty

telling Quadrant III stories from Quadrant IIs if the topics are consequential
but the reporting is only entertaining. The coverage of AIDS education that
began Chapter 5, reporting on Central America in Chapter 4, and coverage
of the potential closure of the Air Force base in Chapter 3 all show elements
of this kind of deceptive mixture.

Profit-minded stations can be expected to emphasize Quadrant III not just
for the wide appeal of such stories, but because news without consequence
often costs less to produce than news that is both informative and entertaining. Stations may even gear discovery to producing Quadrant III stories, by
assigning reporters to haunt courthouses and police stations looking for
emotionally arousing events, or perhaps even creating a celebrity beat.

Quadrant IV: The "hamburger helper" quadrant. Here you'll find events
and issues expected to yield content that is neither orienting nor entertaining.
Such choices have no journalistic value. Some Quadrant IV stories represent
mistakes in judgment or more worthy assignments that didn't pan out. More
often, however, this quadrant represents "filler"—programming-extending
material such as reports of minor accidents, small fires, and minor political
appointments—most without video—that permit stations to extend a newscast over more advertising spots.

From a market standpoint, the low production costs of filler stories may
make them profitable. A station may earn more by extending a newscast
beyond its reporters' capacity to fill it with other kinds of news than by
shortening the news and buying expensive alternate programs such as *Star
Trek* or *Wheel of Fortune* from syndicators. Such inexpensive news may
generate greater return even if it draws a smaller audience than popular
syndicated shows with higher price tags. In fact, Quadrant IV news may
represent the cheapest way a station can fill time between advertisements.[19]
The limited ability of audiences to evaluate quality also may boost the
commercial value of such content.

In sum, this analysis suggests that to maximize *public understanding,* a
news organization should choose most events from Quadrant II, high in
orientation and entertainment value; none from Quadrant IV, low in both; very
few from Quadrant III, high in entertainment alone; and fill in with Quadrant I,
high in orientation alone. To maximize *profit,* however, a news organization
should choose the most events from the cotton candy quadrant, III; few or none
from serious Quadrant I; some—those most interesting and least expensive—
from Quadrant II; and fill in with "hamburger helper" from Quadrant IV.

Note that events likely to yield content of which the public might disap-
prove—such as criticism of U.S. foreign policy—may be high in orientation
value but have a negative entertainment value, that is, consumers might shun
them (and subsequently the source). These would fit Quadrant I.

A caution before reporting the results. The theory and predictions ventured here are exploratory, new rather than tested. Second, news values are latent rather than manifest indicators of underlying logic; they require *judgment* rather than merely *recognition*. Determining the level of social consequence in a story, for example, is inherently more subjective than counting positive or negative adjectives. Even expert journalists rating stories from videotapes they could replay did not agree with a high degree of certainty on all story attributes (suggesting that they too find broadcast news difficult to evaluate). Lastly, the four quadrants are broad. A story that rated a 7 on either dimension is treated no differently than one just past the scale midpoint. Still, the logic of the formulation may prove helpful in revealing underlying dimensions in news selection decisions, particularly when coupled with ethnographic evidence.[20]

Results

The results are summarized in Figures 7.2, 7.3, and 7.4. Differences between the quadrants at each stage are large enough that it is unlikely chance alone can explain the distributions.[21]

Several patterns in the data are apparent. Quadrant I, stories with the worst ratio of benefit to cost from a purely market perspective, is the emptiest corner at each station. Quadrant III, stories with the best benefit-to-cost ratio from an economic viewpoint, however, is not the busiest, except at KMID. At KLRG and KVLG, Quadrant III—the most economically rewarding category—ranks second to Quadrant II, stories with both economic and journalistic reward. This suggests a compromise strategy between business and journalism at two larger stations, and a predominantly business strategy at the mid-sized station.

A simpler way of looking at the results is to combine the proportions of airtime spent in the two high-orientation quadrants for an orientation score and combine the two high-entertainment quadrants for an entertainment score.

- At the mid-sized station, 58% of the airtime was rated above the entertainment midpoint; only 38% above the orientation midpoint.
- At the large station, 72% of airtime was rated above the entertainment midpoint; 53% above the orientation midpoint.
- At the very large station, 63% of airtime was rated above the entertainment midpoint and 55% above the orientational.

At each station, audience appeal was a more important criterion in the sampled newscasts than consequence. Each station took more seriously the commercial demand to enlarge audience. Consequence was not ignored,

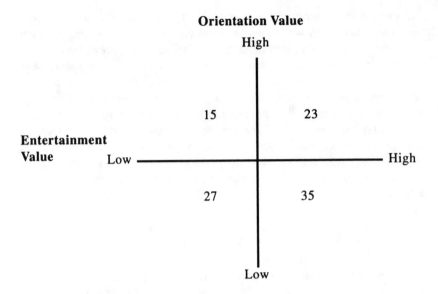

Figure 7.2. Percentage of Newscast Time in Each Quadrant at KMID

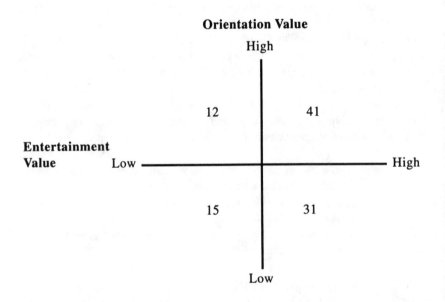

Figure 7.3. Percentage of Newscast Time in Each Quadrant at KLRG

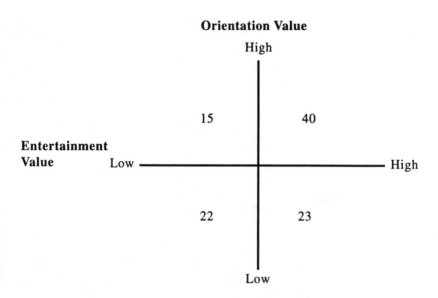

Figure 7.4. Percentage of Newscast Time in Each Quadrant at KVLG

however. At the two larger stations, slightly more than half the airtime sampled was rated above the consequence midpoint.

The flow of events at the large station provided an interesting glimpse into selection decision making. During the course of my visit, teachers in the market's largest school district staged a strike. Here was an event that had great social and personal consequence—it affected not only the quality of education for tens of thousands of students, but it also disrupted the lives of their parents who now faced the possibility of children at home during working hours. The event and its attendant issues also had powerful entertainment value, particularly in the conflict between the teacher's organization and the administration of the school district. Human interest elements were also available in abundance with so many frustrated parents and elated, bored, and under-supervised children. Here was an event at the top of both orientation and entertainment dimensions, a strong Quadrant II type. Whether a station was following a market or journalistic model, we would expect a great deal of resources to be committed to such a story. In fact, a station would ignore or minimize a Quadrant II event only at considerable risk of losing viewers to competitors.

One of the KLRG newscasts sampled came on the first day of the strike. The newscast was quite different from the other three in the KLRG sample in several respects. First, the station broadcast 37% more local news during its hour-long evening newscast than usual. Second, the expert journalists rated 69% of the total news time that evening in Quadrant II. By contrast, the other three newscasts averaged only 31% of their airtime in Quadrant II. On routine news days—those without an event that is consequential in so many of the market's households—KLRG's selection priorities were less attuned to either personal or social consequence. But on the first day of the strike when so much of the market was hungry for orientation, consequence became a far more saleable commodity.

A Second Measure: Volume of Local News

Besides looking at the values in events and issues editors choose to cover, we can step back and ask how stations use their news time. Because stations earn money from the primarily entertaining programs that fill the broadcast day, they could choose to limit, perhaps even eliminate, commercials during the 60 minutes of their premier evening newscast. Each of the stations visited, however, chose to spend the full 16 minutes per hour the Federal Communication Commission then allowed on advertising messages. The remaining 44 minutes were spent on local news, national news from the network, weather, sports, syndicated news stories and commentary, and on banter between news readers. Because each station aired a half-hour of network news, either immediately before or after the local newscast, national stories on the local newscast either repeated the networks or were pieces the network had sent to its affiliates but not considered important enough for the national broadcast. Within the newsroom, stories from the network used in local news were considered filler. In fact, at the largest station, one segment toward the end of the hour was constituted entirely of short network reports. The primary function of this segment was as a time buffer. The section began with 5 minutes of stories averaging only 20 seconds each, and expanded or contracted as much as needed to fill in for stories that fell through or ran shorter than expected, or to accommodate stories running longer than planned.

If airtime devoted to local news is considered the most important use, a rough measure of journalistic commitment would be the proportion of time devoted to local news. Considering that each station promoted its evening newscast as a comprehensive—one explicitly claimed "in-depth"—digest of the important local happenings during the past 24 hours, the volume of locally originated news may come as a surprise. At KMID the local news averaged 17.1 minutes on the evenings sampled, about 29% of the news hour, or just slightly more time than was consumed by advertisements. Boosted by the expanded strike coverage, at KLRG the average was 21.4 minutes. Even at KVLG only half the local news hour was local news, 29.8 minutes.

At all three stations there were other newscasts during the day. So the total local news exceeded the figures reported above. But much of the 30-minute 11 o'clock report at the three stations repeated or advanced the early evening stories, as did the next day's noon report at the mid-sized and large station. The noon report at the largest station was less redundant. The day's premier newscast, the one at which most of the station's resources were pointed, was the early evening program.

Seventeen minutes of news simply cannot cover the important goings-on in a mid-sized market. First consider that the market covers six counties with a total population exceeding half a million persons. Within it lie scores of incorporated towns and school districts, one large state university, and many large and thousands of small businesses. Seventeen minutes of news read at a normal speaking pace amounts to fewer words than cover half a single newspaper page. Although video images add further information, their contribution, if described in words, might not fill the rest of the page. Also consider that the pair of expert journalists evaluating KMID's newscasts rated only 38% of the time devoted to news, including nonlocal, above the midpoint of the orientation scale. You could argue that viewers who relied on KMID's premier newscast watched only about 6½ minutes of information helpful in making sense of their environment.[22]

KLRG served a market of about 1 million households and several million persons. It included 14 counties, hundreds of incorporated towns and cities, two major state universities and a handful of private ones. If 53% of the 21.4 minutes of local news was devoted to stories above the orienting midpoint, just over 11 minutes of journalistic information was broadcast on the evenings sampled. At KVLG, 29.8 minutes of local news were broadcast in the evening. Similarly, if 55% of the 29.8 minutes of local news broadcast on KVLG had high orientation value, then just over 16 minutes of socially responsible news about one of the largest metropolitan areas in the United States was made available during the premier daily newscast.

Were the newscasts sampled atypical? According to the journalists working in those newsrooms, the only unusual newscast was the one during the teachers' strike at KLRG. The results suggest that there's not a great deal of local news on local television newscasts.

Philosophies of News Selection

The key news selectors—assignment editor, news director and assistant news director, executive editor or producer, and producer—at the stations studied came from across the country. One news director was from California, another from New York, and a third from the state of Washington. All of the selectors had graduated from college and some had master's degrees in journalism. They represented a wide variety of universities, including some of journalism's most respected. Given the difference in resources at hand from the mid-sized to the very large station, and the differences in the communities served—from almost entirely agricultural to completely urban, you might have expected substantial differences in their criteria of newsworthiness. Yet in three of the four newsrooms visited (including a station in a very large market used as a pretest for this study), any one of the important selectors could have spoken for all of the rest—with the exception of but a single person—the "experimental" assignment editor at KLRG.

The Role of Consultants

One reason for this orthodoxy is the similar advice given by the major television consultants. One of these firms is Audience Research & Development of Dallas, TX. AR&D, like its competitors, uses the techniques of social science to learn what makes audiences pay attention to local television newscasts. The firms market their general research findings. They also review videotapes of local newscasts and send back detailed critiques and suggestions for change.

AR&D's analysis of one station participating in the study showed some advice of a journalistic nature. In one story critique, the consultant said an earlier explanation of why protesters were opposed to a bird sanctuary would have increased viewer comprehension. The bulk of the comments, however, concerned themselves with techniques for maximizing audience. Many of these suggestions concerned camera angles and other advice that might have improved both the journalism and audience size. But not infrequently stations were advised to ignore or contravene journalism norms. An AR&D memo, for example, listed story topics by "inherent viewer interest levels." The memo read:

> Our research indicates that viewers come to the tube at news time inherently liking some stories more than others. The list will make your hair stand on end. Here it is:
>   VERY STRONG—Humor (stories played for a laugh); Sex (arousal within bounds).
>   STRONG—Human interest; Entertainment; Fires.
>   ABOVE AVERAGE—Science; Disasters.
>   AVERAGE—Environment; Health; Education; Energy; Obituaries; Courts; Sports; Crime; Politics; Ethnic; Weather.

BELOW AVERAGE—Consumer; Government; Transportation; Accidents; Dissent; Economics.

WEAK—Religion; Labor.

Notice how all the soft stuff appears at the top of the list, and the rock hard falls to the bottom? Your viewers are telling you something, whether you want to believe it or not.[23]

AR&D cautioned that the list describes audience interest, not news selection priorities. But in another section of the same memo, the station is told to promise to "satisfy a viewer's basic needs and desires." The strategies that followed, however, appealed to desires only. It was a list of tricks designed to motivate persons to watch, often at the expense of satisfying their information needs. For example, stations were advised to "reinforce" the audience's attitudes. People prefer newscasts that reflect their own biases, the memo argued, so the station should play to them. "We tend to associate with other people who confirm our beliefs, who reinforce why we think what we think, like what we like, want what we want," the memo explained. "It's the old 'birds of a feather' syndrome." By contrast, good journalism challenges the beliefs and preferences of its consumers.

The memo also urged the news department to "reassure" viewers. "It's another perfectly human desire to protect our interests, and to look for reassurance that our fears—whether justified or not—will not be realized," the memo stated. Even justified fears should be downplayed, according to the consultant. "Television news plays a large part in assuring viewers that the world is not coming to an end," the memo continued, "that nothing is going to sneak up and bite them, and—believe it or not—that things ain't so bad." The norms of journalism, by contrast, command a neutral perspective. News is supposed to reveal the world as it is, no better, no worse. And a particular task of journalism is to warn the community about what's going wrong, so that it may be corrected. Suggesting that justified fears be suppressed or downplayed may help create a comfortable buying mood for advertising, but it is the antithesis of news. Other "motivators" to watch mentioned in the memo are "emotional variation" and "diversion."[24] Journalism, on the other hand, may be concerned with manipulating emotion, but only to attract attention to significant issues and events. And rather than diverting people's attention from problems, journalism's task is to focus on problems.

The emphasis on "selling" the news continued in the critiques of specific newscasts. A set of stories about health were praised, not for their objectivity, but for being "positive." "The stories were well written, and there was good use of sound and fine video," the consultant wrote.

But the most impressive thing I noted was the positive aspect of the three local stories—a concerted effort to fight cancer, children who had beaten cancer, and the mall walk opportunity for exercise. Dean Edell [a syndicated medical feature] was the only downer with some doomsaying about noisy toys. I found the whole experience uplifting. It fit right into the "Spirit of [state name],"

a theme the station was using in promotions for itself. The consultant also praised a story about a baby being born from a frozen embryo. "This was an excellent story. It points out that the producer is selecting stories based on interest and even positive impact as opposed to filling the first block with the 'important' stories of the day."[25]

What the Selectors Themselves Say

This emphasis on news as a commodity—something to be sold and let the buyer beware—was the most consistent theme of the qualitative analysis at each of the stations. This part of the analysis is based on interviews with the key selectors mentioned earlier.

AT THE MID-SIZED STATION

At KMID, story selection was almost exclusively the responsibility of the assignment editor. He described his selection criteria this way:

> I look at visuals. I look at interest. News has moved away from coverage of courts, police, fire, city council, boards of supervisors, the governor. In the last 5 years, newscasts have tried to become a *People Magazine*. I still maintain that boring as it may be covering a city council from start to finish, it contains more useful information than any consumer feature. But it's not visual, not exciting and the impact is not immediate. So it's no longer cool to do so. A lot of this [KMID's newscast] is not news. It's entertainment.

AT THE LARGE STATION

The morning "budget" meeting at the large station that opened this chapter gave a feel for the selection debate occurring there. During the month I visited, several theories of selection emerged. The simplest was that of Dave, the "experimental" assignment editor. He stressed the norms of journalism. "The rules of journalism," he said, "are the rules of public service." He criticized his own and other stations' reporting as focusing too heavily on events and not enough on issues and trends. "I don't know what function we serve by covering a big shootout, except that we 'rubberneck' for people. Our [reporters] cover the trees, but not the forest. They don't even know the rest of the forest is there." As a former newspaper reporter, he described himself as a "real heretic here."

At the other end of the spectrum, an almost purely market view was also present, voiced by the producer of the evening newscast. He said viewers (not just in this market, but in others where he had worked) are easily bored. They value entertainment over information, even in newscasts. Giving them entertainment, he conceded, probably harmed society. From his perspective, however, the station had little choice but to provide what the market demanded. He excelled at picking stories, he added, because "I have a short attention span. If I'm bored, I know the viewers will be bored. The viewer at home doesn't give a shit." I asked what he considered boring. "Business and economic stories, politics—certain cities have pretty boring city councils—anything that's hard to take pictures of, and hard-to-explain stories."

The executive editor's viewpoint suggested that the market and technology had much to do with selection:

> TV news is a hybrid thing. We are a medium in which people have a set of expectations above and beyond news. They watch the *A Team.* They watch the *Today Show, Hill Street Blues.* They are all well produced. When they tune in news, they want information, but they still have a set of background expectations that this will be TV. That it will be in color. That it will have some movement.

In his view, because most televised programming is entertaining, even news viewers consciously or unconsciously expect a visual and entertaining program.

At first, the news director's selection theory sounded as if it had been quoted from the norms of journalism:

> People have a very basic psychological need to know what's going on in their community. It's not like the newscast is the only place to get information, but a good reliable daily dose of everything—drawing a picture of the world that has some consonance with the world they see every day.

But the contents of that picture of the world, he explained, depend upon the news medium:

> One day in Seattle, the city council was on the verge of making a set of very important decisions to avoid bankruptcy. The decision was about raising taxes and/or cutting services. On the same day the decision was to take place, there was a five-alarm fire in the Old Town section of Seattle. Traditional journalists would say the city council story was a better, more important story. But that's "newspaperese." It's the kind of story newspapers can tell very well, whereas television can't tell it as well. Where the fire is a TV story from the very beginning. From about 10 years ago, TV stopped playing by print rules.

He implied that the "rules" of print are to publish the significant. The "rules" of television are to disseminate the visually appealing. But what if the visually appealing is not significant?

> Slash and trash? [TV news talk for a selection formula relying on violence and sensation] I'm not here to argue that's not news. When I was young I fought against a story about a parrot in a tree that wouldn't come down. Was it important? Not at all. Was it interesting? You bet! It was grand adventure! I was wrong [to have opposed it]. It was just a damn good story.

What, I asked, was the value of such reporting? He responded:

> The reaction to local news is primarily a gut reaction at its most fundamental level. We're going for somebody's gut and not their head. One of my responsibilities is to attract as many viewers as possible so my station can make as much money as possible.

Another responsibility, he acknowledged, was to the public welfare. But like his producer, the news director doubted that many viewers cared about informative reportage. "There's no use," he said, "preaching to an empty church." He told a story to illustrate the point:

> When I was [a graduate student] in Seattle, I did a documentary as a master's thesis. It was about an important issue and was in depth. It aired on public television and afterwards a half-dozen people called in about it and the public TV people felt that was very good response. But even mindless bullshit on a commercial station got 20 times the call-in response. That told me who was out there watching.

I asked whether journalists had an obligation to inform the public even if a larger audience could be gathered with entertainment. He responded: "We're not in the business of dispensing medicine here. We're not in the business of dispensing information that's good for them whether they want it or not."

AT THE VERY LARGE STATION

The news director said:

> I don't know what consequence means. Take the [Roxanne] Pulitzer trial [a lurid Palm Beach divorce trial that catapulted wife Roxanne to the cover of *Playboy* magazine]. What was the consequence of that? It was the greatest story

in the world! I'm not here to improve society. I'm here to tell good stories. It's television. It's pictures. That's the business!

In fairness, the news director, and particularly his assistant (who several months later succeeded him) often chose more consequential stories than the philosophy above implies. In a long discussion of news selection, the assistant expressed frustration with trying to balance the demands of the market and those of journalism. The latter, he explained, came at the cost of the former. "The industry," he said, "doesn't reward good journalism." When asked how different news production would be if stations were paid on how much the audience learned rather than how large and demographically correct it was, the assistant news director paused, then said, "It would change the whole premise on which we work."

Notes

1. Siebert et al., 1956.
2. The Commission on Freedom of the Press, 1947, p. 21.
3. Massing, 1985.
4. Wenner, 1985, p. 173.
5. Wenner, 1985, p. 173.
6. Donohew, Finn, & Christ, 1987.
7. Donohew, Sypher, & Higgins, 1987.
8. This does not imply that viewers form preferences based on an organized head-to-head comparison of what each station offers. Preferences are determined much less systematically, by sampling what's available, by the preferences of family members with whom one watches, and by the preferences of friends and associates. Common to the selection process for each of these individuals or groups, however, is an evaluation—usually not conscious—of these two general content dimensions, orientation and entertainment.
9. Frazier & Gaziano, 1979, p. 21.
10. Stevens, 1985.
11. See Buckalew, 1969; Galtung & Ruge, 1965; and Ward, 1967.
12. A better approach would have been to combine both television and print journalists in the pool of judges. This would have permitted comparing ratings by medium to establish whether any bias against broadcast news existed among the print journalists. Unfortunately, the Knight program was dominated by newspaper journalists.

At no time did any of the judges make disparaging remarks about television news. And the method of the study—viewing one videotaped story at a time and independently rating it for the intensity of each of the values separately, without being informed of how their scores would be analyzed—may have limited any global prejudice against broadcast news. Further, the analysis was adjusted to the range of scores, countering any tendency by the judges to give consistently low scores. (The method is explained in Note 17.)

13. The specification that issues or events had to be consequential for 5% or more of the households in the signal area gives stations the benefit of the doubt in defining consequence, that is, stories didn't have to affect most, or even many, of the potential viewers to be

classified as consequential. Five percent was intended as a minimum potential audience for a mass medium.

14. Epstein, 1973.

15. Shoemaker, Brendlinger, Danielian, & Chang, 1986.

16. Obviously, this is a less rigorous approach than might be applied by a social responsibility purist. But the analysis has been designed throughout to give local television news every benefit of the doubt.

17. There were several complications in the analysis that required a more sophisticated analysis than a straight average of news values on each of the two dimensions. The major problem was that the orientational dimension contained only two values; the entertainment dimension had five. Second, editors believed that the most obvious values were the ones upon which the audience judged stories, that is, a story with a little human interest, a little conflict, a little unusualness, and so forth, would not attract as much attention as a story with a great deal of human interest, but little or none of the other entertainment news values.

The goal of the analysis was to discover a pattern, a logic, in these gatekeeper's choices. With advice from Professor Clifford Nass of the Communication Department at Stanford, I settled on this approach.

For the Orientational Dimension. There was no reason to expect any one issue or event to have both personal and social consequence, so the higher of the two values was chosen to place the story. Although the journalist-judges rating the stories could have assigned them any value between 0 and 7, in no case was the mean rating of the two judges 0 on both the social and personal consequence measures. And few ratings of either measure exceeded 5.5. Because the point was not to establish an absolute measure, but to divide stories into high and low levels of orientational value, I collapsed the index to a 1-5.5 range. The few outliers above 5.5 were reduced to 5.5. The change created a uniform distribution. This was critical because of the next step.

The next problem was to establish a midpoint. I programmed a computer to create a hypothetical random distribution. First, I chose 7,500 pairs of numbers between 1 and 5.5. Then I picked the higher number of the pair. The mean of these picks of higher numbers was 4.1, rounded to 4.0, the closest value a score could be.

The idea was to establish what the midpoint would be, given my procedure of taking the higher value of the two consequence scores, in a chance distribution. Stories rated at or above 4 on either consequence value were rated as high; those rated 3.5 or lower were placed in the low consequence categories. In other words, by chance alone we would expect half of the picks under this procedure to be above 4 and half below.

This design created a fair and logical midpoint for the distribution. Had the original distribution been used, the midpoint by chance would have been substantially higher, pulled up by the outliers. Given that few scores exceeded 5.5, it would have biased the results against the high consequence categories.

One could argue that this method exaggerates consequence scores. I am more comfortable with that criticism, however, than the criticism in the opposite direction had I decided on a midpoint using the full 7-point scale.

For the Entertainment Dimension. Assignment editors said they tried to consider the relative intensity of all news values in selection decisions. However, in their conversations rarely were more than two or three values—the most salient—mentioned. Given how they thought aloud about the process and their impression that the public paid decreasing attention to less obvious values in a story, I settled on a weighted sum.

Reflecting the belief that salient news values had more to do with attracting audience than the less intense values present, a weighted sum was calculated for the entertainment dimension. The news value coders rated most intense received a weight of 1; the second most intense value, .5; the third, .25; and the fourth, .125. The weighted sum was limited to four terms because there were an average of four nonzero news values per story.

This weighted approach squares with research findings that indicate attention is better captured with salient than non-salient stimuli. Such research is summarized in Ross and Nisbett (1980).

Finding the midpoint of such a weighted sum was similar to the method used for the orientation dimension, with one exception. Instead of simply taking one score—the higher of the two consequence measures—as in the orientational dimension, the four highest scores for entertainment values were weighted and summed. This time the computer was programmed to make 7,500 *sets* of four selections, each randomly chosen between values of 1 and 5.5. The program then computed the mean of the resulting distribution using the weighting scheme above. The midpoint of such a chance distribution was 7.4. Again, scores falling on the mean were counted in the higher category.

18. Stephens, 1988.

19. Ferall, 1989.

20. Some have argued that social scientists should not venture to study questions in which measurement is imprecise. Unfortunately, many of society's most vexing issues are too complex for simple counts of unambiguous markers. If social science is to realize its potential, it should attempt new measures that are less precise. However, it should also call attention to that imprecision and suggest less confidence in the results. In such cases, complementary analyses that compensate for some of the imprecision are almost imperative.

21. At all three stations a chi-square test indicated the four quadrants were significantly different from a uniform distribution, with $p < = .025$.

22. Recall that the 38% figure is based on reviewing national news included in local newscasts, not just the locally originated news. But local news made up the bulk of the stories rated even at the smallest station, so the approximation seems justified.

23. Audience Research & Development, 1984, pp. 12-13.

24. Audience Research & Development, 1984, p. 4.

25. Karl F. Zedell of Audience Research & Development, in a letter to the news director of KLRG, November 18, 1986.

8

The Third Stage of News Production:
Reporting the Story

Although most research about news selection has focused on how journalists decide which events to cover, that's only one of a long sequence of choices. The reporter or writer assigned to gather the story must make dozens of subsequent decisions: Which background material to look up? Whom to interview? Which documents to examine? Where to point the camera to illustrate the story? And once the information has been gathered, there is yet another set of questions: Which quotes to include? Which facts from the documents? Which images from the videotape? And in what order should all the pieces be placed to form a coherent narrative? All of these are the decisions of the third phase of news production.

Case Study: News-Gathering

10:10 a.m. The news-gathering began when a Harvard-educated reporter with 9 years of television news experience I'll call Mark was summoned into the morning news meeting at KVLG, the station with the greatest number of journalism awards in its market, which is among the nation's largest. The executive editor assigned Mark to a story about a city council election in a city of approximately 50,000 persons located in the midst of the metropolitan area KVLG served. The election merited coverage, the editor said, because only 15% of the electorate was expected to vote.

The producer of the evening news suggested Mark take a lighthearted angle on the story, perhaps collecting the excuses of people who didn't intend to vote. "It's got to be stellarly funny," she said. "Given the fact that only

15% of the voters are expected to show up, who are they?" added the executive editor.

10:35. Mark, a photographer I'll call Jim, and I were off to the florist to pick up a flower for Mark's sport coat. After that we began the 45-minute drive to the city holding the election.

11:06. About half-way there Mark glanced over his assignment sheet. He read aloud a three-paragraph note from KVLG's story planner: "Two council seats up for grabs. Three questions: We ask people who do vote, 'why?' . . . Ask officials 'why so few [voters are expected]' . . . and find out what it means to Democracy." Jim, the photographer, suggested finding out which candidates the low turnout might benefit. But Mark said he didn't know the candidates' names or whether they might be available.

11:10. Jim noted the discrepancy between the informational angle of the assignment sheet and Mark's order from the producer to make the story funny. Mark responded: "I can do it hard. I can do it soft. I can do it in between. You make it entertaining. But maybe informing and make a point. It isn't news."

I asked why it's not news. "It's news, but it's not hard news," Mark replied. "It's not the best story, but if you give it a different spin, you can make it a good story."

Noting that other municipal elections were taking place in the metro area today, I asked if Mark would summarize those in his story. He said the question was naive because he had only 90 seconds to tell about this election. "In a minute-and-a-half you want image and you want impact," he explained. "You only need just one good line, just one good quote." He had a line in mind: "In Chicago even the dead vote, but in [this city] not even the dead vote."

11:48. We pulled off the expressway into the first neighborhood in the city and stopped. Mark intercepted two middle-aged women walking down the sidewalk. He told them how "pretty" they looked and then peppered them with questions about whether they voted and why. One of the pair responded that she voted because "this is my city. This is where my children live and my grand-children." Mark pushed in vain for an expression of anger over the low turnout.

11:53. We returned to the car. Mark was disappointed. "Some people are shallow," he said. "You can't always find people who are articulate."

11:54. We found a polling place. Mark exclaimed: "Great! It's empty." Jim took pictures of the empty booths while a poll official explained that suburban polls such as this one were rarely busy at noon. As voters strolled up, Mark asked each the same set of questions about low voter turnout, trying to provoke an emotional response.

12:12 p.m. A man and his wife, émigrés from the Philippines when Ferdinand Marcos was in power, approached the poll. Jim videotaped the following exchange:

Mark: Does it surprise you that not many Americans show up?

Man: Well, most people are working now.

Mark: Why is it important to vote?

Man: Because we have to decide . . .

Mark interjects: Do you actually think your vote makes a difference?!

Man: Of course. We are electing a person to represent us.

Mark: What if I say I'm going to take your right to vote away?

Man: You cannot. This isn't a communistic form of government.

Mark (steps closer to man): I say I will! You'll fight me?!

Man: Of course. It's my right!

Mark: It's like cutting your throat?

Man: (Nods vehemently.)

12:26. Mark grinned. "You've got to get them impassioned," he explained. "You need to make the point [that] people don't realize how important democracy is. We just lucked into this guy!"

Asked about threatening to fight a respondent to provoke a response, Mark responded, "We're not making up the news. We know there's a 15% turnout. We're illustrating the facts." Jim countered that Mark didn't know the facts; in fact, couldn't know them until the polls had closed that evening after the newscast. "You do a story like this at 12 and you can't see a trend developing," Mark conceded, "but I'll make a couple of calls later."

12:30. We began to look for a McDonald's. Mark explained that the voting booths reminded him of the "golden arches," and he wanted to contrast the lunchtime crowd at the restaurant with the empty polling place. Bemused, Jim responded: "You know the Burger King burger looks like a ballot. Maybe we should get a shot of it?"

After 14 minutes vainly looking for a McDonald's, Mark decided to stop in a shopping center to gather more interviews. "Did you vote today?" he called out the window to a middle-aged woman walking with her teenage son. "You're 18, but you don't look it," he quipped as she began to backpedal and her son ducked into a store. As Jim and Mark stepped out the car, Jim rolling tape, the woman retreated toward the store saying she couldn't answer the question. Mark said she looked "fine" and that he wouldn't use her in the story if someone else spoke to him. At first, the woman feigned apathy. Later, she confided that she couldn't vote because her religion forbade it.

1:04. We found a McDonald's. The first five persons Mark stopped said they had voted or would vote. Mark declined to interview them. "People like that ruin the story," he joked. He decided the five were unrepresentative of the electorate. Still, he mused, "this is a problem: When you start out with an angle, it's like you find the things that support the angle."

Mark asked a young man in a black Volkswagen Jetta whether he'd be voting. The man said no, then changed to yes, then taunting the newsman, switched back to no. Just before he roared away, he shouted pugnaciously: "Give me something worth voting for, I'll vote for it!"

1:20. After a stop at city hall just long enough for Jim to gather video of the exterior, we drove to a cemetery. Mark felt it would be the ideal place for his "stand up" narration featuring the joke about the dead voting. However, the cemetery guards appeared unsympathetic and we moved on.

1:48. Finding a polling place, Mark performed his stand up. He said: "In a place like a Chicago or a Manila, the old joke goes that the election was so hot the dead people voted, sometimes twice. But the best thing you can say about [this city] is not even the dead people voted."

"Uh, dead people don't vote," Mark whispered almost to himself as the illogic of his punch line struck him.

1:58. We headed back to the station. Jim explained to me that it is very hard for KVLG reporters to come back empty-handed from an ill-considered assignment. The station didn't gather enough local news to pick just the best stories for the evening newscast. "We hardly ever pull out. . . . We go on [the air] whether it's garbage or not." Mark responded: "It's news because we say it's news. If we didn't see it, it didn't happen." Quality reporting really didn't matter anyway, he continued, because "people just want to be cozy with their favorite anchor team."

Mark became somewhat defensive: "This can be a valuable story. OK, it's obviously meant to be a tongue-in-cheeker. [But] we're doing something valuable. It's a different twist of the voter apathy story."

"We don't even know that yet," exclaimed Jim. "They decided in [the newsroom] that it's going to be a low turnout just because one lady said so. We don't know that. The polls just opened!"

"I think this is going to be a pretty good story," Mark sniffed. "A lot of it will depend on the writing."

"Yeah," replied Jim. "About 99%!"

2:30. Back at the station, Mark defended his strategy:

> I could have talked to a clerk. I could have talked to the candidates and asked how it affects local politics. But there's only 48,000 people in [the suburban city]. If I did it regular, it would have been too specific. It would have been boring.
>
> [So] you make it generic. You find the thread that goes from [a city in the southern part of the market] to [a city in the northern part].
>
> You end up taking one guy to represent those voting. It takes on a kind of symbolism. It's something so compressed. That's a sign of our times. You don't even mention voter apathy. It's a cliché, a turn-off. It's emotion and the signs that convey the real meaning. The facts [only] legitimize your story as being different from fiction.

During the remainder of the afternoon, Mark mixed the sounds and images he had gathered with a narration he would later "voice over" the pictures in the studio. His editors insisted on checking with the city clerk around 4:30 for the latest estimate of voter turnout. The clerk stuck with her low projection. A staff writer checked projections of turnouts in other metro communities for the anchor's "lead-in" sentences to Mark's story. An editor would examine Mark's script on two occasions, but neither time would he see either the videotape or a transcript of what the various sources had to say. In fact, all that would be edited were the few sentences bridging from one video clip to another. What was in between would be known only to Mark until it was broadcast.

On Air. The anchor's lead-in to Mark's story was completed more than 3 hours before polls were to close. It read: "As expected, voter turnout has been dismal so far in today's local elections." No vote tallies were provided. Mark's story implied that the city he visited typified this apathy and the reasons behind it. He began with a quote from the woman who said she would not vote for religious reasons (despite promising the woman that he would not use her in his story if other sources were located). The quote gave her false first answer, apathy. The man in the Volkswagen followed, saying he had nothing to vote for (despite Mark's uncertainty about whether the man had or hadn't voted). The story ended with the upbeat passion of the Filipino immigrant emotionally defending his right to vote in America. The three quotes were framed by Mark's joke about the dead abstaining from voting and the juxtaposition of the empty polling booths with the more popular "golden arches" of McDonald's.

Beyond Anecdotes:
Analyzing News-Gathering

Back issues of such journalism monitors as *Columbia Journalism Review, American Journalism Review* (formerly *Washington Journalism Review*) and *Quill* contain a number of anecdotes like the one above. By themselves, they may be dismissed as a poorly trained reporter having a bad day or perhaps even one bad station in a barrel of 740 healthy ones. To satisfy this concern, I collected 34 case studies at the three stations participating in this part of the research. I selected the cases purposively to represent the best news reporting at each station. Two criteria defined "best": (1) more socially consequential stories—in my estimation—were favored over less important ones; and (2) where each reporter could not be accompanied on assignment, the higher quality journalists—as estimated by the assignment editor—were selected.

You might assess the quality of news-gathering any number of ways. For parsimony I chose to focus on a—perhaps *the*—central norm of news-gathering, the standard of journalistic objectivity. However troublesome objectivity is as a concept, it remains a fundamental norm of journalistic practice in most of the world's democracies.[1] If the most important function of news is to help audiences orient themselves to their environment, Swedish researcher Jorgen Westerstahl observed, "news reporting must be factual and impartial in order to provide a foundation for independent and rational decision-making."[2] The first step analyzes whether reporters gathered the news objectively in each case.

The second step examines patterns among violations of commonly accepted norms of objectivity. News theorists disagree about who or what is responsible for such ills as biased reporting. Is it individual journalists? The news department? Society's "haves" using the news to control society's "haven'ts?" This analysis will help us decide.

Two secondary analyses were also conducted. Both concerned how the newsroom was organized to assist the reporter's news-gathering. This allocation of persons and other resources reveals what managers value and what is less important. First I looked at how stations stored past reporting to provide background for current coverage. Second, I analyzed the process of quality control over stories.

Conceptualizing Journalistic Objectivity

The concept of journalistic objectivity is a pain in the south parts. As Westerstahl noted: "The use of the term 'objective' in the phrase 'objective news reporting' is unfortunate in that it implies theoretical problems regarding the nature of knowledge, problems that philosophers have been disputing for centuries."[3]

The key problem, of course, is that no account of reality is independent of the perceiver. Anyone who has witnessed the breakup of a love affair knows that each party has a different explanation for why. All seeing is based on the particular perspective and purposes of the seer. Robert Hackett applied this thinking to news: "No longer can we simply assume the possibility of unbiased communication, of objective and detached reporting on an allegedly external social and political world."[4] Every news account, he explained, should be considered the result of a "structured orientation" that reflects influences on its production.

> [These influences] may indeed include partisan favoritism or political prejudices, but they also include criteria of newsworthiness, the technological characteristics of each news medium, the logistics of news production, budgetary constraints, legal inhibitions, the availability of information from sources [and] the need to tell stories intelligibly and entertainingly to an intended audience.[5]

Hackett's argument resembles the case I made for a theory of news in earlier chapters. Both arguments are based upon the notion that people, including reporters, can't help but be subjective. They can't divorce themselves from the particular "lenses" of their own histories and purposes. Nor can they report without regard for the purposes of the organizations that employ them. As a result, their reportage reflects a particular ideology—a set of explanations for how things work, for what is real and what is illusory, for what is valuable and what is worthless.

Obviously, the foregoing doesn't mean that people can never agree on what is true and false. But it does mean that what they call true and false may be judged quite differently by persons seeing through different ideologies—say persons from different social classes.

Although acknowledging that "news, after all, is fundamentally and inherently ideological," Professor James Ettema has argued that journalists are nevertheless right to apply some reality standards to their work. Although he rejected "truth" as unworkable, he suggested that journalists follow a "practical wisdom," an effort to justify fact claims with as much evidence as practicable.[6] Ettema relied on media sociologist Michael Schudson, who argued that journalists ought to adopt a "mature subjectivity," that is "firmly grounded in the process of screening tips, assembling and weighing evidence, fitting facts, and attempting to disconfirm the resulting story. In the end," wrote Schudson, "these exercises yield a degree of 'moral certainty' about the convergence of facts into a truthful report."[7]

Westerstahl provided a framework for this practical wisdom based on the canons of journalism adopted into Swedish broadcasting regulations. The framework consists of a set of craft norms defining journalistic objectivity. No claim is advanced, however, that true objectivity is possible. Westerstahl's typology is adopted here—with some modification based on the foregoing discussion—because it facilitates systematic analysis of newsgathering cases. Westerstahl's conception of journalistic objectivity is also more complete than other conceptualizations I considered. As Hackett noted, some researchers have limited objectivity to accuracy, or to balance, and neglected important considerations such as impartiality and relevance.[8]

Westerstahl thought of objectivity as having two components: factuality and impartiality. A story is factual, he argued, if it is true and relevant. A story is impartial if all sides to the issue—if there are sides—are balanced and the presentation is neutral. Not all of these subrequirements of journalistic objectivity need be met in each story, and application of these standards may vary somewhat from one story to the next.

TRUTH

For Westerstahl's criterion "truth," I'll substitute Ettema's notion of justifiably factual. An account is justifiably factual if accepted journalistic standards of care with facts are applied. Specifically, the account must be accurate: There would be little significant discrepancy between the reporter's account of an event and that of a disinterested observer (from the same culture) accompanying the reporter. Second, fact claims by sources that are at odds with what the reporter already knows are checked with another source, or against the evidence available. Third, allegations of wrongdoing must be substantiated—either coming from the proper authority or checked against another source in a position to know. Fourth, the names and positions of all sources, except those promised confidentiality, must be supplied so viewers can evaluate their claims.[9] Finally, adequate evidence must be supplied to justify conclusions drawn or implied by the reporter that are not common knowledge.[10]

RELEVANCE

Westerstahl defined *relevant* with only one sentence, as "a description that allows the audience to understand the course of events."[11] From his examples, *relevant* appears to mean two things: (1) the description of the information/event contains at least enough information for viewers to discern what has happened, that is, the journalistic question of *what* has been answered, even if *why* and *how* have not; and (2) all elements of the story are directly related to, or in some way develop, its theme. Relevance does not require that the story be complete.

BALANCE

"Balance" is required "only when news reporting deals with conflicting parties."[12] A balanced story is one where all major sides are given appropriate access to the audience. At a minimum, a source representing each side to an issue must have been offered a chance to comment and the gist of that response included in the story.

NEUTRAL PRESENTATION

Reporters are restricted from both positive and negative value judgments. Impartiality "implies that the report not be composed in such a way that the reporter is shown to identify with or repudiate the subject of the report"[13] or any party in the story.

Note that Westerstahl's typology of journalistic objectivity is far from a summary of good journalistic practice. It says nothing about what is newsworthy, for example, or how news should be presented to generate the widest public interest or understanding. Rather, the typology is a statement of *minimal* care to be taken with information presented as news.

Judging Objectivity

Just as news reporting can contain no truly objective reporting because of human limitations, neither can social science. What I aim for in my description and interpretation of these case studies is the same "mature subjectivity" that Schudson urged on journalists.

Theories of News Content

Examining more than 100 studies of how news content is selected, Professor Pamela Shoemaker and her associate Kay Mayfield found five quasi-theoretical explanations for what becomes news.[14] The first theory is essentially journalistic—content reflects social reality (what people with similar cultural "lenses" would agree is reality) with little alteration. The second theory holds that news-gathering routines distort this social reality. The third says content is shaped by the personal biases and backgrounds of journalists. The fourth argues that news content results from social and institutional pressures both within and outside the media firm. The last holds that content is controlled through ideology by social elites and used as a tool for social control.

Collapsing these somewhat, I propose four categories of journalistic objectivity norm violations. Violations may reflect one or more of the following:

1. Personal biases of the journalist;
2. The self-interest of the media firm, its parent corporation, or major investors;
3. The self-interest of societal elites outside the media firm, corporate parent, and major investors;
4. Human error.

To decide which of these explanations best fits a particular objectivity violation is tricky business. As we saw in the case study beginning the chapter, journalists may describe their work as following craft norms. But actually they may conform to a different, even incompatible logic. And the station may take the work and present it as news, when in fact it is a collage of images—some of which are artificial—held together by something—in this case a joke—from the imagination of the reporter. The best way I can think of to navigate such a maze is to examine whose interests are advanced by the violation. This "by their fruits you shall know them" approach assumes that although mistakes happen, most news-gathering behavior is purposive, that is, goal oriented, regardless of whether the journalist or the news department acknowledge these goals.

This method of placing objectivity violations isn't perfect. Even with case studies rich in detail, there is frequently insufficient evidence to pinpoint what caused a particular violation. Suppose, for instance, that a reporter with a personal bias against environmentalists wrote a story favoring the timber industry. But the bias was shared by the news department because it believed the industry was more popular than its environmental opponents. It may be difficult to know whether the departure from objectivity represented personal bias, corporate self-interest, or both. If timber was a powerful local industry, it may be even more difficult to rule in or out external elite influence, particularly of an ideological nature, as a cause of the violation. The logging industry may have so dominated the town's information, that the public—including its journalists—sees the industry view as the "true" view. To feel comfortable identifying an explanation, one would need further cases in which the interests of the reporter, station, and timber industry conflicted. While the case study approach adopted here provides depth, it sacrifices breadth.

Below are descriptions of each of these four categories of objectivity violations:

VIOLATIONS REFLECTING
A JOURNALIST'S PERSONAL BIAS

Either consciously or unconsciously, the journalist imposes more of his or her own personal view on news content than objectivity norms permit. The story fails standards of justifiable factuality, relevance, balance, or impartiality so as to promote the journalist's personal view.

For an objectivity violation to be classified as reflecting personal bias, it must match the expressed personal view of a reporter or editor. Although there was no attempt to gather personal histories or inventory attitudes of the reporters and editors shadowed in the present study, each was asked to describe his or her thinking process during news-gathering, an approach similar to David White's classic "gatekeeper" study.[15]

VIOLATIONS REFLECTING
THE SELF-INTEREST OF THE MEDIA FIRM,
ITS CORPORATE PARENT, OR MAJOR INVESTORS

Either consciously or unconsciously, journalists violate objectivity norms to favor the interests of their media firm, its parent corporation, or major investors.[16] Violations may help or harm the interests of other parties, such as influential news sources, advertisers, politicians, societal elites and non-elites, depending on whether the self-interest of such groups coincides or conflicts with those associated with the media firm.

Where journalistic norms of objectivity have been disregarded, the market approach described in Chapters 4 and 5 predicts violations would be motivated by an effort somehow to improve the profitability of the media firm and/or its corporate parent. So we might see protection or promotion of large advertisers, the media firm, its corporate parent, or the interests of major investors. More subtly, we might expect news-gathering behavior that reduces production costs by taking shortcuts, such as careless handling of information—failure to confirm allegations, check dubious claims, support conclusions, weigh evidence, gather all sides to issues, or attribute opinions. We might also expect efforts to increase audience through exaggeration, or appeals to emotion or aesthetics.

VIOLATIONS REFLECTING
THE SELF-INTEREST OF EXTERNAL SOCIETAL ELITES

Either consciously or unconsciously, journalists violate objectivity norms in ways that legitimate the interests of the powerful, or question the legitimacy of individuals, groups, or organizations opposing the powerful. Violations may help or harm the media firm's self-interest or its corporate parent's, or major investors' depending upon whether they coincide or conflict with elite interests outside the media firm and associated enterprises. The elite, or powerful, as defined by Peter Dreier, hold "the top positions in the institutional structure of the society."[17] Practically, the elite of a community would include the politically powerful such as the mayor and members of city council, the advisors and financiers supporting political leaders, as well as prominent owners and top managers of retail and manufacturing businesses, large farms, real estate, or mineral resources.[18]

Within the newsroom, the primary mechanisms of control are ideology and management. Shoemaker and Mayfield defined *ideology* as a "body of doctrines or beliefs that guides a particular individual, class or culture."[19] A second important characteristic of ideology is that for its adherents it seems natural, normal, or "the only proper way of doing something." Ideology is promoted as beyond question.

Ideologies may be broad, such as favoring capitalism or communism, or specific to a particular object or individual. The ideology of the powerful is seen as paving the way for domination of other classes not through coercion, but rather by persuading both press and public to accept an interpretation of events that favors the powerful. Management works first to hire and promote journalists with the "proper" ideology and secondly to censor or constrain, perhaps dismiss, those who think independently.

VIOLATIONS REFLECTING HUMAN ERROR

Unconsciously, journalists violate objectivity norms. Although most studies of news selection have concluded that newswork is purposive, any study of individual cases of news-gathering should take human error into account. As former *Washington Post* publisher Philip Graham observed of news work: "The pressure of time makes mistakes inevitable."[20]

For a normative violation to be classified as simple error, it must have an accidental, rather than purposive quality. In other words, the error is not part of a pattern of objectivity violations within the case study, nor does the journalist appear to be conscious of the violation. These are what information scientists call "random errors."

Note that such errors also may indicate organizational deficiencies. Television news is produced not by individuals, but by corporations. If there is no quality control mechanism to correct reporters' mistakes, there is a problem with the organization as well. In normative journalism editors are expected to hold reporters to exacting standards of accuracy.

Results

Across the three stations, 14 of the 34 stories analyzed—about 40%—followed norms of journalistic objectivity. Twenty—about 60%—failed to meet one or more objectivity requirements. Contrary to expectation, the more resources and time stations could devote to news-gathering, the *greater* the percentage of stories with violations. At the mid-sized station, 5 of 15 stories contained violations. At the large station, 10 of 13 stories violated objectivity norms. At the largest station, five of six stories monitored violated norms. (At the larger stations reporters spent more time on stories, thus fewer could be examined during the study period.)

Some of the reporting, however, met the highest journalistic standards. Consider this case at KVLG, the station in the very large market. At 10:30 a.m., the assistant news director asked two members of the station's investigative reporting team to find background information about a local hospital that had recently refused emergency treatment to an indigent. Their strategy was to find the name of the corporation that operated the emergency room, then to learn what other businesses the corporation ran and whether there had been government or media investigations of impropriety in the corporation or its subsidiaries. The director of the team and one of his field producers—who acts like a reporter except that he doesn't appear on camera—huddled with the librarian to begin their search. They connected to Nexis, using a computer communicating through phone lines to distant databases. Their investigation included a phone call to "Disclosure Inc.," which operated a file of the public records of the federal Securities and Exchange Commission, which regulates stock transactions. They also called a local health department, which was supposed to list the names of persons or corporations owning more than 10% of any local licensed medical facility. They checked the accreditation committee of the hospital trade association in Chicago. They called the attorney general's office in Ohio, where they had learned the hospital corporation was headquartered. By 4 p.m. they had created an informational graphic that accompanied a local report about the hospital. The graphic showed a map of the United States that marked all of the places where complaints had been lodged against the corporation. A second graphic showed quoted excerpts from some of the investigations of these complaints. Some alleged mob domination of the corporation.

Theoretical Explanations for Objectivity Violations

Objectivity violations in all 20 stories were classified as serving the self-interest of the media firm, its parent corporation, or investors. Four violations also served the interest of societal elites. One also showed personal bias and two also showed human errors.[21] (The total exceeds 20 stories because 6 were classified in more than one category.)

To give a flavor of these violations, examine some examples from each category:

PERSONAL BIAS

At the mid-sized station, a reporter was asked to develop a local angle on a wire story about a statewide strike that ended with winery workers accepting a loss of income and benefits. On the drive to a local plant owned by the state's largest winemaker, the reporter said unions in his native Ohio Valley had driven industries away with excessive salary demands.

Upon reaching the winery, in a total of 9 minutes of interviewing, the reporter addressed questions to 10 employees entering or leaving plant property. Most of the questions probed whether the workers felt the strike had been a mistake. Five employees responded. All but one disagreed with the direction of the question and said the strike had been justified. The reporter's story, written in the photographer's car on the 10-minute return trip to the station, concluded that "many winery workers" were questioning the value of the strike and featured the comments of the single employee taking that position. This conclusion may or may not have been accurate, but there was no evidence for it in the wire story that served as background or from 4 out of 5 of the reporter's informants—none of whom were union leaders. This story exhibited the personal orientation of the reporter, served the interest of societal elites by delegitimizing the union, and demonstrated the self-interest of the station through its failure to insist on proper care with facts, specifically on providing evidence for reporter generalizations.

SELF-INTEREST OF THE MEDIA FIRM, ITS PARENT CORPORATION, OR MAJOR INVESTORS

Because these were so numerous, examples of varying severity are provided, one from each of the three stations.

At the mid-sized station, the assignment editor gave several pages from an inch-thick packet of press releases from city hall to a reporter he asked to cover an issue at a city council meeting that morning. It was a time when both public and private employers were discussing routine testing of their workers for drug use. At the meeting, councilmembers argued the merits of mandatory versus voluntary testing to determine whether municipal employees were using illegal drugs. The reporter felt unprepared for the assignment because he hadn't covered this issue before and was unfamiliar with the city council. Still, he was able to complete his 106-word script during the 15-minute trip back to the station.

He began the script as his news director had taught him, with a tantalizing question: "How serious *is* the drug problem among city employees?" [The italics represent his verbal emphasis.] It was a question no one at city council had raised, however, and one his story wouldn't answer, for the next line began: "We won't know soon or easily . . . " The lead violated factual standards because it assumed that there was, in fact, a drug "problem" at city hall when the point of the council discussion was about how to determine *whether or not* employees used drugs. Suggesting that a drug problem of potentially "serious" magnitude existed among city workers serves the media firm's interest in attracting audience at the expense of the public's accurate perception of the city council meeting.

At the large station, one reporter generated four stories about the second day of a teachers' strike. Three had factual errors and one abandoned neutrality. Here is how the noon and evening newscast stories were gathered. Before dawn, the reporter was asked to stake out a particular elementary school because an anonymous female caller said parents there would stage a demonstration in support of teachers. Shortly after 8 a.m. reporters from two other television stations arrived, also tipped by a single female caller. Although many moms and dads dropped off children, only two parents joined the teachers' picket line. In the meantime, each of the three reporter and photographer teams attracted a swarm of students. "The problem is, as soon as we show up, it turns it into an entirely different situation," the KLRG reporter said. "We make it chaotic just by being here." At 8:33, a working teacher announced that school had started and students should enter their classrooms. Some heeded the call, but more continued to pursue the three television crews.

At 9 a.m., the KLRG reporter was permitted to move inside the school. He found it calm and orderly, until students noticed the camera. He quickly restored order with his booming broadcaster's voice: "OK you guys," he shouted, "you have a teacher to watch." When the reporter emerged from the school at 9:16, the other reporters had left. All but a few students had rejoined their classes, supporting the reporter's suspicion that the journalists' presence had created the disorder that would later be reported as reality.

Returning to the studio, the reporter learned little about other schools in the district. The staff was not large enough, the assistant news director said, to call or visit a sample of the schools to check on conditions. So the reporter called the school district headquarters, which provided little new information and no word of disorder in any of the schools.

Despite a notebook full of comments from parents expressing little apprehension about sending their children to school, almost no evidence for either parent or student support for teachers, no evidence for disruption within the school, a concern that students outside were reacting mostly to the presence of the television crews, and having visited only 1 of 74 schools—the one expected to be the most atypical in terms of confrontation—the reporter's script described "a mob scene," in which "school administrators were unsuccessful in their efforts to round up students after classes started." The report claimed "parents are becoming increasingly concerned about what effect the strike may have on their youngsters," and "parents concerned about the situation arrived a half-hour before the first bell rang to join the picket lines, and to tell other parents it's time to start dealing directly with the district headquarters. The parents want a settlement now." By using the single elementary school in his narrative, but mixing in information about the district in general, he implied that events at that school were typical of the entire district.

There was one allusion to the influence of cameras in the noon broadcast. The final paragraph of the script read: "Once the cameras left, many students did return, though some said they hope it's more worth their while today than it was yesterday." The paragraph was dropped from the evening report, but other elements of the story and the morning video were repeated. This story served the media firm's interest in building a large audience. But by creating a false and alarming report, it misled the public.

At the very large station, a reporter was asked at mid-morning to gather local reaction to a position paper about new fertilization and birth technologies that was released in Rome by Pope John Paul II the day before. The reporter was handed an 11-sentence wire service report on the paper. It said the Pope condemned the use of surrogate mothers (women who are implanted with fertilized eggs from the natural parents) and "test tube" fertilization (a process in which sperm and egg cells are mixed in vitro—in glass—outside of the body, then implanted in the mother's womb).

The reporter, a 15-year veteran with a master's degree in journalism, began by trying to line up an interview with a Catholic theologian willing to go on camera and explain the Pope's position. He learned that local church officials had just received word of the document and wanted a day to study it. They promised an explanation at a press conference called for 9 a.m. the next day. Rather than holding off on the story until either he could see the document or obtain a more complete description of it, or asking for an off-camera description, the reporter began to search for a Catholic fertility researcher or an infertile Catholic couple to whom he could tell what he knew of the papal paper and gather a reaction.

The reporter called the public relations officers of the area's major hospitals and medical centers asking them to locate either a Catholic researcher or couple willing to go on camera. One called back 20 minutes later with a woman born Catholic but since converted to Judaism who had undergone the in vitro technique. The editor said no, however. The interview had to be with a practicing Catholic. At that point the assignment editor produced a crumpled press release retrieved from his trash can. The paper was from a small local hospital calling attention to the anniversary of its in vitro fertilization program. "These little hospitals are desperate for publicity," the reporter said while dialing their number. "They'll prostitute anybody to get it." As expected, the hospital was eager to have the reporter visit. In fact the station with the most popular early evening newscast was there now. And the hospital had scared up a Catholic woman for both stations to interview. The reporter asked to go straight to the Catholic woman and her newborn, but the hospital public relations agent insisted on a tour of the hospital's facilities as the price of the personal interview.

While waiting for a photographer to become available, the reporter turned to the wire story about the papal announcement, highlighting several paragraphs. He explained that he would rely on the network newscast to cover what the document said. (The network, however, aired no report.)

At the hospital the photographer and reporter toured the in vitro program with a doctor who was aware of the Pope's paper, perhaps from the just concluded interview with the other station's reporter. The doctor agreed with the Pope that important ethical questions were involved and that there were abuses of human life going on, although not at his hospital. He predicted that the papal statement would have little effect on American fertility practice.

During the subsequent interview at the home of the new mother, the reporter asked: "You must have some feeling about . . . what the Vatican is saying. Can you tell me about your personal feelings about that?" The woman responded that she considered infertility an illness and would "do anything" to have a baby. "As a practicing Catholic," the reporter asked, "how do you resolve that with the leadership of the Church?" The woman said that babies are miracles in themselves. She and her husband didn't attend mass often, she said. She was not particularly concerned about the Pope's view. The reporter directed the photographer to shoot religious symbols around the house. Finding a wedding picture of the woman and her husband at the altar, he motioned to the cameraman. "Great! Made for television," he said.

As broadcast, the story did call attention to a newsworthy event, the papal paper. The mother's eloquent defense of her actions added poignancy and one woman's rationale. And the doctor's comment that he foresaw no changes in his practice as a result provided important reaction from at least one member of the fertility medical community. Although the story contained many elements of excellent journalism, it subtly violated norms of factuality. By insisting on using a Catholic woman as the focus and by emphasizing her connections to the church, the mother was presented as typical of infertile Catholic women. Logically, one person cannot represent so large and diverse a group; she could only stand for herself. The only value of searching for a Catholic woman was symbolic. Further, neither the reporter nor others at the station tried to discover whether her view typified infertile Catholics.

The story also lacked balance because it ignored the Church's side of the issue, not even giving the rationale for advising against artificial solutions to infertility contained in the wire and newspaper stories. The reporter did ask for a Catholic spokesperson to go on camera. But rather than holding the story for a day to attend the press conference, or asking for an off-camera briefing over the phone, the story proceeded. In fairness, the station did air a story from the press conference the following day. The second-day story rectified the imbalance, but there was no further attempt to assess the impact of the Pope's paper on infertile Catholic couples and no attempt to examine how it might affect either Catholic fertility researchers or such research going on at Catholic universities.

Such an informational approach was never his intention, the reporter explained afterward. "Reporters are film-makers," he said. "We're making little films. It has to have flow, a beginning, middle and end . . . a well-rounded, complete production. Newspaper reporters are information-oriented. They are trained to get a whole lot of information. They ignore the production side. That's because they don't understand it's the production that's important."

Had information been the focus, the station would have answered journalism's two central questions: What's really happening and what does it mean to the community? The answer would have begun with a transcript of the Pope's paper, or at least a summary longer than the 11-sentence wire story. The press conference called by Catholic theologians to explain the document might have been the ideal starting place. What the paper meant could best be tracked by its impact on medical research by Catholics and perhaps at Catholic universities, among infertile Catholic couples, and among ordinary Catholics—who might be concluding that together with the Church's ban on birth control and abortion, the distance between themselves and the moral teachings of the Pope had widened. Tracking down even one of these impacts would have cost considerable reporter or field producer time, however, even if leaders of one or more of these groups might be found to speak for the whole. The interview with the lone Catholic mother might be included in an informational story, but only as an element of human interest. It could not be the story's backbone.

SELF-INTEREST OF SOCIETAL ELITES

The clearest examples of such news-gathering were described in detail at the beginning of Chapter 2, so I'll merely remind you of the salient features here. Both stories were gathered by staffers from the large station who traveled to Latin America. The first story was reported in El Salvador and the second in Nicaragua. In both cases the sources reporters interviewed and what the journalists saw were more critical than supportive of the U.S. government's role. The news director explained that such reporting put him in a bind. Were the reports to reflect even an implied criticism of U.S. policy, the station might lose viewers with the opposite political view. In both cases parts of the story vital to public interpretation of the events were deleted. These stories were classified as serving the interests of elites because they censored information that tended to delegitimize U.S. government support of both Nicaraguan "Contras" and the government of El Salvador. The literature of ideological control of media by elites suggests a special antagonism toward Marxist or Communist efforts, particularly those involving force against capitalists.[22] The story was also classified as serving organizational self-interest because, according to the news director, the censorship was intended to avoid driving away any viewers.

HUMAN ERROR

At the large station, a reporter specializing in health issues overstated the cost of a new piece of medical machinery that destroys kidney stones with sound waves. Although her sources said the machine and room it required cost $2 million, the reporter told the public it cost $3 million. The story was classified as human error because the mistake appeared to be inadvertent. The reporter also called the machine a "marvel," violating neutrality and serving the station's own interest in maximizing audience.

Secondary Analyses

ORGANIZATION OF THE NEWSROOM— INSTITUTIONAL MEMORY

News production in all three newsrooms was remarkably similar. Almost every story originated with the assignment editor who commanded a small staff—from two to five persons—whose job it was to discover what was happening in the community. Only a handful of reporters actually worked "beats" (topic areas such as courts, the environment, city hall, etc.), even at the two stations in the very large market. The practical result was that reporters had little experiential background, little history, to give context to their news-gathering.

The usual remedy for such a problem is a background file of past stories reporters can quickly call up by subject and reference. While all stations kept the scripts the news anchors used and most kept reporter's scripts, these were stored by date rather than subject. To find a back script, someone in the newsroom had to remember the date the story ran. But even if someone's memory was so precise, scripts contained only the reporter or anchor's words, not those of news sources. In effect, there was no complete printed record of what any of the stations had previously reported. Video records were both more complete and better referenced. At the mid-sized station, a computer log had been initiated 6 months before my visit in which the "major" stories of the day, in the assignment editor's opinion, were kept in a videotape file. These files were referenced by subject. No reporter knew how to access the computer at the time of my visit, however. Both of the larger stations had a computerized or paper list of past stories, usually referenced by the subject of the visuals. At the large station, entries to the list were lagging about 6 weeks behind, however. Only KVLG had a librarian to help find file stories. This station was the only one to have an on-line data base search facility and a local newspaper on microfiche (and indexed by subject).

At all three stations a journalist seeking to know what was already reported about a topic would have to identify a person, place, or subject involved and look up that name. From there she would be directed to a closet of numbered videocassettes. She would take the cassette to an open editing bench or VCR and spin through the tape looking for the appropriate newscast and story. Useful segments could then be copied onto blank tape, or the reporter could hand-copy notes or quotes by transcribing the tape. I saw only one reporter attempting this rather laborious procedure and the tape she wanted was missing from the shelf.

The lack of reference to background reporting did not appear to be a function of the labor or time involved, however. Even at the very large station with the librarian to assist, few reporters referenced prior reporting. The librarian said his work was almost exclusively retrieving images on videotape—or older shots on film—to illustrate stories where fresh pictures were unavailable. The primary reason for ignoring past reporting, reporters said, was that their stories were too brief to include background.

ORGANIZATION OF THE NEWSROOM— QUALITY CONTROL

Although journalism places high value on getting information to consumers quickly so they can make informed decisions in timely fashion, accuracy receives even greater emphasis in every ethical code. This is because inaccurate information is the antithesis of journalism. It destroys journalism's reason for being—to enable comprehension of current issues and events and thus empower citizens. Some news departments have created mechanisms for controlling this essential quality. Most newspapers, for example, require at least one editor to read all copy before publication. Most also retract errors in subsequent issues and penalize reporters who make repeated errors. Newspapers also have "letters to the editor" sections for those who wish to criticize coverage. A few papers have ombudsmen who may judge the standards of its reporting. These measures may not ensure accuracy, but they do demonstrate some institutional concern.

At none of the stations visited did editors review the complete stories reporters created. Scripts were read, but what sources said in videotaped interviews and whatever else the camera captured was almost never checked. The exceptions were the Latin American series that originally contained words and images critical of the U.S. government's allies. Reporters were occasionally asked about what their video contained or what sources said, but the routine practice was to review only the script. Certainly reviewing a videotape is more technologically cumbersome than editing in print, but it is no less important. In addition, no station had a policy of retraction or correction. Such policies are apparently not part of local broadcast orthodoxy.[23] No reporter could remember a staff member being disciplined for inaccurate reporting. No station aired opposing viewpoints from viewers during a newscast. No station employed an ombudsman. Such consumer representatives are apparently limited to a small number of newspapers.[24]

The principal means of quality control at each station was a "postmortem"—a critique of the early evening newscast by the news director. These sessions—which typically included the assignment editor and producer, and at the larger stations, the executive producer and assistant news director—focused on two types of problems. The primary concern was technical flaws, such as a delay in the start of a videotaped section of a story, "jump cuts"—a by-product of hasty editing in which two similar scenes are spliced together but the principals' positions have slightly shifted, giving the appearance they've jumped[25]—"flapping lips"—in which a source is speaking but the sound has been stripped—and the most dreaded defect—when the screen temporarily goes black. A second concern was "missed stories." News directors monitored competitors' newscasts and compared story topics. Because the treatment of stories—what reporters call the "angle"—differed little from one station to a competitor, that was rarely a focus of comment. Differences in facts also might be questioned here, but this did not occur in the postmortems I attended.

Discussion

OBJECTIVITY ANALYSIS

These findings suggest that organizational and corporate self-interest strongly influence news content resulting in a surprisingly high percentage of violations of journalistic objectivity standards. Human error and personal bias provide only marginal explanations for departures from objectivity.

Economist Edward Herman and linguist Noam Chomsky's theory that news is propaganda serving the interests of society's elites while undermining the interests of poor and middle-income groups receives only limited support, most notably the suppression of criticism of U.S. policy in Latin America. Presumably elites favor the status quo, yet stories suggesting that an IRS complex and City Hall are drug dens or that chaos reigns in the schools, or that housing developers and the county planning commission were responsible for an Air Force base closure, would appear to undermine rather than legitimize the establishment. Creating alarm about public and private institutions may destabilize the status quo, but it seems to help the media firm by enlarging audience. Further, failing to corroborate the substance of alarming stories saves the news department time and money. It also avoids the need to tone down or, worse, reject the story and pay for gathering a replacement. Contrary to Herman and Chomsky's thesis, there may be a fundamental conflict between the news department's interest in attracting audience through negative news and elites' interest in legitimizing the established hierarchy of society.

News historian J. Herbert Altschull's theory of news as propaganda that serves the media's "paymasters"—in this case advertisers—is difficult to rule in or out with such a limited number of cases. No objectivity violations that specifically protected or promoted advertisers or their products were observed in the 34 case studies. My selection bias for the most consequential topics, however, prevented me from accompanying reporters on a series of stories at KMID about the making of a prime-time network miniseries featuring the city in which KMID is located. According to KMID's advertising director, the stories were designed to boost interest in the drama that KMID was to broadcast in several weeks. The ad director crowed that KMID was able to sell its advertising spots on the miniseries at record rates. Such reportage, obviously, fails impartiality standards. In this case, KMID was not boosting the interests of advertisers so much as it was helping itself by hyping the network program. However, KMID also produced an entire newscast, during my visit, at the county fair in which anchors and several stories shamelessly plugged the fair, a major advertiser at KMID during that month. Reporters at both the large and very large station recounted instances of the news department protecting or promoting advertisers in the poll I described in Chapter 6.

Another obstacle to ruling out Altschull's theory with a study of news-gathering is that if it's true, one would not expect reporters to be assigned stories critical of important advertisers. Nothing in this study contradicts the general critique of U.S. news media that they ignore newsworthy issues in the private sector. The proper conclusion might be that Altschull's theory has more limited applicability in commercial news than scholars such as Shoemaker and Mayfield supposed when they used Altschull's critique as the integrating principle for all theories of news content.[26] Even if media firms protect their sponsors, only a moderate proportion of newsworthy issues and events in a metropolitan area would be affected. As news media continue to be bought and merged into larger corporations, however, they will acquire a number of "cousin" sponsors—funders of other businesses owned by the parent corporation. The more these become exempt from critical coverage, the more Altschull's theory will explain.

ANALYSES OF NEWSROOM ORGANIZATION

The analysis of how newsrooms were organized, particularly the lack of quality control, deserves comment. In only 2 of the 20 violations could the reporter alone be faulted. Editors couldn't have known, for example, the actual cost of the kidney machine. In the other cases, however, the structure of the news department either encouraged distortion or failed to correct obvious omissions and errors. For example, when the reporter at KMID implied that most winery workers were unhappy with their union, he did so without presenting any evidence. Had the station a mechanism for quality control, the reporter would have been forced either to support the claim or drop it. Likewise, a fraudulent claim of multiple witnesses of employee drug use at the federal office complex (described in Chapter 3) would have been exposed had an editor asked to see tape or notes. At KLRG, editors agreed in a postmortem of the first day's teacher strike coverage that they had overplayed the lack of order. But they repeated the error the next day—selecting as typical the school they believed most likely to render dramatic and controversial events. And it was the news director, not reporters, who censored indications of a U.S. role in Central America's problems. Defending his action, he cited an economic loss—viewership—as justifying objectivity violations. KVLG editors could not have known that the interviews in the low voter turnout story were staged, but the premise of the story—treating a serious civic problem humorously—was imposed by the producer.

What was most striking about these violations was that they went largely unnoticed within the news departments. Not only was quality control minimal, grossly distorted or irrelevant reports often received praise from editors.

OBJECTIVITY VIOLATIONS BY LEVEL OF RESOURCES

An unexpected finding was that the newsroom with the least resources had the best record of objectivity. If creating an objective newscast were management's aim, one would expect quality control to increase with the station's resources. Yet among observed cases, the opposite occurred. Objectivity violations rose from 33% of the reports at KMID, to 77% at KLRG, and 83% at KVLG. The ethnographic record suggests that at KMID reporters—tasked with three or more stories per day—had too little time to embellish reports in ways that might lead away from objectivity. A closer look at stories at KMID that upheld objectivity norms reveals a pattern of minimal reporting. Most of these topics were simple events and light features requiring little or no fact-checking or gathering of other sides. At the larger stations, where reporters had 4 to 8 hours to gather a story, objectivity violations were so routine they constituted standard practice.

WERE OBJECTIVITY NORM VIOLATIONS SERIOUS?

Two of the 20 could certainly be considered minor. In one case a photographer asked seated winery strikers to march. In the other, the cost of the kidney stone disintegrator was exaggerated. The 18 other violations, however, were likely to have broader impact on how local society understood its environment—whether an Air Force base was to be closed because county officials failed to keep housing far enough away from runways, whether winery workers were angry at their union for calling a strike, whether a major federal office complex was a drug den, whether the United States was spending more than a million tax dollars a day to support or suppress freedom in Central America, whether schools were safe or places of chaos during a teachers' strike, whether a computer company could transfer technology to a competing nation. These results, particularly given the sampling preference for the ablest reporters and the more serious story topics, suggest a set of unwritten rules governing news-gathering that often contradict journalistic standards.

The "Rules" of Local Television News-Gathering

The 34 case studies of news-gathering plus interviews conducted at the stations indicate a surprising uniformity of assumptions and practice. The primary difference from station to station was the level of resources available, not the preferred method of news-gathering.

Taken together, four interlocking rules specify how market logic organizes local television reporting. All rest on the assumption, prevalent in each newsroom visited, that most viewers are either not able or don't care to distinguish between normative journalism and nonnormative presentations. The first three rules are designed to attract the largest possible audience. The fourth attempts to minimize reporting costs.

1. *Seek Images Over Ideas.* Moving images give television its comparative advantage over print and radio news. Gathering the video part of the story is more important than the facts and opinions expressed in the story. The more arresting the video, the better. "Talking heads"—video of sources speaking—is inferior to video of action, but preferable to no video at all. As a corollary, all interviews have to be videotaped. Even sources granted anonymity should be videotaped, with their voices and faces electronically altered. Sources, regardless of their importance, who are unwilling to go on camera should rarely, if ever, be used. Phone interviews, no matter how efficient for gathering information, are not appropriate for television.

2. *Seek Emotion Over Analysis.* Emotion is more appealing than thought. It's also more visual. And it's more parsimonious; emotion can be captured with a 2-second visual of someone crying or laughing, while analysis requires time-consuming background, argument, and counterargument. With its combination of moving visuals and natural sound, television is better equipped to convey emotion than its competitors.

Corollary A: Avoid complexity. Because viewers watching for entertainment have short attention spans and not every viewer is interested in every story, no report should exceed 120 seconds. In such a compressed period of time, you can't do justice to complexity. Plus, facts, particularly statistics, are a turnoff; they're MEGO—"My Eyes Glaze Over." Complex issues are better left to newspapers where there's more space, people can skip over what doesn't interest them, and they can consume at their own pace or even re-read.

Corollary B: Dramatize where possible. Stories with a beginning, middle, and end, rising and falling action, and perhaps an archetypal struggle such as good with bad, giant against the diminutive, are more likely to capture attention than more explanatory journalism that seeks to establish factuality and probes the implications of issues and events for the community.

3. *Exaggerate, if Needed, to Add Appeal.* Although it's risky to inaccurately report easily verified information such as sports scores or the location of an accident, more interpretive information affords considerable latitude. Select reporting sites, video, and quotes not for the typical, but for the extreme or provocative. However, present them, at least implicitly, as if they

are representative. Choreograph the actions and words of those on camera, if necessary, to enliven the story. Ignore or downplay elements of events and issues that undercut their appeal. Never allude to holes or weaknesses in the interpretation of events reported; present the story as authoritative and complete as of the time of the newscast.

4. *Avoid Extensive News-Gathering*. Any story, regardless of topic, can be gathered and prepared for television in 3 hours, or at the most, 8. Don't spend time gathering background information from previously broadcast stories; there's only time in the story for the most recent information. Don't script questions in advance of meeting sources; it's not worth the time and you may over-gather information you can't fit into a 1- or 2-minute story. Gather few or no documents such as position papers, speeches, fact sheets, or analyses by sources; they can't be used on camera and, again, there's not time for the detail they may introduce. Don't travel to more than one or two sites; you don't have the time. Don't interview more than a few sources; you won't be able to put them all on the air. Don't spend more than a few minutes with each source. Long sound bites bore entertainment-oriented viewers. Don't shoot more than 30 minutes of videotape; you'll have too much tape to edit. Don't bother checking dubious fact-claims; viewers pay attention to feelings more than information; and you may feel obligated to drop provocative elements of the story if the claims are false.

Conclusion

Recall for a moment the results of the analysis in Chapter 7. At the two larger stations a bit more than half the airtime devoted to news was rated high in orienting consumers to their communities. At those stations there seemed to be "info" combined with the "tainment." Even this limited optimism must now be questioned. When the panel of journalists rated 53% of KLRG's newscast and 55% of KVLG's as having social or personal consequence, it assumed the stories were put together following accepted journalistic standards. As these cases have demonstrated, some, perhaps many, of the stories rated consequential may have been illusory. This fear that consequential elements in many of the two stations' stories were there by hype rather than by honest news-gathering gains support beyond the case studies from the selection pattern in the mid-sized station. At KMID, where journalists had the least time to hype and most often followed the minimum requirements of objectivity, only 38% of news time was rated above the orientation midpoint.

When analysis of the discovery and selection of events and issues is combined with examination of how they are covered, market logic's domination of journalistic logic becomes almost complete. Even the most prestigious station with the greatest resources often produced a collage of video and commentary about those current events likely to turn the most heads that was designed with far greater regard for interesting than informing or educating viewers. While the station promoted its newscasts as the best journalism in the metropolitan area, and the content may have looked like and sounded like news, this research suggests that much of it was an illusion. Or worse, a deception.

Notes

1. Christians, Rotzoll, & Fackler, 1987.
2. Westerstahl, 1983, p. 407.
3. Westerstahl, 1983, p. 403.
4. Hackett, 1984, p. 253.
5. Hackett, 1984, p. 253.
6. Ettema, 1987.
7. Schudson, 1978, p. 192.
8. Hackett, 1984.
9. This implies that anonymity should be granted to sources only when information of value to the public would not be available if the source were named.
10. This list is my own, but it conforms to standards promulgated in widely used reporting texts such as Mencher, 1987, see chap. 2; or style books such as Lippmann, 1989, see chap. 1 by Benjamin C. Bradlee.
11. Westerstahl, 1983, p. 416.
12. Westerstahl, 1983, p. 417.
13. Westerstahl, 1983, p. 420.
14. Shoemaker, 1987.
15. White, in Dexter & White, 1964.
16. A major investor is defined by the Securities and Exchange Commission as one whose holdings constitute 5% or more of the parent corporation's outstanding shares.
17. Dreier, 1983.
18. Obviously, top executives and major shareholders of media firms and their affiliated companies are members of the elite, at least locally. But members of the elite can have conflicting purposes as well as cooperative ones. With news media, owners may profit by selling sensational stories of villainy in other parts of the establishment.
19. Shoemaker, 1987, p. 4.
20. Goldstein, 1985, p. 241.
21. To check the reliability of my matches of violations and categories, a second evaluator undertook the task. She placed 16 of the 20 stories in each of the same categories, an agreement rate of 80%.
22. Herman & Chomsky, 1988.
23. None of the research I reviewed for this book mentions a retraction/correction policy at any U.S. station. Some, however, may exist.
24. Emerson Stone, 1993.
25. Gaye Tuchman (1978) explained editors' aversion to jump cuts as originating in how easily viewers can identify them as errors and as indicators that something has been edited out. They damage the illusion that the report is uncut reality, what Tuchman calls the "web of facticity," newsworkers attempt to create.
26. Shoemaker, 1987.

9

The Journalists Respond

O n the first day of observation at each station, I asked the news director
to describe the station's news mission and how it was being accomplished. And on the last day I reviewed preliminary findings with the news
director and other key journalists, asking for their own interpretations of
newsroom behavior. At each station the representations offered at the beginning and end of my visit differed as starkly as noon from midnight.

First Impressions

The early evening newscast at the mid-sized station, KMID, began with a
fast-paced collage of local images: the most inspiring buildings from the
city's skyline, a sailboat breezing on a lake at sunset, brightly colored hot
air balloons drifting over green fields. The number and variety of images
suggested that the station's cameras skimmed over the entire area and
uncovered a world of excitement. The accompanying music throbbed with
drama—the kind of music played in the background of key action scenes in
the movies. It connoted urgency and climax until it ended abruptly as the
camera zoomed in on a tailored, handsome man and woman both smiling
then turning serious, "Good evening, I'm . . . "
The building where this newscast originated is modern with large white
satellite dishes reaching skyward for information. Inside the news director's
office a plaque hung from the wall, a "certificate of merit" for "best news"
from the Associated Press Television-Radio Association. In a collection of
videotapes sat the legendary Edward R. Murrow's "Harvest of Shame"
broadcast. The news director, a trim and handsome young man, used to

anchor the evening newscast. On my first morning of observation, he explained KMID's news philosophy:

> We provide a solid hour of news with very little fluff element, a meat and potatoes newscast—tell me what's going on in my backyard and tell me what's in it for me? . . .We're not only asking the four W's [who, what, where, when] but why something is important, an interpretation.
>
> We're not a hype station. We don't go "live" if there's no reason to. The most important story is often not the most interesting and the most visual, but we'll still lead with that. We never neglect the hard news story even if it's uninteresting.

The news director said the basics of journalism—getting information, talking to people, using the phone—are the same as in newspapers. "Certainly we don't go into as much detail. [But] we go through records. We sit through meetings." The principal difference between KMID's reporting and that of the local newspaper, he explained, was that KMID reporters "boiled down" the same amount of information into a more concise story.

Behind the Facade

Unfortunately, almost every aspect of KMID's news operation would prove illusory. That very evening the entire newscast was broadcast live from the county fairgrounds. This occurred not because of an event that required instantaneous coverage, but as a promotion of the fair and the chance for a more interesting visual backdrop. From a journalistic viewpoint the decision caused problems. Deadlines for all stories were advanced because of the technical dislocation of remote broadcasting. And the fair became the focus of the news with stories planned about "carnies"—the exotic people who travel with the fairs from town to town—and "the vegematic man," and a medical segment from the blood pressure testing booth, and perhaps a podiatrist to stand next to "the footsie-wootsie machines." Not only fluff, but a payback for the fair's advertising on KMID.

Although it is normal for an individual or organization to fall somewhat short of its goals, behavior that contradicts those goals hints at deception, or perhaps schizophrenia. By the end of my month of observation the station routinely violated nearly every precept of reporting about which the news director boasted. When confronted with the contradictions between his words and the station's deeds, he acknowledged the facade. But he blamed costs or the audience for the discrepancies. For example:

- When told that no reporter was observed checking government or private records or sitting through more than 20 minutes of a meeting, the news director said, "We can't just sit through the entire meeting," because of the cost of committing a reporter and photographer for a substantial part of the day.

• When told the presence or absence of visuals appeared to powerfully influence story selection, he responded: "The visual promise does have an effect on what we cover. You want to get the most for your money, so, yeah, we gravitate toward the more visual stories."

• When asked why the profiles his station prepared of political candidates routinely repackaged snippets from the candidates' own political advertisements rather than presenting original reporting, the news director said: "Time. That is the big thing hitting us. Yes, we could analyze these charges, and analyze in depth the 10 to 13 [local] races. Any given week with full staffing we could delve into these things. [But] in politics, so many candidates and so much goes on so quickly, it's hard to get it covered as one would ideally like to do."

• When asked why KMID relied on the newspaper to dig up and report so many stories rather than independently covering the community, he replied, "Our general rule of thumb is that one half the people who watch us have not read the [local daily newspaper]. So we don't worry too much about copying the [newspaper]."

• When confronted with his own rule that no story run more than 105 seconds, too little time to present all sides to an issue or complex matters, he replied: "In TV generally the pace is fast—bam-bam-bam. We like to do that too." He explained, "If you [the viewer] don't see something you like right now, you may see something next that attracts you."

• And what about the commitment to important news, even if it's dull? At the end of my visit, I asked the news director what he would do if by improving the journalism of his newscast it lost two ratings points? (A ratings point is 1% of the area's households with television. Given the size of the audience KMID was drawing to the early evening program, the loss of 2 ratings points would represent a substantial decline in the station's viewership, about 25%.) "If we did something new," he replied, "and it backfired and we could trace it to that, we'd make some changes, or repackage it, maybe put a spoonful of sugar with the medicine. I can't imagine [an improvement] that vitally important. We're not so egocentric that we'd say, 'they ought to take [their medicine].' "

The clash of outside journalistic image with inside business reality at KMID recurred at each of the other stations in the study. News directors' portrayals of news production changed radically between my first visit, as an outsider, and these exit interviews. At the outset, only one news director explained the logic of news production in other than public service terms.

That one said he had learned to think "with a cash register in my head." He refused to permit my access to the station, arguing that he did not want his reporters to think about news values or journalism while gathering stories. Instead, he wanted them to think about ratings. He instructed his reporters to imagine that he was placing a certain number of viewers in their hands at the beginning of their story, he explained, and he wanted all of them back at the end. In each of the stations where I was admitted, economics steadily displaced journalism over the course of the visit as the primary explanation for news production. "You've got it," said the news director at the station serving as the pretest for the study. "The purpose is to make as much money as possible." An assistant news director who later became director lamented that "the industry doesn't reward good journalism."

Although few of the journalists questioned the accuracy of the preliminary findings, there was a great deal of discomfort—and some disagreement—with the generalization drawn from those findings: Economic norms usually dominate journalistic norms when the two conflict. The most common discomfort reaction of those interviewed went something like: "I know you're right. But I hate to think of myself that way." The most common disagreements varied little from station to station. They can be grouped into six claims:

1. It's fruitless to preach to an empty church. We do the best we can with a public that won't sit still for serious news.
2. Television is inherently an entertainment medium. This is because news programs are surrounded by entertaining shows with a certain pace and quality of production that create an expectation of newscasts. It's also because television is a "feelings" medium; it transmits not only what was said, but how it was said.
3. Television is inherently an action rather than information medium. Because it's a visual technology and the pace is controlled by programmers rather than viewers—who can't "reread" what they don't understand the first time—television is unsuited for abstract or complex information. It favors action over ideas and issues.
4. The public, not journalists, should decide what constitutes quality journalism by the decision whether to watch. It is simple arrogance for journalists to force their standards on the public.
5. All television need do is headline the news. For most people, television is just one part of a daily news cycle that includes supplementary information from radio and newspapers.
6. We do the best we can with the limited resources that stations possess.

Each of these claims deserves analysis. But first notice what's common to all of them. *None argue that local television news meets high standards of journalistic quality,* at least as defined in the craft's ethical codes. All six either place the blame for journalistic shortcomings outside the news department, or they imply that television is "a different kind of animal" than print—for which journalism codes were first developed. These differences, they imply, are great enough for TV news to merit its own set of rules.

You Can't Preach to an Empty Church

Of all the reasons given for why local television news falls short of journalistic standards, the idea that the public won't sit still for serious news is the most widely cited not only by news directors and journalists, but by media critics and the public as well. The notion's appeal rests on the fact that attracting as large an audience as possible is a fundamental goal of journalism. And it rests on the apparently limited popularity of serious news programs such as *The MacNeil/Lehrer News Hour.*[1] In each of the newsrooms I visited, the idea that serious stories—those that are complex, lack compelling visuals, or analyze rather than arouse—bore, and thus drive away, viewers was taken as a given. Indeed, one news director presented the results of research undertaken by consultants as evidence.

To analyze this claim, let's expand the metaphor of preaching to an empty church. Suppose a minister sought to fill her church by adding entertainment to the liturgy. Incorporating pleasurable activities, such as singing, might build attendance in ways that enhance the spiritual experience. Other efforts to attract people, such as including a popular secular singer, might begin to replace worship time with something else. To the extent that the entertainment displaces worship, full or not, her church takes a step away from its sacred mission and toward a more secular one. At some point, the church risks becoming something different. And if churchgoers think they're getting right with god, they may be deceived. Something similar can happen in a newsroom.

Stations are paid for the size of the audience of potential customers they deliver to advertisers, not on how much viewers learn about current issues and events. So the decision to seek the largest number of viewers becomes a commercial, not a journalistic, one as what's merely interesting replaces what's important. As I argued in Chapter 5, except in time of crisis, the market for serious news is a subset of the public attention market. The latter is larger because it also includes those who watch for entertainment.[2]

It may not be realistic to expect serious journalism to attract as large an audience as entertainment-oriented news. Still, the more that watch a quality newscast the better. I've argued that the fundamental purpose of journalism is to maximize the public's understanding of its environment. That means the most gain in knowledge by the largest number of persons. Mixing elements likely to draw attention with those likely to impart knowledge best serves this primary goal of journalism, what I called Quadrant II stories in Chapter 7.

But such narratives must pass a test: Do the attention-attracting elements serve the informative? For example, did the emotional response of the Filipino emigrant in the vignette beginning Chapter 8 help explain the problem of low voter turnout, or was it included simply for its audience appeal? The analyses in Chapters 7 and 8 suggest that local television stations are willing to turn the "church" into a circus in order to fill it.

The analogy between church and news breaks down here. Even the dimmest worshipper would take notice—more likely, alarm—if a rabbi or preacher herded elephants and trapeze acts into the sanctuary. As we have seen, the substitution of entertainment for news is more subtle, particularly when the topic of the story is serious but the treatment is merely appealing. According to years of surveys, the public trusts what it sees on local newscasts to be news. The potential for deception is greater in front of the set than in front of the sanctuary.

Those who drafted American-style democracy assumed not only a public that would do the work of keeping informed about the important issues and events of the day, but one that would debate the issues and their solutions in a "marketplace of ideas."[3] But even in an 18th century America of rural villages and multiple local newspapers in which the distance between political decision makers and the governed stretched across many fewer people than today, public participation in politics has never approached the ideal. In the first days of the nation the majority of the public was excluded on the basis of their gender or race or lack of property or education. Although each of those exclusions has now been remedied and some level of literacy has spread to much of the adult population, public knowledge of and participation in the political life of communities and the nation remain disappointing. As Professor Jay Rosen noted:

> Well worn research . . .shows how rarely citizens participate in public life, how little they know about current issues or how alienated they feel from politics (Neuman, 1986). Such figures will always cause the general public to appear a "phantom" as it did to Lippmann (1925). Indeed, if we continue to ask the question Lippmann (1922, 1925) asked, "Is the general body of citizens informed and engaged in public life in the manner democratic theory assumes?" the answer will usually be "no" (Schudson, 1983).[4]

So journalists' dismal assessment of the public's interest in serious news may have some validity. But by playing to public apathy and creating the illusion that news consists of just what's entertaining, news departments attempting to please the market may discourage the public from seeking rigorous and analytical news reports. Many viewers may be more than willing to go along with a definition of news that makes no demands on them. And as they do, the audience for serious news diminishes even for news departments trying to follow the norms of journalism. Instead of decrying a lack of public involvement, argued Rosen, news departments ought to join with other segments of society in building it by orchestrating public discussions of community problems and goals.[5]

Television Is Inherently an Entertainment Medium

A second reason television journalists employ to defend making newscasts entertaining goes like this: When people sit down in front of a television, they are conditioned to expect entertainment. News won't hold their attention if it is too dissimilar. There is no question that entertainment—soap operas, game shows, situation comedies, cartoons, dramas—dominates the broadcast day of all but public television stations. But as we saw in Chapter 2, local news programming has begun to claim a significant, and growing, portion of the day's programming. Despite entertainment's predominance, there is no evidence that viewers cannot shift their perspective in order to watch a serious news program.

In fact, huge numbers of Americans put their televisions to informational tasks from time to time. For instance, the four debates between presidential and vice presidential candidates in October of 1992 drew 41.6% of television households—a Super Bowl-sized audience that ranged from 81 million to 88 million viewers.[6] The debates were not without entertaining elements—confrontation, celebrity, Ross Perot's country humor—but the video was relatively static, little more than still pictures of "talking heads," the audio was often monotonous, and the main topic—government—is generally considered boring by television consultants. Not only did viewers use their televisions for information, they seem to have learned a great deal about the candidates' issue positions.[7] Television does present entertainment very well because, unlike print with its lines of abstract symbols, its representations are lifelike and concrete. But that vividness also serves the presentation of information very well as we shall see in the next few pages.

A second rationale for applying television in an entertaining fashion is the claim that TV is a "feelings" medium. Media sociologist Joshua Meyrowitz argued that television has an inherent emotional track that print lacks. For example, a televised speech always includes more than the words of the speaker. It also carries the speaker's accent, mannerisms, voice quality, emphases, facial expressions, and body language. All of these may be reported in a newspaper if the reporter chooses to spend words on them, Meyrowitz noted, but they also may be separated from the content of the speech and left unreported. Television has an advantage over print in conveying emotion accurately and efficiently because the writer needs extra words to describe them and may not do them justice. But that attribute does not *limit* television to feelings.

In fact, viewers may understand a speech more readily for hearing the speaker's emphases and cadences than readers who see only the words in print. Television can be superior to print both cognitively and emotionally. An advantage in presenting emotion does not denote a deficit in conveying thought. Summarizing research on the effects of emotion on the mental processing of news, Barrie Gunter wrote: "Arousing content (e.g. humour) can affect attention to information and, when related directly to the central concepts of a presentation, can also improve learning."[8] However, if emotion is not carefully keyed to the core elements of a story, it can distract viewers and disrupt learning.[9]

Television's Pacing and Visual Characteristics Make It a Better Medium for Action Than for Information

Just as television has an advantage over print in presenting emotions efficiently, it can simulate motion while print cannot. (Note that print is also a visual medium: It cannot be received by another sense. But it's a static visual medium.) For events whose importance lies in the characteristics of the actions taken, television has an advantage in efficiency over print. A newspaper reporter may write about how a fire crew saved a family's life or how a multiple car collision looked, or how people in a besieged city live and die, but no matter how skilled a writer she or he is, the account can never be as accurate or efficient as moving pictures of the event. This is because the writer must rely on the reader's imagination for images rather than on the reality in front of the camera. Television's pictures also have a validity in the public's mind that word pictures do not. Television beats print in presenting news in which a description of some action is essential to the story.

Sometime in the future, when news departments may choose between transmitting stories in audio-visual or text and photo format, it will make sense to segregate events for more or less visual coverage. In the meantime, however, television's visual advantage does not justify displacing consequential nonvisual information with what is less important but more dynamic or aesthetic. Those who rely on TV news may be misled into thinking that only what is interesting to watch is newsworthy.

Television is inherently a visual medium. But that can make it more, rather than less, effective as a vehicle for information. Pictures—moving or still—can help viewers understand and remember the news. Summarizing research on video news, Gunter wrote, "Depending on how they are used in news programmes alongside accompanying news narratives, pictures may enhance or impair memory and comprehension."[10] When images match the verbal narrative of news stories, understanding is enhanced. Gunter explained:

> The meaning of a news story is carried in the narrative. News comprehension therefore depends on effective processing of the story text. Cognitive research has shown, however, that memory for pictures tends to be better than memory for words. Furthermore, pictures tend to be well remembered even long after presentation. There is evidence, also, that because they are more readily processed than words, pictures may "drown out" the verbal content in television news. Dhawan and Pellegrino (1977) found that pictures are encoded to a deep semantic level of processing faster than verbal materials. There is evidence that pictures and pictorial representations in broadcasts can enhance memory and comprehension of information.[11]

More recently, Doris Graber titled her research into the impact of visuals on television news learning, "Seeing Is Remembering." She concluded:

> Despite the stereotypical and brief appearances of most pictorial images, viewers' recall of TV news stories was enhanced by visuals, especially those that are personalized through unusual sites and human figures.[12]

Can television accommodate abstraction and complexity? News programmers define *complexity* as the intricacy of the topic of a news story—how much information is necessary for the typical viewer to make sense of it. About two thirds of the journalists I interviewed said the abstraction and complexity of certain kinds of stories—typically about the economy, government, social trends, or stories relying heavily on statistics—were suitable for print, but not for television.

The notion that television is a poor medium with which to explain abstract or complex topics is widely held even outside of broadcast newsrooms. For example, in his provocative book, *Amusing Ourselves to Death,* Neil Postman argued that television creates a discourse of images to replace the discourse of words that prevailed in the age of print. Images, he argued, are poor vehicles for abstraction compared to words. Images, particularly photographs, are concrete and specific, yet their meaning is open to interpretation by the viewer. Words, however can describe ideas that have no form or physical substance, and they are specifically defined in dictionaries. Further, we have rules requiring words to be arranged in the logical order of sentences. And rules exist for grouping sentences around one theme for a paragraph and ordering paragraphs into logical essays. Finally, we have the rules of evidence for deciding if a claim is true. An image-based medium like television, Postman wrote, follows not the logic of proposition and argument, but a subjective aesthetic that subordinates reasoning to feeling, the abstract to the concrete, and blurs the distinction between truth and falsity when images are manipulated to persuade—as in advertisements—but are presented as real. In sum, television is not suited to a serious informational role.[13]

Postman's argument is complex and intriguing. But it is based on two assumptions that are questionable, particularly for quality newscasts. To be effective, the argument requires either that television has no audio narrative track or that the words, sentences, and the logic of exposition of such a track are so dominated by the visual aspects of television that they carry no meaning.

But as Gunter observed, television news carries meaning not just in its images, but also in reporter and anchor scripts. In television newswriting, the audio and visual can be constructed to reinforce each other, providing a redundancy that can make complexity easier, rather than more difficult, to convey.

As an example of this synergism, television journalist Bill Moyers once interviewed Postman for a Public Broadcasting Service documentary titled "Consuming Images." Moyers ran a video clip of a McDonald's advertisement showing a father and his young daughter enjoying the bonding experience of a lifetime at the restaurant. At the same time Postman made an argument that the idealized image of the father and daughter might seduce viewers into accepting an assertion that would be preposterous if made in words: that taking your child to McDonald's will transform you into a wonderful parent and your child into an adoring daughter or son. The *combination* of Postman's audio track and the video clip created a more powerful teaching device than print alone. The McDonald's advertisement demonstrated that television could realize Postman's fears that TV creates a new kind of "language." But Moyers's documentary showed how video can enhance the understanding gleaned from words alone, when the two are orchestrated for the purpose of instruction.

It may not be helpful to ask whether television or print is a superior learning tool. The two are very different media. Each has unique advantages and disadvantages. Researchers John Robinson and Dennis Davis recently listed some of television's advantages:

Unlike . . . radio format, TV simultaneously engaged both the eye and the ear, the same sense modalities that most people use to learn naturally from their own environment and experiences. Unlike print media, television was thought capable of effectively communicating news images and information, regardless of the audience's level of literacy.

Second, TV news producers take great pains to make their stories visually appealing, to present news instantaneously, and to make viewers feel they are a part of the events shown. New computerized graphics present technical and statistical data in compelling formats.

Third, broadcast organizations routinely employ news researchers and consultants to keep news producers up-to-date on what audiences like and do not like about the news. Continuous feedback also comes from broadcast ratings services, which monitor the public's daily use of its TV sets.

These advantages should make television an ideal medium for the "information age."[14] But television also has disadvantages as a learning tool—beyond those mentioned by Postman:

- The inability of the viewer to control the program's pace means you can't slow down or re-view difficult parts, nor stop to fit the new information into your mental "files" or schemas—rules of thumb about how something works.
- Television programs are briefer than their print counterparts, and therefore impart less information. For example, a half-hour newscast contains fewer words than a single newspaper page.[15] And news documentaries contain less information than news magazines or books.
- Viewing is often a social activity with potential for distraction, while reading is solitary—more conducive to concentration.
- Although a certain level of effort is required to make sense of printed words—and thus enjoy reading—television can be enjoyed with only minimal attention.

These drawbacks make complexity difficult to convey, but not impossible. Print's advantage over television in permitting the reader to set the pace can be minimized—although not eliminated—by careful programming. When a news account deals with complexity, it makes sense to slow down the speed of narration, to increase verbal and visual redundancy, to repeat key points, perhaps even include interludes for thinking.[16] No technological barrier prevents employing any of these strategies in a newscast. However, a newscast designed so explicitly to convey information might seem plodding and bore those watching primarily to be entertained.

Time constraints that once required newscasts to be brief are diminishing. The diffusion of cable systems with scores of channels has already set the stage for both national and local all-news channels. Pay-per-view financing through cable may make it feasible to produce news content targeted to small, specific audiences. Finally, videocassette recorders afford viewers greater choice over when they will watch newscasts, making them as time-convenient as newspapers.

Although friends or family may sit together in front of the television, the experience need not be distracting. As long as all agree, each may devote full attention to the screen. In fact, the presence of others may even aid your understanding if there's opportunity to ask about terms or elements in the story you don't understand, or the reactions of others cue you to meanings you would have missed viewing alone. Further, research indicates that discussion of an idea may help place and imprint the knowledge gained from a story in your mind.[17]

If used properly by both programmers and viewers, television can be a powerful informational medium. Levy recently concluded:

> Television . . .does have some unique advantages in conveying information. When it slows down and repeats its message (much as TV commercials do), no communication medium can match it, particularly for portraying a sense of "being there," of experiencing a dramatic or historic event. Indeed, television is unsurpassed as a meaningful information source when its pictures are dramatic and unequivocal in the message they transmit—as with the Challenger disaster or the pro-democracy demonstrations in Beijing.[18]

The Public Should Decide What's Quality Journalism

The argument that the public acting through the market should be the final arbiter of what's newsworthy and how news should be presented is the backbone of market journalism. Its attractiveness lies in putting to use in journalism the same mechanism that has led to constantly improving products at stable or lower prices when applied to many other goods and services. But markets do not work equally well with all types of products.

In Chapter 5, I argued that letting the public decide the standard of quality for journalism had more potential to sabotage than serve the public interest. This is because media firms serve four kinds of customers—the audience, sources, advertisers, and investors. The last three are in much better position to conduct informed transactions than the first. Most of the public is simply not able to evaluate the quality of a product that by definition is unknown or "news" to it. Further, where their news alternatives are as similar as peas in a pod, consumers have little basis for discriminating high from low quality.

Advertisers and sources, who are contracting for public attention, however, can know with considerable precision what they are getting for the money or information they offer. Some sources and most advertisers enjoy a buyers' market. If they don't get what they want, they can go elsewhere. Investors' rights to information about a firm's financial condition are guaranteed by the Securities and Exchange Commission. And their choice of alternative investments is at least as long as the stock pages of the *Wall Street*

Journal. Unless their demands are met, they too can go elsewhere. To the extent that the interests of advertisers and sources differ from audiences, news firms wishing to maximize return to stockholders must serve those interests over the public interest. Chapters 6, 7, and 8 showed how at each stage of news production the optimal decision for the market harmed more than helped the public interest.

Putting aside all high falutin' theoretical reasons for why there is a contradiction between news content that serves the public and that which serves the market, there is a more practical reason to disbelieve the claim that the public knows best: Not one of the journalists below the level of news director who was interviewed at the end of the study believed the claim to be true. In fact, they believed the opposite—that quality journalism would empty the "church." The argument that the public is the best judge of quality journalism directly contradicts the first reason given for why television news is the way it is—that the public won't sit still for quality journalism.

Television journalists' tolerance for this contradiction may seem surprising because at each station the public's news judgment was constantly ridiculed. Viewers were often referred to by derogatory names such as "Billy Bluecollar," "Joe Sixpack," or "your average wrestling fan," and characterized as having short attention spans and more curiosity about the personalities reading the news than the news itself. Clearly, journalists saw through the equation of news quality with popularity. But good reasons exist for ignoring this contradiction. To question the wisdom of the market would put reporters at odds with managers and managers at odds with owners. It would also shatter the illusion that comforted all three groups: that the newscast was a public service.

Television's Proper Role Is to Headline the News

Every television journalist interviewed said the ideal newscast should cover events in abbreviated form. Television's job is to "boil down" the information available and capture the main points of a story. Secondary details should be left to other media. Part of the logic underlying this theory holds that the local newscast is just one of a variety of sources the average citizen uses to keep informed. A veteran reporter at the largest station explained it this way:

> The news business is a cycle and each medium has its own [part]. Joe Sixpack gets up in the morning. . . . He picks up the morning newspaper. The newspaper is a re-hash of yesterday. He travels in his car and gets the headlines. The radio gives him the headlines of what's going on today. He gets to work and in the course of office conversations, talks about the stories that interest him. Then

that night he goes back home and hears more headlines [on the car radio]. He goes home and turns on the TV set because he wants to know more about that story. The TV gives him more than the radio because it's got pictures. Then he picks up the evening paper and gets a complete write-through. So each medium has its place in our daily life.

The reporter's description of a news consumption cycle accurately describes the habits of some—although it's difficult to imagine "Joe Sixpack" acting so diligently. But this theory contains a number of assumptions:

1. The average person receives news from a variety of sources—radio, TV, newspapers, other persons.
2. These news sources will cover essentially the same stories, yet either each will add a different piece of the full account to create an aggregate whole, or one source used by all (the newspaper, in the reporter's example) will report the story in depth.
3. The stories covered by the various media will contain the most important information of the day.
4. The stories will be accurate.

If all four of these assumptions are met, then television coverage of events that goes little beyond the headline does society no harm. In fact, by calling attention to newsworthy issues and events that may be pursued in depth elsewhere, such coverage provides a service. But a 1990 survey conducted by the Times Mirror Center for the People and the Press indicated that only about half—49% of a national sample—used more than one source of news on a daily basis. Only 43% said they read a newspaper the day before they were surveyed.[19] If radio and television content themselves with little more than headlines, only the shrinking proportion of society that uses the paper to fill in the details behind those headlines is likely to possess knowledge in depth. And here lies a corollary assumption—that newspapers are a depth medium. In fact, led by *USA Today,* many American newspapers are shrinking articles to better serve a market of consumers with little time for reading.[20] As newspaper readership continues to decline and as printed stories contract, so does the validity of the assumption that viewers will use the paper to fill in details of important stories television introduces.

With both print and broadcast news departments seeking to sell to the attention market, Assumptions 3 and 4 also face jeopardy. The data in Chapters 7 and 8 suggest that local stations may neither select the most important issues and events to headline, nor report them accurately. Similar logic applies to radio and newspapers following the market model of journalism. All news media might be expected to pursue those events with the highest payoff in audience that cost the least to discover and report. Television newscasts may headline only the day's most attention-grabbing and obvious events, and do so in a way that makes them more compelling than they are. And rather than contradict such a glitzy news agenda with a longer and more sober accounting of what's important—whether it's exciting or not—radio and newspapers may follow the newscasts' lead.

We Do the Best We Can
With the Station's Limited Resources

When I first heard this reason used as a justification for journalistic shortcuts or norm violations, I assumed that it meant: "We do the best *for the public, that is, the best journalism* we can with limited resources." But as my analysis of market logic proceeded, a second meaning arose: "We do the best *for investors, that is, the most profitable programming* we can with limited resources." First let's examine for whom these media firms do their best and then ask whether newsroom budgets stretch the station's resources to their limits.

If serving the public by maximizing citizens' understanding of their surroundings were the goal, then any news department—large or small, print or broadcast—ought to make compromises with journalistic norms only when a failure to do so would jeopardize the media firm's ability to turn a profit sufficient to cover the community in the future.[21] Further, such compromises ought to be undertaken with the logic of triage, that is, compromises with the greatest potential to thwart public empowerment should be made last. Finally, no practices that would obstruct the goal of reliably informing the public or that would misinform the public would be ethical. A news department that routinely misinforms would cease to be a "news" provider. For society's good, it would be better if such a firm closed its doors.

At the first, or discovery, stage of news production, the news department of a media firm with extremely limited resources would be expected to uncover news independently only on those beats most necessary to a citizen's understanding of the community, such as local and regional government. Because municipal and county councils hold most of the responsibility for local government decision making, they would be the most essential points of news generation for the community. This is not to argue that decisions made by state legislatures and the federal government do not profoundly affect local citizens. They do. But local news departments can collectively— and therefore less expensively—support information-gathering at higher levels of government through cooperative news organizations such as the Associated Press. And for local stations that air national network newscasts, what happens at the federal level need not be their primary concern.

At the second, or selection, stage of news production, the news department of a media firm with very limited resources following the norms of journalism would select only those events and issues that promised to be most consequential for the largest number of consumers. Merely interesting stories that might consume a local reporter's time would have to be forgone so that the essential informing mission could be served. At the third, or reporting, stage, if scarce resources force a choice between the informative and the entertaining aspects of a story, the first must take precedence. And rather than send reporters and photographers from story to story across the signal area, fewer, more in-depth stories might conserve resources. Obviously, all reports should follow the fundamental norm of objectivity, that is, they should be factual and impartial. Scarce resources cannot justify inaccurate stories with correctable biases. The danger of misleading the society is too great.

As we saw in the last three chapters, the data for local television give weak or no support to even a scaled-back model of journalistic practice. The only beats consistently worked by reporters at all three stations were courts and police. And the stories aired from those beats suggested that these two were staffed as economical access points to dramatic events, rather than as part of an attempt to systematically understand and report on how two arms of the community's justice system work. No one was assigned at any of the stations to uncovering news of local government. Instead, the stations relied on other news media for investigative reporting of government and on the press agents of local boards and councils to play the civic watchdog. Selection practice at all three stations favored stories high in entertaining values over those high in consequence. And, particularly at the larger stations where reporters had more resources—principally time—to gather information into stories, objectivity norms were violated routinely. Taken as a whole, the evidence supports a model in which the media firm attempted to maximize the return to investors on the resources it received.

The notion that local stations are operated to maximize profit rather than public understanding gains further support from an examination of earnings reported by the National Association of Broadcasters. As noted in Chapter 6, figures for 1985, the year before the study began, showed a median pretax profit on gross revenues of 15.8% per year for stations of KMID's size and type, 30% for large stations like KLRG, and 39% for stations as large as KVLG.[22] Compare these figures to the national manufacturing average of 9%.[23] By 1990, growth in broadcast television's advertising revenues had flattened or declined and the audience had fractionated with the spread of cable television and videocassette recorders. But even in these more difficult financial times, mid-sized stations like KMID earned median pretax profits of nearly 14%; large stations like KLRG made 29%, and very large stations earned more than 36%.[24] Even during a deep national recession, the least profitable type of station in the study was earning half again as much return as the national average.

Further, the percentages are based on large volumes of gross revenues. The typical network-affiliated station in the 10 largest metropolitan areas earned an annual median profit of more than $30 million.[25] In all but the smallest markets and the smallest stations in larger markets, stations could expand the resources devoted to news and still maintain a handsome profit. In fact, a 1992 survey conducted for the Radio-Television News Directors Association indicated that at about three quarters of all local stations responding, advertisements airing during the newscast alone earned more than the cost of the news. And at another 16% of stations, newscast ads broke even with news expenses.[26]

Conclusion

Local television journalists and editors present their work both to viewers and to themselves as a public service that serves the market. But their actions demonstrate daily the fundamental contradiction between serving the marketplace of viewers and serving the public. To protect themselves from confronting this contradiction—and placing themselves in opposition to superiors and ultimately investors—newsroom employees enlist a set of justifications for their performance.

They tell each other they would create better journalism if the public would pay attention; or if television weren't inherently better suited to entertaining than informing; or if television weren't so visually oriented that ideas and abstractions are technologically inappropriate; or if television could handle enough complexity for people to really learn from it; or if television generated enough money to support a serious news operation. Or they say television's role is only to pique people's interest so they can read about it or listen to it elsewhere. Or they say the public ought to choose what's news by its viewing decisions and journalists should simply follow the common taste. Although each of these reasons for mediocrity has some merit, neither individually nor collectively do they justify the practices observed. But they do succeed in masking the subordination of the public's interest to the short-term interest of investors.

Notes

1. Some caution should be exercised in interpreting national audience ratings for *The MacNeil/Lehrer News Hour*. Over the years, the Federal Communications Commission gave

UHF licenses to most public television stations. Because UHF signals don't cover as much territory as VHF (channels 2-13), programs carried on UHF channels may reach only about half of a market's households. News researcher Guido H. Stempel III, argues that in comparing the popularity of *MacNeil/Lehrer* to network newscasts, it would be wise to double the *MacNeil/Lehrer* numbers to compensate for the technological difference (personal communication, December 3, 1992).

2. Note that entertainment should still be portrayed as news to differentiate it from openly entertaining competing programs, and thus retain the viewer watching news from a sense of civic obligation.

3. The Commission on the Freedom of the Press, 1947, chap. 1.

4. Rosen, 1991, p. 269.

5. Rosen, 1991.

6. Herbert, 1992. I don't mean to imply by this comparison that politics is as popular as football. The presidential debates owe some of their enormous audience to their rarity (as does the Super Bowl). The point is that consumers can and do use their TVs for serious, as well as entertaining, programs.

7. Zhu, Milavsky, & Biswas, 1993.

8. Gunter, 1987, p. 69.

9. Gunter, 1987.

10. Gunter, 1987, p. 71.

11. Dhawan & Pellegrino, 1977; Gunter, 1987, p. 71.

12. Graber, 1990, p. 134.

13. Postman, 1985.

14. Robinson & Davis, 1990.

15. Robinson & Levy, 1986.

16. National Public Radio's *All Things Considered* and *Morning Edition* programs innovated the use of musical interludes between stories. In doing so, they broke a taboo against "dead air" devoid of narration. Why couldn't a television news program introduce similar musical dividers between stories, perhaps with the program logo or summary of key points in the previous story or in the newscast as visual background?

17. Rosen, 1991.

18. Levy, 1992, p. 70.

19. *The American Media: Who Reads, Who Watches, Who Listens, Who Cares?* (Times Mirror Center for the People and the Press, 1990). Each of the percentages quoted was from a question about media used "yesterday," rather than the more general question about media used "regularly." I chose the more conservative numbers because of research showing that people tend to exaggerate their news consumption when questions are asked generally.

20. Stepp, 1991.

21. McManus, 1992.

22. Stanley, 1986.

23. Udell, 1978.

24. Helregal, 1991.

25. Helregal, 1991.

26. Stone, 1993b, p. 8.

10

So What?
Market Journalism's Effect on Society

We Are What We Eat

My focus has been on how news is produced rather than what happens to those who consume it. The two are closely related, however. The public can't get out of the news what's not put into it. Nutritionists sometimes claim that "we are what we eat." To some degree there is an analogy in the relationship between the health of society and the "nutritional" value of the information it consumes. Even if you dismiss the idea of the news media as a "Fourth Estate" of government as a romantic ideal,[1] citizens nevertheless depend upon the media to enable them to meet their routine civic obligations—electing scores of local, state, and national officials, and deciding referenda and bond issues.[2] As sociologist Gaye Tuchman observed: "The news media set the frame in which citizens discuss public events and . . . the quality of the debate necessarily depends on the information available."[3]

It is difficult to assess the social impact of market journalism with precision. No one has determined what proportion of American news media has abandoned normative journalism for a market approach. For that half of American adults who rely on two or more sources of news, the weakness of one may be offset by the strength of another. This is most likely at the national and global levels of reporting where the competition is greater and more diverse, including sources such as public radio and television that are at least partly protected from market forces because of the way they are funded (although this distinction erodes as federal financing decreases). We cannot take much comfort, however, from the continuing availability of some normative journalism. The spread of market journalism from local television into network news and newspapers coupled with the decline of daily newspaper reading among young adults make empirical assessment of market journalism's impact on society urgent. This chapter reviews what society can expect from market journalism if current trends continue and some of the evidence for these expectations.

In Chapter 5, I defined normative journalism as information about current issues and events designed to provide the greatest increase in understanding for the largest number of citizens that the resources of the media firm permit. Such content serves the public good. By contrast, market journalism is information about current issues and events designed to serve the profitmaximizing interest of the firm, often—but not always—at the expense of the public's need to understand its environment. The market serves the public most in times of crisis—a flood, earthquake, tornado, or civil insurrection—when informative news is demanded by a broad cross-section of the market. On routine news days, however, market journalism is analogous to junk food. Just as a bag of salted french fries and a juicy burger are widely appealing but nutritionally barren or unhealthy, news filled with meaningless sound and fury may boost ratings, but starve society of useful information.

Four Social Impacts

Compared to normative journalism, market journalism is likely to have at least four social impacts, all of which reinforce each other. Researchers have begun to find evidence for the first effect. Evidence for the second is suggestive. The last two are more speculative and shall only be mentioned. The four are:

CONSUMERS ARE LIKELY
TO LEARN LESS FROM THE NEWS

This is because there is less of consequence presented and the presentation doesn't facilitate learning. As junk food pushes healthier fare out of our diet, junk journalism *displaces* at least some of what's important with what's merely interesting.

When news departments that derive most—or all—of their income from advertising seek to maximize audience, they must create content that attracts more than those who consume news primarily for information. I argued in Chapter 4 that such firms must operate not in the market for news, but in the larger public attention market. To attract such consumers, content must be entertaining; such as emotionally arousing, unusual, about celebrities, visually compelling, and so forth. In televised news with its limited time available for a newscast and the inability of consumers to select among the stories offered, entertaining content must displace at least some informative content when the same content cannot serve both functions—which, as we saw in Chapters 7 and 8, is much of the time.

In print the displacement is less severe. Space in a newspaper is less scarce than time in a broadcast day. Entertaining content can be added to the informative. In print the size of the "news hole," the space allocated to news, rises with advertising "lineage," the space allocated to ads. The volume of advertising rises with the circulation among potential customers.[4] To the extent a newspaper can attract such new readers by adding entertaining content to the informative, it can add such material without displacing information. However, if a newspaper wishes to maximize return to investors, some displacement can be expected. That's because, as we saw in Chapters 6, 7, and 8, it costs more to discover and report objectively on the significant events and issues than to produce merely interesting content. Some informative content such as that from public hearings, press conferences, and government meetings, however, is inexpensive to gather and may attract the interest of parts of the readership. Uninterested readers can skip to other articles they find more appealing without withdrawing their attention from the media firm's product. In contrast to television, localized information carries only the penalty of additional news-gathering cost.

If people are to learn from the news, not only must there be informative content, but it must be presented with sufficient context and in a logical order to permit consumers to make sense of it. In television, maximum learning may also require a slower pace and more repetition for complex subjects. But television news departments following the market model are likely to eschew the logical presentation, context, pacing, and repetition necessary to broad learning from newscasts because advertisers pay for the quality of the audience that is exposed to their commercials, not for the quality of the newscast and the resulting amount of learning that takes place. Making a newscast more informative may drive away the entertainment-oriented viewer. Again, the problem is less severe in print, where readers control pacing and repetition. However, contextual items such as the pros and cons of proposed civic actions, the history of issues and events, and explanation of the processes of government or business consume reporter time and lengthen newspaper stories to the point where they may disappoint and intimidate readers searching for short, entertaining articles.

In summary, news departments following the market model can be expected to displace some—in print—and much—in broadcast—of the informative with the entertaining at all three stages of news production. At the discovery phase, a daily effort might be made to uncover issues and events where there is a high probability of finding the dramatic, violent, or unusual—

such as the courts and the police. Less effort could be expected visiting locales such as the halls of local government where important but dull information originates. Such a passive approach is unlikely to uncover official wrongdoing. No effort may be made to discover improprieties on the part of powerful businesses and industries that advertise or are owned by another arm of the media firm's parent corporation. Displacement occurs most noticeably at the second stage of news production: Issues and events are likely to be selected for their audience appeal and availability more than for their consequence. Less obvious is displacement at the final stage, reporting. Even when important topics are selected, they may be covered in entertaining rather than substantial ways.

Evidence

Few studies explicitly compare market journalism content with normative journalism. However, a growing body of systematic and anecdotal evidence supports the conclusion that market journalism contains less informative content than would be expected from normative journalism and that the content presented is less intelligible.

In Television. Chapters 6, 7, and 8 documented both of these conclusions. The total volume of the local news hour devoted to local news after commercials, sports, and weathercasts had been deducted was just 17 minutes at the mid-sized station, a fraction over 21 minutes at the large station, and 30 minutes at the largest station. When you consider that only 38% of that news time was devoted to content judged high in consequence at the mid-sized station, only 53% at the large station, and 55% at the very large station, the volume of news available each day to help consumers understand their communities was very small. At all three stations, the proportion of news time rated above the midpoint on the entertainment scale substantially surpassed the percentage rated above the midpoint on consequence. Turning heads was more important than filling minds.

Chapter 8 provided evidence from reporting case studies that indicated little effort was expended to gather or present background, context, or explanatory material in either the video or narrative portions of news stories. Even within stories with consequential topics, the effort to build audience caused reporters to displace much of the information viewers needed to make sense of the story with emotional or other entertaining content. Although reporters could cite instances where information harmful to advertisers or the stations was ignored or censored, none of the stories analyzed dealt with these interested parties.

Other research, gathered from stations across the nation over the past decade and a half, demonstrate a similar lack of consequential news or context, or both. As market journalism has gathered force over time, the results of the research have grown more negative. Newer studies show more sensationalism than older ones.[5]

Most studies focused on the selection stage. Analyses of the topics of local television news were conducted by Joseph Dominick, Alan Wurtzel, and Guy Lometti in New York; William Adams in Pennsylvania; Jung Ryu in Cincinnati; Tim Wulfemeyer in San Diego; David Dozier and Richard Hoftstetter in San Diego and Houston; Ira Eisenberg in San Francisco; Phyllis Kaniss in Philadelphia; and Karen Slattery and Ernest Hakanen, replicating Adam's study in Pennsylvania.[6] The researchers generally found that from one third to more than half of the stories were reports of unlinked and unplanned events such as crimes, violence, and disaster, more likely to attract audience than explain the community to itself.

Eisenberg quoted an anchorman at San Francisco's most prestigious station: "Broadcast journalism is going down the tubes. We're not doing news anymore. We're doing scandal, celebrity gossip, and cutesy animal stories. It's become just a formula to build an entertainment audience."[7] Slattery and Hakanen's 1992 replication of Adam's Pennsylvania study is worth reporting in some detail because of its breadth—early and late evening newscasts at 10 stations located across the state were surveyed—and because it provides the most direct evidence that the displacement of consequential news by sensational content may be growing.

The authors used the same content categories as Adams did in 1976, at the same stations, at the same time of the year, with both years containing presidential elections. Both studies classified "government and politics" as "all stories dealing with public policy issues, elections, campaigns, and activities of governmental bodies and political organizations." "Sensational and human interest stories" were those covering "crime, violence, natural disasters, accidents and fires, along with amusing, heartwarming, shocking, or curious vignettes about people in the area."[8] Both focused only on local news.

Not only did Slattery and Hakanen find that at each station in the four metropolitan areas surveyed—Pittsburgh, Scranton-Wilkes Barre, Harrisburg, and Johnstown-Altoona—that the sensational/human interest category had grown and local government and political coverage had declined, but that the latter category was sometimes reported with "embedded sensationalism/human interest," rather than in an informational manner. In addition, "the shift in coverage from public affairs to sensationalism/human interest was especially pronounced for lead stories (those stories which begin during the first three minutes of a newscast)."[9]

For the early evening newscasts, governmental coverage dropped from 64% of news time in 1976 to 19% in 1992. Sensationalism/human interest using Adams' categories grew from 12% in 1976 to 41% in 1992. When sensationalism/human interest elements embedded in other categories of reporting were counted, sensational news content jumped to 48% of news time in 1992 for Pittsburgh stations, and 56% for stations in the three other cities.[10] Late evening newscasts showed similar results.

Other studies examined the context with which news was delivered. James Bernstein and Stephen Lacy recently reviewed past research about news of government. Both their own study, conducted in Michigan and Oregon, and earlier studies showed a lack of depth, particularly in stories originated by the station itself.[11] David Altheide, who conducted case studies of local television news production in San Diego, showed how the imposition of television news-gathering routines and particularly the abbreviation of reports decontextualizes events:

> In the process of presentation, the world of everyday life is transformed for news purposes. The effect is to take an event out of its familiar circumstances and surroundings and meanings, and then embed it in a foreign situation—a news report. Thus in order to make events news, news reporting decontextualizes and thereby changes them.[12]

In her study of Philadelphia television news, Kaniss observed a news presentation logic oriented toward maximizing audience by concatenating the most compelling video with the most emotional or unusual sound bites, rather than trying systematically to describe an event or issue. She wrote:

> While one television reporter claimed that leading with the best video was simply a technique "to get people hooked and interested" in order to present important information, the need for effective video may influence the angle of a story and alter the meaning of the news. As one reporter presented the problem: "You have to use the best video first and that often makes for a very convoluted story." Another local television journalist described the difference between a newspaper story and a television news story: "Instead of an inverted [pyramid] order in the newspaper, where the most important information comes first, television news stories have the formula of a mini-drama, with rising action, climax and denouement. Television stories stress action, not background facts."
>
> The need for good sound bites also influences the way local television covers the news. Often, the sound bite which makes it to the air is not the comment that best summarizes the speaker's position, but the one which captures the most emotional, dramatic, or controversial remarks. "Catchy" comments are often taken out of context, with the result that positions may be distorted and peripheral points may get more coverage than central arguments in a policy debates.[13]

Network television has also been found to displace the important with the merely interesting. For example, a study of coverage of the 1988 presidential campaign conducted at Harvard University's John F. Kennedy School of Government drew two conclusions specifically critical of TV reporting:

> The production demands of television, which place a premium on symbolic visual elements and powerful emotional moments, have come to dictate the daily activities of presidential candidates and to drive out the extended explanation of issue positions.
>
> Television, with its emphasis on the individual candidate and his or her skills in projecting a message, has contributed to the decline of political parties . . . and abetted the rise of a personality-based politics which tends to diminish discussion of issues.[14]

Given the content and presentation of television news, it should come as no surprise that research has repeatedly shown that viewers learn little from it. Mark Levy recently summarized research conducted primarily in the United States on learning from commercial newscasts as follows:

> Public opinion polls, laboratory experiments, and observations of people watching television in their homes reveal a remarkably consistent set of findings. TV news is not doing a very good job of informing the public.[15]

Although the responsibility for such poor performance might lie with the medium itself, with the audience's use of the medium, with the news department's use of the medium, or some combination of the three, researchers blame news departments the most. Three recent books—*The Main Source,* written by University of Maryland researchers Mark Robinson and Mark Levy; *News That Matters,* by University of Michigan researchers Shanto Iyengar and Donald Kinder; and *Poor Reception,* by British researcher Barrie Gunter—all reached or supported a similar conclusion: While there are differences between television and print as informational media, and there are differences in the way audiences use them, the news department contributes more to the failure of audiences to learn much from televised news than either the medium or the audience. Television journalists either lack the knowledge necessary to create newscasts that viewers can readily understand to make sense of their environments, or their firms choose not to create such programs.[16]

In Print. In print, the trend toward market journalism has also tended to reduce both the volume of consequential news and the amount of context stories include. In surveys of newspapers, Leo Bogart showed how larger portions of the news hole have been reserved for photographs, particularly on front pages where news stands the greatest chance of being read. On the remaining space he found more entertainment-oriented features and less information-oriented news.[17] In a 1991 survey of newspaper editors, Carl Stepp reported a movement away from government coverage toward lifestyle features:

> Perhaps nothing crystallizes the issue better than what is happening with government coverage. Traditionally newspapers have accepted the role of providing citizens with reliable, if unsexy, coverage of public affairs like zoning boards and subcommittee hearings. But many editors concede that the routine government story has been one clear casualty of the move toward reader-friendly journalism.[18]

Doug Underwood and Keith Stamm surveyed more than 400 journalists at 12 West Coast newspapers. Journalists indicated increasing reader and market orientation that manifested itself in loss of depth in stories and displacement of informative news with "softer," more featurized reporting. Underwood and Stamm's review of earlier research suggested similar trends nationwide.[19]

Even the nation's prestige press has been criticized for displacement. The Harvard campaign study mentioned above concluded:

> The press has generally adopted too much of an insider's approach to its campaign coverage. The insider's perspective is rooted in an overemphasis on the most obvious and enticing part of the campaign: the "horserace" drama of which candidate is ahead and who is likely to win. "Horserace" coverage leads to more stories about strategy than about substance.[20]

As television continues to increase in popularity as a news source, and newspapers change to adopt to the market journalism formula, the American public can be expected to become even less informed than it is now. And now, according to a 1988 study commissioned by the John and Mary Markle Foundation, is a time of "political apathy and striking political ignorance [on the part] of average Americans."[21]

CONSUMERS MAY BE MISLED

A diet heavy in junk food may do more than displace nutritional meals. The salt, fat, and cholesterol may damage health themselves. Likewise, when what builds audience or assists the interests of the media firm's investors or sponsors replaces what's important or unbiased, society suffers more than a shortage of useful information. It is misled. At best a partial picture of reality is substituted for the whole. At worst, what's presented is distorted in ways that can lead members of the public to grief. An example from an unlikely source, one of America's most respected journalists, illustrates the problem. National Public Radio commentator Daniel Schorr confessed the following to the 1990 graduating class of journalism students at the University of California at Berkeley:

> I found it easier to get on the [CBS] Evening News with a black militant threatening violence than with a moderate appealing for a Marshall Plan for the ghetto. So I spent a lot of time interviewing Stokely Carmichael and H. Rap Brown. In 1968, a few months before his assassination, the Rev. Martin Luther King told me that nonviolence in the civil rights community was in danger of losing out because networks, by giving such exposure to irresponsible militants, were electing them as the leaders of American blacks.[22]

The market impulse, which was powerful even during the 1960s when normative journalism was the stated goal of network news, created a subtle reward system that encouraged reporters to substitute the radical for the representative.[23] While the majority of African Americans may have supported King, people watching Schorr's reports were led to believe that the civil rights movement had shifted toward violent leaders. Such a misperception could have diminished white support for extending civil rights to people of color as well as disillusioning moderate African Americans.

In routine coverage, market journalism affects news production across all three of its stages producing two kinds of distortions, those of omission of newsworthy information and those of inclusion of the non-newsworthy.

Evidence

In Television. As we saw in Chapters 6 through 8, both types of distortions occurred at the stations studied. With the exception of the investigative unit at the largest station, stations spent little staff time to discover potentially newsworthy issues and events. They relied more on outsiders—individuals and institutions with their own agendas—to bring information to their attention. As a consequence, they presented a picture of the community missing much of what was occurring beneath the surface.

Chapter 8 indicated that 60% of the stories analyzed failed to meet minimal standards of journalistic objectivity. Surprisingly, at the two largest stations, where reporters had both more experience and more time to gather stories, the rate of violations rose to more than three of four stories. Although some violations were trivial, many substantially changed the nature of the story. U.S. involvement in the tragic civil wars of Nicaragua and El Salvador was censored, for example. One city government was accused of a drug problem as was a major federal agency's installation. The closing of an Air Force base was blamed on developers and county planners. Winery workers were portrayed as dissatisfied with their union. Schools were described as places of chaos during a teacher's strike. All of the objectivity violations served the self-interest of the station or its parent corporation, usually through exaggeration to build audience or reporting shortcuts. Approximately 12% also served the interests of other elite interests in society. None of the case studies of reporting involved sponsors. But other coverage observed at the mid-sized station demonstrated a marked commercial bias, labeling as news stories giving publicity to the county fair and to a network miniseries about to air in prime time on the station. And at both the mid-sized and large station, reporters cited instances of protecting advertisers from adverse coverage.

Kaniss's content analysis of Philadelphia television news and interviews with reporters revealed similar types of distortion resulting from the stations' decisions about news discovery, selection, and reporting. She found a passive system for uncovering newsworthy information that gave an advantage to those powerful enough to employ public relations officers: "The limited number of reporters and the lack of a beat structure makes local television news reporters particularly dependent on easily accessible sources for their story ideas."[24] The picture stations painted of local and state government was distorted by a selection bias for the sensational: " 'Sexy' versus 'snoozer' government stories receive more play."[25] At the reporting stage, she found that appealing story elements often displaced the significant ones: "When government and policy is covered, the need to adopt a 'sexy' or 'humanistic' angle may displace important information."[26]

Kaniss concluded her study this way:

> In summary, local television news tends to give relatively low priority and limited time to governmental news and to focus on the relatively sensational aspects of government stories when they are covered. Complicated budgetary stories are reduced to packages of a few minutes in length or, when lacking in effective video, to stories read by anchors in less than a minute. Television reporters are less interested in probing whether new proposals are sound than in capturing an emotional sound bite on camera or covering an activity-filled demonstration, no matter how small the numbers.[27]

At the network level, Robert Entman analyzed differences in coverage between scandals that are inexpensively discovered and reported and entertaining versus those expensive to track down, complex and difficult to report, and dull to watch. The first scandal was "Billygate," the revelation that President Jimmy Carter's colorful brother had been hired as a representative of Libya's interests. The second scandal never received enough attention to merit a "gate."

It was the indictment of President Ronald Reagan's Secretary of Labor Raymond Donovan on fraud conspiracy involving organized crime. Entman argues that the misadventures of Billy Carter, who appeared to have little or no influence over his brother, were far less important than the charges against Secretary Donovan. Yet ABC, CBS, and NBC gave "Billygate" far more coverage.[28] Providing the most popular news at the least cost misled the public from a focus on an important scandal to a preoccupation with an irrelevant one.

In Print. As print news departments move from normative to market journalism, cases of distortion appear to be increasing.

Edward Herman and Noam Chomsky analyzed the content of such publications as *The New York Times, Time,* and *Newsweek.* They contrasted, for example, coverage given to victims of then-Communist governments with that accorded victims of governments backed by the United States. They found jingoistic distortions both of omission and inclusion that benefited both news firms and other powerful persons and institutions in U.S. society at the expense of others both at home and abroad.

A number of case studies of distortions have been published. Researcher Jane Ciabattari examined how *Time* magazine failed to cover the news of its merger with Warner Communications immediately after it occurred, despite the fact that the agreement made the new company the world's largest entertainment and communication company. When *Time* did write about the merger, it did so from a point of view biased toward the new mega-corporation rather than in the more critical fashion of normative journalism.[29]

Columbia Journalism Review published an internal management memo to the staff of the *Contra Costa Times,* one of a chain of Lesher Communication newspapers in the San Francisco Bay area. The memo ordered that a Gay Freedom Day parade never again be covered on the front page because past coverage generated complaints from readers and top managers. The memo acknowledged that the parade had attracted between 140,000 and 230,000 persons but explained: "There are some topics that warrant extreme care; they include, but are not limited to: family life, children, animals, homosexuals, religion, AIDS, abortion, sexual bias, etc. Readers have opinions on these topics and others, and they are angry and vocal when their beliefs are damaged." The memo then required that stories "about gays and their activities" must gain special advanced approval from top management if planned for the front page.[30] Market journalism seeks to please more than inform its audience.

Across the nation a spate of instances where newspapers omitted reporting critical of powerful advertisers and ran positive content, some of which was composed by the advertisers themselves, has recently been reported.[31] Researcher Elizabeth Lesly found that many newspapers had acceded to

pressure from realtors to adopt a favorable attitude toward house buying and
the use of real estate agents. She quoted the real estate editor of Knight-
Ridder's *Boca Raton News:* "I prefer to tell the good story, the happy story.
I don't go looking for termites—that's not my role. I've never run out of
good stories to write." The editor defended the paper's positive orientation:
"We're a business. [And] as newspapers change, there is a much closer
interaction between ads and news than [there] used to be."[32]

Researcher Steve Singer reported on a national trend toward favorable
coverage for automobile advertisers. In some cases newspapers even turned
over automotive "news" sections to their advertising departments. Singer
quoted Frank Daniels III, executive editor of the once-proud *News and
Observer* in Raleigh, NC:

> [The auto section is designed] to create a marketplace for advertisers. It doesn't
> make sense to do it [write critical articles] to piss off advertisers. . . . At this
> stage, there isn't a single bit of advertising that isn't important. As a group, auto
> dealers are our third-largest advertisers.

When asked where consumers might get objective information about
cars, Daniels responded: "There are other places to get information, like
Consumer Reports. I would never look to newspapers to decide what
model to buy."[33]

Stanley Cohen examined how slow even the elite newspapers were to
report on the Savings and Loan scandal. He quoted respected *Washington
Post* economic columnist Hobart Rowen: "The media more or less instinc-
tively reach for stories of sex, politics and intrigue ahead of the more
pedestrian financial issues. That's the way it is." Cohen concluded that the
omission of such important economic stories was "because editors and
reporters had been emasculated by marketing strategies that assume that no
one will read anything more substantive than the saga of a sex orgy involving
a member of the political establishment."[34]

The effort to tailor news to economically desirable consumers has gone
further in print, but has also begun in broadcast journalism, according to
former journalist Ben Bagdikian:

> Executive editors throughout the country are being trained not to select news of
> interest to their community as a whole, but only for those people who live in selected
> neighborhoods that have certain characteristics wanted by major advertisers.
>   The practice of selecting news in order to make advertising more effective
> is becoming so common that it has achieved the status of scientific precision.
> . . . The result is the rapidly growing exclusion in standard American newspa-
> pers and broadcast operations of the activities and interests of the less affluent
> and the older people who live in the circulation area.[35]

In four editions of his book, *The Media Monopoly,* Bagdikian has documented scores of incidents in which newspapers and magazines served their investors, advertisers, and the market, but deceived the public.[36] Martin A. Lee and Norman Solomon called attention to numerous other cases of journalism's move toward market standards in *Unreliable Sources: A Guide to Detecting Bias in News Media.*[37] And every other month, *Columbia Journalism Review's* Darts and Laurels section adds new cases of distorted reportage.

NEWS SOURCES MAY BECOME MORE MANIPULATIVE

Normative journalism actively seeks consequential information from all sides of issues and seeks to establish the validity of what sources claim. But market journalism seeks the least expensive content that generates the largest audience. Market journalism rewards sources who "feed" the media saleable content and penalizes those without "spin masters" to promote them, as well as sources who would be honest and those who might try to explain complexity. Roger Ailes, Ronald Reagan's highly effective media advisor, said:

> There are three things that the media are interested in: pictures, mistakes and attacks. That's one sure way of getting coverage. You try to avoid as many mistakes as you can. You try to give them as many pictures as you can. And if you need coverage, you attack, and you will get coverage. It's my "orchestra pit" theory of politics. If you have two guys on a stage and one guy says, "I have a solution to the Middle East problem," and the other guy falls in the orchestra pit, who do you think is going to be on the evening news?[38]

Michael Deaver, who orchestrated the Reagan campaign and White House, elaborated on this type of manipulation in a conversation with Bill Moyers:

> We absolutely thought of ourselves when we got into the national campaign as producers. We tried to create the most entertaining, visually attractive scene to fill that box, so that the cameras from the networks would have to use it.[39]

But pictures were not the whole of it. Almost every aspect of a "photo opportunity" was manufactured with the twin purposes of selling to the media and selling the candidate. The Harvard study of the 1988 campaign noted:

> These "manufactured news" pieces work because they also are ideally suited to the needs of the television news producer, who is the critical target of the campaign's daily strategy. These theatrical set-ups are easy to cover and easy to get back to the home station or network by deadline time. For both television and print journalists . . . there are more incentives to use these fresh, sure-fire

"hot button" images and quotes than to dig up independent, meaningful stories that take more time.[40]

The emphasis on attention-getting content also sabotages the presentation of complexity. Candidates who wish to explain issues in depth appropriate to their difficulty may be denied the time in media that value short lively quotes, or "sound bites," averaging 10 seconds.[41] In a world of such extreme brevity, candidates are encouraged to dodge issues and substitute slogans for solutions. As Robert Entman observed: "Elites who want to succeed politically cannot afford to debate complicated truths."[42]

Market journalism creates an exchange in which candidates win favorable exposure in return for entertaining "news" that serves media firms' bottom lines. The deal advances unscrupulous politicians and boosts the income of owners of news firms, but it penalizes political figures who can't afford sophisticated promotion or are unwilling to compromise their ethics. More importantly, the public becomes an un- and misinformed loser.

THE AUDIENCE BECOMES
MORE APATHETIC ABOUT POLITICS

Despite rising levels of education, the percentage of Americans eligible to vote who exercise their franchise knowledgeably appears to be declining. Entman noted, for example, that 45% of the public was unable to name any congressional candidate in their district in 1956; in 1984, 68% failed. "If there are any trends in the data," he concluded, "they are not toward more knowledge or voting."[43] Although there may be many reasons for this decline, such as the disintegration of political party infrastructure, it seems plausible to think the news media also bear considerable blame. Several arguments have been advanced. One holds that the public feels alienated from a politics that appears to be played by insiders in the media, government, and industry. The Harvard study of press coverage of the 1988 presidential election makes this case:

> Public frustration builds when what appears on television to be personal political communication turns out to be empty staged events and "insider" news about the process behind the scenes, rather than news about matters connected to peoples' lives. People say they feel manipulated equally by the candidates and the press, and they don't know whom to believe.[44]

The Markle Commission reached a similar conclusion:

> American voters today do not seem to understand their rightful place in the operation of American democracy. They act as if they believe that presidential

elections belong to somebody else, most notably, presidential candidates and their handlers.[45]

My personal view is that while some citizens are put off by the process of politics and media coverage, more of the public blithely follows both the path of least effort and the lead of market journalists in paying attention primarily to the entertaining aspects of news. Many people have accepted an uncontested and increasingly uniform commercial definition of what's news. Such citizens don't take seriously the burden of informed democratic participation in large measure because the news portrays politics as irrelevant to their lives. Consequently, these citizens are blindsided by the results of political processes they don't understand. They become victims. Their informational powerlessness builds apathy. And that makes them both less eager and less able to comprehend serious reporting.

Conclusion

We can now answer the questions raised in Chapter 1 about market journalism and more specifically local television news. First, the effort undertaken to satisfy the audience, whether in broadcast or print, is not democracy of the one-person-one-vote variety. Market journalism values the attention of the wealthy and young over the poor and old because news selection must satisfy advertisers' preferences. In fact, rational market journalism must serve the market for investors, advertisers, and powerful sources before—and often at the expense of—the public market for readers and viewers. To think of it as truly reader- or viewer-driven is naive. Second, market journalism may indeed help integrate factions of society because of its popularity; it provides a common focus. But, as we have seen, it is often an integration of informational poverty. Finally, the stations in this and other studies did not add entertainment to information creating "info-tainment" so much as they displaced and often distorted information in favor of whatever they believed would attract attention at the least production cost. Most of the time, market journalism is an oxymoron, a contradiction in terms.

Notes

1. See, for example, Gitlin, 1980, or Schudson, 1983.
2. Verba & Nie, 1972.
3. Tuchman, 1978, p. ix.
4. Udell, 1978.
5. Slattery & Hakanen, in press.

6. Adams, 1978; Dominick, Wurtzel, & Lometti, 1975; Dozier & Hofstetter, 1985; Eisenberg, 1990; Kaniss, 1991; Ryu, 1982; Slattery & Hakanen, in press; Wulfemeyer, 1982.

7. Eisenberg, 1990, p. 93.

8. Slattery & Hakanen, p. 19.

9. Slattery & Hakanen, p. 13.

10. For parsimony I have rounded all statistical estimates to the nearest whole number. All contrasts between the 1976 and 1992 surveys were statistically significant at the .01 level, according to the authors.

11. Bernstein & Lacy, 1992.

12. Altheide, 1976, pp. 24-25.

13. Kaniss, 1991, p. 108.

14. Hume, 1991.

15. Levy, 1992, p. 69.

16. Gunter, 1987; Iyengar & Kinder, 1987; Robinson & Levy, 1986.

17. Bogart, 1982, 1992.

18. Stepp, 1991, p. 24.

19. Underwood & Stamm, 1992.

20. Hume, 1991, p. 8.

21. Hume, 1991, p. 53, quoting from Buchanan, 1991, p. 58.

22. Schorr, 1990.

23. Epstein, 1973.

24. Kaniss, 1991, p. 106.

25. Kaniss, 1991, p. 122.

26. Kaniss, 1991, p. 120.

27. Kaniss, 1991, p. 130.

28. Entman, 1989, ch. 3.

29. Ciabattari, 1989.

30. Document, 1989.

31. Collins, 1992.

32. Lesly, 1991, p. 22.

33. Singer, 1991.

34. Cohen, 1989.

35. Bagdikian, 1990, p. 232.

36. Bagdikian, 1990.

37. Lee & Solomon, 1991.

38. Runkel, 1989, quoted in Hume, 1991, p. 77.

39. Moyers, 1989.

40. Hume, 1991, p. 44.

41. Hallin, 1992; also see Adatto, 1990.

42. Entman, 1989, p. 20.

43. Entman, 1989, pp. 25-26. Caution should be exercised before calling two data points a trend, however. Entman's conclusion should be considered only suggestive.

44. Hume, 1991, p. 36.

45. Markle Commission on the Media and the Electorate, 1990, p. 8, quoted in Hume, 1991, p. 37.

11

Where Do We Go From Here?

How Did We Get Here?

Problem-solving goes best when the nature of the problem is well understood. Seeing market journalism as something entirely new misunderstands it. The trend toward letting the market decide what's news stems from the intersection of a rapidly accelerating trend that began perhaps six centuries ago with the decline of feudalism, and an inherent dilemma of news production that is as ancient as the serpent's news to Eve about fruit from the Tree of the Knowledge of Good and Evil.

The historical trend is commodification—the creation of a monetary price and market for virtually every aspect of human experience. Profits have long been earned on provision of food, shelter, and a variety of material goods. But during the last five decades public services previously funded by taxpayers or nonprofit institutions such as recreation, sport, art, hospital care, even education have been set to the task of earning profits.[1]

The eternal dilemma of news is the tension between representing reality as accurately as humans can, and misrepresenting it in favor of those who control the production process—be they tribal chieftains, popes, kings, war lords, government officials, or corporations. The dilemma is the same for individuals. We have to choose daily between straightforward and manipulated renditions of *our own* experience—our personal news—that we tell superiors, colleagues, those we supervise, and our family and friends. Do we selectively tell the truth, embellishing here and there, or do we disclose the whole story regardless of the cost to our ambitions?

Whether interpersonal or mass mediated, news is a powerful instrument of social control. This is because news defines the reality upon which people act. Struggle over control of news is inevitable. In this chapter I'll examine five general approaches to managing this struggle so it benefits the public.

Antecedents of Market Journalism

For most of human history, news has been shaped by the leaders or rulers of the territory in which it circulated. Production of news did not begin to move into the hands of business until about the time of Gutenberg in the 15th century. Within 200 years, the German inventor's presses were widespread in Europe. But most were still firmly under control of kings, lords, and parliaments.[2] In 18th century Europe and North America, however, the printing press, with its power to vastly reduce the cost of spreading knowledge, became an instrument through which business and other interests wrested control of news from rulers. The American Revolution, which resulted in a separation of government from news, was perhaps the signal event of this struggle.

Freed from official control, however, American newspapers were not free to tell the news as truthfully as possible. The political parties that supplied much of the funds for early American news enterprises shaped the news as powerfully as any government officials. But their control over the press was fractionated among contesting parties. The more educated members of the public could evaluate the differing accounts to make sense of current events.[3] The partisan press, however, constituted only a brief interlude in the underlying movement of news toward business control.

The commodification of news began in earnest in the United States during the first third of the 19th century when rising literacy and the invention of the steam engine made possible the mass or "penny" press. Then, as now, serving the market was not the same as serving the public. News historian Frank Luther Mott wrote: "Bad taste, coarseness which sometimes became indecency, overemphasis on crime and sex, and disreputable advertising were outstanding sins of these papers."[4] Such "lowest common denominator" fare served the American mass market of the middle and late 19th century well. The new nation swelled with immigrants. And education, though nearly universal for children, rarely continued past adolescence. But not infrequently, the press served the public as well, with investigations of government fraud and business trusts.

Although news had been liberated from government and party control, news was rarely free of the self-interest of the businesses that produced it. Sensationalism, publicity stunts, and the outright fabrication of news crafted to build circulation blighted the commodity press, culminating around the turn of the 20th century with the "yellow press" circulation wars between William Randolph Hearst and Joseph Pulitzer. The excesses of those years helped plunge the nation into war with Spain and fostered an imperial role for the United States,[5] whose legacy still plagues much of Central America and the Philippines.

Partly in reaction to yellow journalism, the first codes of news ethics were established in the 1920s and slowly spread through the industry.[6] The proliferation of such codes, however, did not necessarily alter journalistic practice. In 1947, The Commission on Freedom of the Press, chaired by University of Chicago Chancellor Robert M. Hutchins, concluded: "The press is . . . caught between its desire to please and extend its audience and its desire to give a picture of events and people as they really are."[7]

After World War II flattened nearly all of the world's industrial capacity except America's, the United States entered a period of enormous economic expansion. The news media rode the crest of the boom. The news industry sprouted an entirely new wing—television journalism. Although the number of daily newspapers declined, their volume and quality increased.[8] So did their profits and payrolls.[9] Television news added tens of thousands of additional jobs and made celebrities of network journalists. College enrollments in journalism programs boomed and a new field of study, communication, was founded in American universities. Once a trade peopled by reporters and editors with high school educations, journalism reached toward professionalism. Even the smallest papers and stations began to demand a college education of would-be reporters.[10] Journalism had entered a golden age.

But underneath the improvements in journalistic products, the structure of the industry was changing. Two related trends were under way: concentration of independent media firms into fewer and much larger corporations that often owned non-news businesses as well; and the movement from family to public ownership of media properties.[11] The first trend placed greater control over the public's perception of reality in fewer hands. The second trend caused news firms to compete for investors' dollars with other types of ventures. Both trends caused news to be treated as any other business, rather than as a special enterprise with public responsibilities commensurate with First Amendment privilege.

Since entrepreneurs such as Benjamin Day founded the Penny Press in the 1830s, ownership of newspapers and later broadcast companies lay in the hands of families. Because each family had only limited numbers of members and news firms generate a large volume of money, news firms earning profits equaling as little as 5% of their gross income from advertisements and subscriptions made their owners wealthy. While enough to enrich a few family members, such profits, if splintered into thousands of shares, would not be great enough to attract many investors. News firms hoping to sell stock on Wall Street had to boost profitability enough to meet or beat offerings from other companies.

Smart businesspeople such as Al Neuharth saw fortunes to be made in converting inefficient family-owned newspapers into modern businesses. Neuharth's Gannett Corporation began to buy newspapers that had no competitors. Taking advantage of these monopolies, Gannett was able to boost advertising rates to the most the market would bear. New production technologies and a huge crop of recruits from journalism schools whose idealism made them willing to work for low salaries cut labor costs. Business school-trained managers introduced modern management techniques into newsrooms. As a result, Gannett generated profits that became the envy of Wall Street.[12] Other media corporations followed suit. The sheer profitability of news firms accelerated their acquisitions by larger corporations.[13] The news had become golden to investors as well.

But sooner or later every boom goes bust. Asia, led by Japan, and Europe, led by Germany, rebuilt their industries, eroding U.S. dominance. Technological advances created a global economy in which U.S. firms moved manufacturing jobs abroad, taking advantage of lower wages and fewer environmental restrictions in developing nations. Domestic economic growth slowed.

As the economy soured, so did the advertising spending that has increasingly become the lifeblood of news corporations.[14] Meanwhile, the rapid increase in the value of media properties since the 1950s led to an expansion of supply, principally in UHF and cable television systems offering consumers scores of new channels. By the mid-1980s, the television audience had fractionated enough that the three principal networks lost a third of their viewers.[15] With increasing competition and the end of the economic boom, the greater market orientation of the news industry began to make itself felt in both print and broadcast newsrooms. Because profitability, not public service, is the primary investment standard, publicly traded corporations faced pressures to produce competitive profits regardless of the effect on news quality.

The underlying dilemma of the commercial news media—the tension between serving the public and serving the interests of owners—again became evident. This time, however, many news firms have corporate cousins to protect from public scrutiny. And the rhetoric of journalistic responsibility has been replaced with the rhetoric of accountability to markets among advertisers, audiences, and stockholders.

Five Possible Solutions

Critics of the press have offered a variety of solutions to the problem of media profit-making at public expense. Two of those solutions—the most widely advocated ones—ignore the concept of markets. Indeed, they discount the economic structure of the news business entirely. The third invites government to regulate the market. The fourth foresees a technological rescue. The fifth attempts to use the market itself as a lever for higher quality.

EDUCATING JOURNALISTS
TO BECOME PROFESSIONALS

The most widely employed strategy for combating the commercialization of news—and a variety of other journalistic ills—is to instill in students a greater sense of professionalism. Ethical standards are inculcated by journalism educators, by professional groups such as the Radio and Television News Directors Association and the Society of Professional Journalists, and by mid-career educational experiences such as the Knight and Nieman fellowships. All of these are important actions to improve the quality of journalism. But by themselves, they are likely to prove ineffective for reasons first mentioned in Chapter 2.

Journalists, as the courts often have ruled, are not independent professionals, but employees.[16] Journalists are not as free to follow professional norms as are doctors, lawyers, architects, and others. Journalists are not paid by those who consume their services. Neither are they licensed nor disciplined by peers. And news departments, unlike hospitals, universities, and elementary schools, need not meet professional standards for accreditation. While professionals serve clients—acting on *their own* interpretation of the client's best interest—employees serve the market—accepting the *customer's* interpretation of what's best. The key customer, in this case the advertiser, is always right.

A reporter or editor in a profit-maximizing media firm who subordinates market standards to those of journalism may be tolerated about as long as a counter clerk at McDonald's who refuses to sell fried food. There is simply no evidence professionalism can restrain corporate demands for profit. Bagdikian recently pointed out that American news media have never had better educated or more professional journalists than they have today, yet bottom-line oriented executives are increasingly moving their organizations away from quality journalism.[17]

APPEALS TO THE SOCIAL CONSCIENCE
OF MEDIA OWNERS AND MANAGERS

Much of mainstream media criticism published in academic journals and trade magazines has argued that the news business has a duty to serve society implied by the First Amendment to the Constitution in print, and directly stated by the Federal Communications Act of 1934 in broadcast. Often these critics have tried to demonstrate that news media could improve their products without sacrificing profits, or at least without undue sacrifice. The Hutchins Commission took this approach in 1947. The Commission argued that while playing to mass tastes may maximize profit, quality journalism has always sold well.[18] Then, as now, there is no evidence that good journalism is unprofitable. Indeed, newspaper chains with a reputation for quality, such as Knight-Ridder, remain highly profitable. Low quality journalism may be even more profitable, but responsible journalism hardly threatens a firm with bankruptcy. The industry enjoys a choice.

Asking any business to accept average profits when extraordinary returns are possible, however, conflicts with a central tenet of capitalist faith: that the common good is most reliably secured by harnessing self-interest rather than altruism. Almost five decades ago, the news industry met the Hutchins Commission's report with hostility.[19] More recently, broadcasters uniformly opposed FCC regulations seeking to impose civic responsibilities.[20] And neither the Commission nor the government, nor critics who have followed have succeeded in heading off the trend toward market journalism. Media owners, more and more of whom have no background in journalism, cannot be expected to accept arguments that market theory breaks down for commodities such as news.[21]

A second reason why appeals to conscience cannot be expected to effect change derives from the trend toward stockholder ownership of news corporations. Even news corporations that esteem journalistic standards face pressures to conform to profit-maximization. Because most stockholders have little knowledge of or interest in journalistic performance, their loyalty is bought not with public service, but with maximum return on investment at an acceptable level of risk. Firms that practice normative journalism also may hazard hostile takeover by outside investors because they are not earning the maximum short-term profits.[22] Although such takeovers have declined with investor confidence in the high-risk "junk" bonds used to finance them, some threat remains. If outside investors are able to buy even a significant minority of shares, they may be in position to force out managers following a longer-term profit strategy that resulted in quality journalism.

Recently, the desire to please stockholders caused even Knight-Ridder, the nation's second largest newspaper company, to tarnish its reputation for quality when it redesigned the *Boca Raton News* in Florida to please the market. The newspaper's editor told a *Washington Post* reporter: "If readers said they wanted more comics and less foreign news, in a market driven economy, I'm going to give them more comics and less foreign news."[23] In fairness, however, Knight-Ridder is also experimenting with a strategy of educating the market by stimulating a sense of community. The hope is that people who feel a stake in their communities will read newspapers.[24] More about that later.

INCREASED GOVERNMENT REGULATION OR FUNDING

No other American business has such great public responsibility and so little accountability as news. For example, if the computer industry turns out junk, society may be inconvenienced, but our basic freedoms won't be jeopardized. The same is true of most other businesses. Without reliable information, however, self-government becomes impossible. Further, the importance of the news media to an informed citizenry is growing as the influence of political parties wanes.[25]

Despite the magnitude of their role, news media experience few of the checks and balances placed on less vital industries. In most industries, the U.S. government has, at least in theory, subordinated private to public good. That is, government at various levels has reserved the right to constrain firms from profitable activities that legislators decide harm the public. The exercise of that right may be spotty and inconsistent. But there are examples of intervention, such as the breakup of the American Telephone and Telegraph Company in the interest of promoting competition.[26]

Government also oversees the quality of many industrial products. Meat, fish, and vegetables as well as all construction projects must be inspected. Automobiles have to meet standards for economy, safety, and emissions. Gasoline pumps and grocery scales are inspected for accuracy. Alone among industries, the products of the news business—particularly printed news—enjoy protection from most government regulation by virtue of the First Amendment. Although broadcasters are licensed by the government and required by law to act in the public interest, the Federal Communications Commission has rarely protected the public from shoddy reporting.[27]

A few critics have argued that greater regulation might improve broadcasting. Robert Entman, for example, makes the point that the Fairness Doctrine—which required airing local issues and giving equal time to all sides—pressured stations into more public affairs reporting than now occurs in its absence.[28] Changes in government tax policy also offer promise. Incentives for holding stock for a period of 5 to 10 years might expand the profit horizon of managers, making it easier for high quality news departments to survive.

There are also blue-sky alternatives. I would like to propose a tax credit for informed voting. Citizens could opt to take a brief quiz during their visit to the polls. If their knowledge of the candidates and issues was proficient, they could qualify for a $50 tax credit. Tax laws subsidize other behaviors thought beneficial to the nation such as owning a home, and they penalize "sins" such as tobacco and alcohol consumption. Why not reward informed voting? And if some of the half of eligible Americans who routinely don't vote turn up at the polls, so much the better.

More news scholars have advocated government funding of news media—either publicly or privately owned—than the kind of regulation until recently imposed by the Federal Communications Commission. Government money, with few strings attached, these critics argue, would eliminate or reduce market pressures to promulgate only popular news content. The quality and independence of such shows as the Corporation for Public Broadcasting's *The MacNeil/Lehrer News Hour* and National Public Radio's *All Things Considered* and *Morning Edition* are offered as examples of noncommercial news programs. Were funding expanded for these newscasts, some have argued, they could afford better coverage and higher production values that might attract larger audiences. Government subsidies for commercial news media such as exist in some Western European nations have also been proposed.

The downside of all strategies for increased government presence in news production is the difficulty of insulating editorial judgment from the influence of those who make funding decisions. There is, however, some evidence that some European nations have been able to subsidize news media without compromising their integrity.[29]

NEW TECHNOLOGIES

Led by advances in computers and new transmission technologies such as fiber optics and satellites, technology is changing the news environment in significant ways:

1. Previously Distinct Technologies Such as Printing and Broadcasting Are Merging. Most newspaper text and graphics now go through a digital electronic form—and are sometimes sent over airwaves to remote printing facilities—before publication. New display technologies are making it easier to read text on screens, and screens more portable and convenient.

2. From Media Scarcity to Abundance. The change is most apparent in the multiplication of television channels available with modern cable systems. But broadcast stations have also proliferated and the first national newspapers have appeared. Computerized data compression techniques suggest that the telephone line could soon become a major source of news.

3. From Content Geared for Mass Audiences to Content Tailored for Groups or Individuals. The abundance of media has made it feasible to "narrowcast"—serve niches in the audience. Sports addicts can watch ESPN. Those interested in government can watch C-SPAN. In print, computerized typesetting and production facilities have lowered the cost of zoning for particular circulation regions.

4. From One-Way to Interactive Media. Cable systems are acquiring the capability for two-way communication. And telephone utilities are exploring the installation of high-capacity fiber optic lines to households. These developments make possible an "information utility" through which consumers could "talk back" to news departments, giving opinions and ordering news from many sources.

What do these changes portend for news? Ithiel de sola Pool has argued that the number and variety of communication channels will, by themselves, diminish the tendency toward "lowest common denominator" programming.[30] Were news departments to adopt "niche" strategies of competition, one might expect an effort to corner the upscale market advertisers covet with a high-quality news product. Proponents of this view point to *The New York Times,* the *Los Angeles Times,* and other major newspapers as exemplars of how high profits can coexist with high journalistic quality. This may indeed be an option in very large markets where the number of persons able and willing to discriminate between high- and low-quality journalism is large enough to support the cost of excellence and an exceptional bottom line. The smaller the market and the more the media firm depends upon advertising, however, the less likely a quality niche strategy is to yield extraordinary returns.

Anthony Smith foretells an "electronic Alexandria"—virtually unlimited knowledge available from the world's news media and libraries through a network connecting to a home computer.[31] Once in place, such a network of high-capacity coaxial or fiber optic cable would enable transmission of text, photos, graphic information, and video at a fraction of the cost of imprinting and distributing physical products like paper or magnetic tape.

Such a network could become the foundation of an information utility with two-way capacity. Those wishing to produce their own television programming could feed it directly into the network. With no need to spend tens of millions of dollars on distribution through broadcast facilities or presses and delivery trucks, those who wish to produce news may no longer have to join the staff of a station or a newspaper. Freelance reporters who tap into the existing network to offer specialized and general information might escape organizational profit demands. News might be sold on a pay-per-story basis from reporters or experts working for themselves. Freed from the costs of paper, presses, and distribution—which constitute more than half the expenditures of most newspapers—print news departments might reinvent themselves as electronic news services.

If households are connected to interactive networks, residents could select only what they wanted, thus excluding many commercials. Moving from an advertiser-supported to a subscriber-supported system changes the news transaction. Currently, because news departments are rewarded equally for marginally interested consumers and news aficionados, it's efficient to mix large amounts of entertainment into the news to maximize audience. But if consumers must bear the full cost of news directly, rather than enjoy an advertising subsidy, many marginal consumers may opt out. Those who remain are likely to want news of higher journalistic quality. If they are willing to pay for it, journalism could be reinvigorated.

Much of the literature of new technologies for producing and delivering news is giddy with enthusiasm. The drawbacks have been little explored. Some difficulties, however, can be readily anticipated. News will still be a commodity even if price joins taste in determining what is watched. As choice in programming expands, consumers who might have watched or read news for lack of an alternative may abandon the news altogether. And if news departments in stations and newspapers are replaced by individual journalists and groups of reporters, consumers will experience even more difficulty evaluating which sources are trustworthy.

RESHAPING PUBLIC DEMAND

By educating consumers and stimulating civic participation, it may be possible to use the market to improve the quality of its offerings. The virtue a market-based news system enjoys over one controlled by government or by a few media barons, after all, is that it must respond to consumer demand. If producing quality journalism were to attract the largest audience, news departments should compete to produce such news, unless the cost of greater quality exceeds the added revenue from the larger audience. An approach that educates consumers and stimulates their appetite for quality news also avoids government control and empowers citizens to reclaim the means of exercising self-government.

Consumer Education

Public perceptions especially of the credibility of news media may offer a lever for change. Many news departments believe their reputation for accuracy is crucial to their success not only as a news provider but also as an advertising carrier.[32] If enough consumers stop believing a firm's news, they might abandon it, provided a more credible local alternative exists. The loss of such savvy consumers would reduce audience size and probably diminish the desirability of the remaining audience's demographics. Further, if many believed a firm's news to be substantially inaccurate, its advertisers would also lose the factual environment that by association adds to the credibility of advertisements placed in reputable news media. Any erosion of the news department's market share among consumers and advertisers would quickly draw the attention of profit-conscious managers.

Although consumer education may provide the safest and most powerful force for improving news, it's also the most difficult to mobilize. Even highly educated members of the public have come to enjoy entertaining news. And, as we saw in Chapter 5, discerning the quality of news is not like squeezing avocados or kicking tires. Further, those in the best position to critique the accuracy of other qualities of news—journalism organizations like Sigma Delta Chi and the Newspaper Guild, and journalism-school faculty researchers—often find themselves depending on the industry for jobs or funding. On the other hand, journalists—defined as those who wish to investigate and explain a community to itself—have little future in a market-driven news industry. And preparing students for such a future would represent a questionable allocation of university resources.

Despite the intimidating magnitude of a task like reeducating public taste, there are examples of dramatic shifts in consumption of and attitudes toward popular products in the wake of education campaigns. The percentage of Americans who smoke, for example, has declined substantially since the 1960s. The antismoking messages were helped by federally mandated warnings and advertising bans in broadcast media. But less organized and privately funded alterations of the information diet of Americans have also produced substantial opinion and behavior changes. Over the past three decades Americans have become more diet- and exercise-conscious, and polls show much greater environmental concern than previously.

Any effort to educate the American taste in news would have to be broad-based and prolonged. The schools, elementary through university, would provide a natural launching pad for such an effort. In fact, some school districts are already teaching children how to analyze advertising in order to protect themselves. Many universities now offer courses that take a critical view of the media, particularly the news media.

Although it might jeopardize some industry funding, communication and journalism department faculty could localize research, examining the quality of hometown and state news. Such research could help the public discriminate between nutritious and junk journalism. Public radio and television broadcasters and cable companies with under-used channels may be natural distributors of such research were it presented vividly. Journalism professional organizations and enlightened managers in both broadcast and print also might publish such reports. Quality news departments might be eager to promulgate research rating local news: They have a direct economic stake in the public perception of good journalism. Finally, citizens such as you can use simple assessment tools like the ones provided in Appendices A and B to rate your favorite local newscast or newspaper. (Be sure to mail the station or paper your results!)

Stimulating Civic Participation

Professor Jay Rosen and others have recently captured the attention of some media managers with a call for "public journalism." Building on research that shows that the extent to which people feel an involvement and stake in their local communities predicts newspaper readership, Rosen has argued that news media can serve both the public and their own interest by adopting a "public bias."

> Journalists should try to make politics "go well," so that it produces a discussion in which the polity learns more about itself, its current problems, its real divisions, its place in time, its prospects for the future. By their commitment to such a discussion—and the sort of politics that would produce it—journalists might distinguish themselves from other actors and reclaim some of their lost authority in the American public sphere.[33]

As an example, Rosen proposes the experience of Knight-Ridder's Columbus, GA, newspaper, the *Ledger-Enquirer*. In 1987, the paper's editors planned a series of articles titled "Columbus: Beyond 2000" that sought to assess the community's problems and prospects. Reporters not only sought to identify issues by talking to experts, they also canvased a cross-section of residents in their homes. The result was normative journalism of high quality. But, Rosen relates, Columbus was a demoralized community with a history of racial division and low-wage industries. The paper received little response to its series. If the *Ledger-Enquirer* were to realize its hope of empowering the public, it would have to go beyond an informational role.

Under the leadership of its remarkable publisher, the late Jack Swift, the newspaper's editorial staff initiated a series of meetings—beginning with backyard barbecues—to stimulate public conversation about the community's problems. Town meetings, the creation of a "United Beyond 2000" civic organization and establishment of "friendship networks" that crossed racial and class lines resulted. The newspaper became politically active, but remained nonpartisan. It adopted a public bias both in its reporting and in community organizing.[34]

The idea of such "public journalism" is exciting, and the support Knight-Ridder provided the Columbus project and later more limited efforts in Charlotte, NC, Wichita, KS, and San Jose, CA, is promising.[35] However, as Rosen himself conceded, "media owners may, in their own way, oppose a more serious, public-minded press."[36] If media owners are reluctant to pay for normative journalism, they may resist spending even more to staff community organizing efforts. Further, a publicly biased news medium might alienate some investors, advertisers, and sources with its coverage.

Conclusion

Efforts to curb junk journalism through an emphasis on professionalization both in journalism training and in organizations of reporters and editors should continue, but they would need to wield economic clout, perhaps through unionization, before management is likely to respond. Appeals to the social responsibility of media owners seem unlikely to succeed so long as those owners are distant stockholders who believe they are insulated from the civic consequences of poor quality news. Any government enforcement of news quality risks censorship and contravenes the First Amendment. Government funding of public or private news organizations might be a valuable idea, however, provided that funding decisions aren't made by the subjects of the reporting. Government incentives to boost citizen information-seeking and political participation would presumably foster the demand for quality journalism. New "narrowcasting" and cable technologies may make "lowest common denominator" news programming less profitable, but there is no guarantee of high-quality journalism in speculation about the effects these technologies may come to have. Increasing public awareness of the consequences of junk journalism may be the surest route to a healthier information diet. It uses market forces without requiring potentially dangerous regulation. Education also emphasizes the duty citizens owe themselves to keep informed. Unfortunately, such a project would require a massive commitment from many persons and institutions over a long time in order to succeed.

Whatever time and trouble such an effort would require, however, would be a bargain compared to the alternative. As Walter Lippmann observed 70 years ago:

All that the sharpest critics of democracy have alleged is true if there is no steady supply of trustworthy and relevant news. Incompetence and aimlessness, corruption and disloyalty, panic and ultimate disaster must come to any people which is denied assured access to the facts. No one can manage anything on pap. Neither can a people.[37]

Notes

1. Schiller, 1989.
2. Stephens, 1988.

3. Mott, 1962.

4. Mott, 1962, p. 243.

5. Mott, 1962, p. 527.

6. Schudson, 1978.

7. The Commission on Freedom of the Press, 1947, p. 57. If you haven't read the Commission's report, *A Free and Responsible Press,* treat yourself to it soon. Nothing more important about journalism has been written since this slender volume.

8. Bogart, 1992.

9. Bagdikian, 1990.

10. Cook, Gomery, & Lichty, 1992, see introduction.

11. Bagdikian, 1990.

12. Squiers, 1993.

13. Bagdikian, 1990.

14. Coen, 1991.

15. Auletta, 1991.

16. Mintz, 1993.

17. Bagdikian, 1990.

18. The Commission on Freedom of the Press, p. 91.

19. Abel, 1984.

20. Miller & Kim, 1993.

21. Stepp, 1991.

22. Squiers, 1993.

23. Kurtz, 1991.

24. Rosen, 1991.

25. Entman, 1989, chap. 7.

26. Pool, 1983.

27. Ferall, 1989.

28. Entman, 1989.

29. Hilliard, 1992.

30. Pool, 1983.

31. Anthony Smith, 1980.

32. Although research on credibility and media attention has yet to clearly bear them out.

33. Rosen & Taylor, 1992, p. 10.

34. Rosen & Taylor, 1992.

35. See, for example, Oppel, 1992.

36. Rosen & Taylor, 1992, p. 31, endnote 25.

37. Diamond, 1975, p. xiv.

APPENDIX A:
RATING THE "NUTRITION"
OF NEWSCASTS

Obviously, you don't have time to follow reporters around and check how accurately they record happenings and source comments. You may be aware of some kinds of events and issues stations ignore, but there may be many more you would have no way of detecting. Evaluating the quality of news is difficult for viewers. Still, there are certain patterns in the news that distinguish between market and normative journalism. The following analysis should yield a rough idea of the quality of your favorite newscast if you've picked a typical news day. To slow the newscast down enough for analysis, you should videotape it, then play it back one story at a time.

Some Ground Rules

a. Skip the sports and weather segments. Our focus is on news of social-civic value. (But if a weather or sports story is included in the news segments, i.e., told by the news anchors, then do rate it.)

b. Skip stories that don't have a specific local or state connection, that is, national and international news that isn't explicitly tied to your state or metropolitan area. National and global news is presented in greater depth on network newscasts. Such content is primarily used as inexpensive filler on local newscasts.

c. Skip extremely brief stories; those less than 20 seconds long. You'll be busy enough evaluating the major stories.

I. News Topics

The primary purpose of the news is to *explain* how your environment is working so that you can make good decisions, particularly civic decisions. Place each story analyzed in the *single category* that best matches what the whole story is about. Note that the core theme of a story will be that part of it to which the greatest amount of time is devoted. Place the number of minutes and fractions of a minute (in seconds) in one of the following categories based on whether the story's core is about:

Category	Time of Stories
1. A specific crime or police investigation or court action (any single event is likely to impact on only a few persons; issues and trends have wider effect and go in Categories 10 or 11.)	—
2. A specific accident, fire, or disaster	—
3. Heart-warming events or people experiencing basic human emotions such as sexual desire, love, joy, anger, sorrow, hatred, etc. Examples may include missing children or spouses, demonstrations, disputes, reunions, intrigues, romances, animal stories, etc.	—
4. What's primarily unusual, unexpected, or ironic	—
5. What's primarily amusing or entertaining	—
6. The lives of the rich, famous, or notorious	—
7. How the schools (K-university) are or ought to be performing, or how they are supported or led, or about teaching or other issues relevant to educational quality.	—
8. Business or economic conditions or trends (News of specific firms goes in Category 14, unless the firm is a major local employer or a bellwether company in some respect)	—
9. Health, fitness, scientific discovery	—
10. Important social trends such as civil rights, housing, crime, the environment, etc.	—
11. State and local politics or government	—
12. How to do something practical such as plant a garden, search for a job, etc.	—
13. Wise purchasing of goods and services	—
14. Other topics	—

Add the number of minutes and seconds in Categories 7-11. Although good stations will contain information from other categories, 50% or more of the entire broadcast (including commercials, sports, weather, banter, etc.) ought to fall into Categories 7-11 if journalistic standards are being observed. After all, the newscast has very little time to cover what's important in the thousands of square miles its signal reaches. Market journalism will empha-size Categories 1-6, sports, weather, and news gathered by other than the station's own reporters.

II. Quality of Reporting

Now, let's look within the same stories. Good journalism demands that reporters penetrate the facades of public relations officers, uncover what's really going on, and explain it to us. Even when newsworthy topics are covered, market journalism normally fails to go below the surface because of cost. Market journalism also practices misdirection—where a newswor-thy topic is selected, but covered in a way designed to gather audience attention rather than to inform viewers. Such reporting focuses more on the sensational and emotional aspects of a story rather than a careful explanation from which viewers can learn something about their community. Market journalism favors short stories. Elements likely to be considered boring or complex are often left out.

Give each story a score for each of the following characteristics. Then figure an average for all stories for each characteristic. Don't worry about the amount of time the stories consumed.

1. OBJECTIVITY

  a. Does the reporter maintain a neutral stance so you can't tell what her or his personal feelings about the topic are?

0	1	2	3	4	5
Shows personal feelings				Neutral	

  b. Does the reporter give all sides to a controversy a chance to summarize their side of the story? (Skip this question if event or issue has no more than one side.)

0	1	2	3	4	5
One sided				All sides represented	

  c. Does the reporter help you evaluate source comments by giving additional factual evidence for or against arguments sources raise?

0	1	2	3	4	5
Offers no assistance				Offers additional facts	

2. INFORMATIONAL RICHNESS

  a. Are the sources quoted providing content that is more factual or reasoned, or more opinionated or emotional? Factual interviews tend to be with experts,

leaders, and officials. The answers are usually specific and impersonal assertions of what's real, or logical arguments. Factual interviews tend to be
unemotional. Opinion interviews, in contrast, tend to be with everyday
people, perhaps those affected by the event covered. Opinion answers provide
personal observations about the advantages or disadvantages of what's real.
Opinions are often delivered with considerable feeling. Although emotional
opinions have their place in news, most source comments should be factual.

Most quotations in the story are:

0	1	2	3	4	5

Opinion or emotion   Fact or logic

b. How many sources are quoted? The more viewpoints expressed, particularly
those from sources who might be expected to fall on opposing sides of issues,
the greater the potential for learning.

0	1	2	3	4	5

< 2 sources   >3 sources but < 5   > 5 sources

c. Is the background provided sufficient to understand the event or issue reported in the story? Adequate background means that someone unfamiliar
with the subject, say an infrequent viewer, should be able to understand what
is occurring. Context includes explanation of technical or trade terms and
processes, what precedes or may follow as a consequence, pros and cons, and
so forth.

0	1	2	3	4	5

Little context   Abundant context

3. VALIDITY OF THE REPORTER'S ANGLE ON THE STORY

Because news time is limited, reporters take angles or approaches to
stories that emphasize certain facts about an issue or event and diminish the
salience of others. An angle is valid to the extent that it fits the viewers'
information needs and that reporter interpretations and conclusions are
supported by evidence. We'll evaluate only the adequacy of support for
generalizations the reporter makes on his or her own (as opposed to conclusions sources may make).

Adequate support means that in your opinion the average person would
accept the evidence offered as justifying the conclusion. For example,
statements such as "Neighborhood residents oppose development of this
property," should be supported by reference to a systematic poll or perhaps
the assessment of a neighborhood association leader; a gathering of protesters or comments from bystanders is insufficient. Only conclusions that most
readers would accept as general knowledge may be presented without
evidence.

Most reporter generalizations are:

0	1	2	3	4	5

Unsupported   Well supported
by empirical evidence   by empirical evidence

III. Rating the Newscast

You should now have one percentage from Part I, and seven averages, one for each characteristic mentioned in Part II. The percentage of substantive news—categories 7-11—is probably the most important. If the newscast does not address serious topics, it matters little how it treats those topics in Part II's analyses. The percentage of time spent on substantive stories should be no less than 50%. Scores below that point indicate a substantial entertainment bias in news selection.

In Part II, average scores on all seven indices should be at or above 3. If not, even though the station may be choosing newsworthy topics, its reporting is shortchanging your understanding of them. Scores below 3 suggest market journalism.

IV. Taking Action

If your analysis suggests that you are viewing market journalism, consider:

1. Checking out another source of news, another station or a newspaper.

2. Complaining to the station's general manager with the specifics of what you found. The rule of thumb in the newsroom is that one letter represents about 100 viewer opinions.

3. Developing alternate sources for the most consequential news. This may mean asking members of organizations such as PTAs or neighborhood associations to attend government or school board meetings and report their events for newsletters.

APPENDIX B:
RATING THE NUTRITION OF
YOUR NEWSPAPER

You don't have time to follow the press around and check how accurately they record happenings and source comments. You may be aware of some kinds of events and issues the press ignores, but there may be many more you would have no way of detecting. Nevertheless, market journalism has some more obvious traits. The following analysis may help you notice them.

Let's give your newspaper the benefit of the doubt. Choose a Sunday edition to rate. That's when newspapers showcase their best writing and thinking. For parsimony, limit your perusal to stories beginning on two pages—the front page and local news section front page. That's where the local staff's best work can usually be found.

I. News Topics

The primary purpose of the news is to *explain* how your environment is working so that you can make good decisions, particularly civic decisions. Instead of counting stories, let's measure their column inches (how long they would be if all the columns containing a story were placed end to end). If the story "jumps" to an inside page, be sure to measure all of it. Also include "sidebars"—related stories published next to the main story—as if part of the main story.

Put the column inches for a particular story in the single category that best matches what the whole story is about. Note that the core theme of a story will be that part of it to which the greatest number of column inches are devoted.

Measure the length of stories about:

Category	Column Inches
1. A specific crime or police investigation or court action (any such specific event is likely to impact on only a few persons; issues and trends have wider effect and go in Categories 10 or 11.)	—
2. A specific accident, fire, or disaster	—
3. Heart-warming events or people experiencing basic human emotions, such as sexual desire, love, joy, anger, sorrow, hatred, etc. Examples include missing children or spouses, reunions, demonstrations, intrigues, romances, animal stories, etc.	—
4. What's primarily unusual, unexpected, or ironic	—
5. What's primarily amusing or entertaining	—
6. The lives of the rich, famous, or notorious	—
7. How the schools (K-university) are or ought to be performing, or how they are supported or led, or about teaching or other issues relevant to educational quality.	—
8. Business or economic conditions or trends (News of specific firms goes in category 14, unless the firm is a major local employer or a bellwether company in some respect.)	—
9. Health, fitness, scientific discovery	—
10. Important social trends such as civil rights, housing, crime, the environment, etc.	—
11. State and local politics or government	—
12. How to do something practical such as plant a garden, search for a job, etc.	—
13. Wise purchasing of goods and services	—
14. Other topics	—

Add the number of column inches in Categories 7-11. Although good newspapers will contain information from other categories, 70% or more of the total column inches on the pages you analyze ought to fall into Categories 7-11 if journalistic standards are being observed. After all, the front page and local news front are the newsiest locations in the paper. Market journalism will emphasize Categories 1-6.

II. Quality of Reporting

Now, let's look within the stories. Good journalism demands that reporters penetrate the facades of public relations officers and uncover what's really going on. Market journalism normally fails to go below the surface because of cost and focuses more on the sensational and emotional aspects of any story rather than a careful explanation likely to lead readers to learn something about their community. Market journalism favors short stories with elements likely to be considered boring or complex left out.

Here focus your analysis only on stories produced by your local newspaper, that is, exclude stories from wire services such as the Associated Press, as well as stories from other newspapers that are reprinted in yours. Locally originated stories will have a "byline" under the headline identifying the reporter by name and under the name, your paper's name will appear.

Give each story a score for each of the following characteristics. Then figure an average for all stories for each characteristic.

1. OBJECTIVITY

a. Does the reporter maintain a neutral stance so you can't tell what her or his personal feelings are about the topic?

0   1   2   3   4   5

Shows personal feelings   Neutral

b. Does the reporter give all sides to a controversy a chance to summarize their side of the story? (Skip this question if event or issue has no more than one side.)

0   1   2   3   4   5

One-sided   All sides represented

c. Does the reporter help you evaluate source comments by giving additional factual evidence for or against arguments sources raise?

0   1   2   3   4   5

Offers no assistance   Offers additional facts

2. INFORMATIONAL RICHNESS

a. Are the sources quoted providing content that is more factual or reasoned, or more opinionated or emotional? Factual interviews tend to be with experts,

leaders, and officials. The answers are usually specific and impersonal assertions of what's real, or logical arguments. Factual interviews tend to be
unemotional. Opinion interviews, in contrast, tend to be with everyday
people, perhaps those affected by the event covered. Opinion answers
provide personal observations about the advantages or disadvantages of
what's real. Opinions are often delivered with considerable feeling. Although emotional opinions have their place in news, most source comments
should be factual.

Most quotations in the story are:

0	1	2	3	4	5
Opinion or emotion				Fact or logic	

b. How many sources are quoted? The more viewpoints expressed, particularly
those from sources who might be expected to fall on opposing sides of issues,
the greater the potential for learning.

0	1	2	3	4	5
< 2 sources		>3 sources but < 5		> 5 sources	

c. Is the background provided sufficient to understand the event or issue reported in the story? *Adequate background* means that someone unfamiliar
with the subject, say an infrequent reader, should be able to understand what
is occurring. *Context* includes explanation of technical or trade terms and
processes, what precedes or may follow as a consequence, pros and cons,
etc.

0	1	2	3	4	5
Little context				Abundant context	

3. VALIDITY OF THE REPORTER'S ANGLE ON THE STORY

Because news space is limited, reporters take angles or approaches to
stories that emphasize certain facts about an issue or event and diminish the
salience of others. An angle is valid to the extent that it fits the readers'
information needs and that reporter interpretations and conclusions are
supported by evidence. We'll evaluate only the adequacy of support for
generalizations the reporter makes on his or her own (as opposed to conclusions sources may make).

Adequate support means that in your opinion the average person would
accept the evidence offered as justifying the conclusion. For example,
statements such as "Neighborhood residents oppose development of this
property," should be supported by reference to a systematic poll; a gathering
of protesters is insufficient. Only conclusions that most readers would accept
as general knowledge may be presented without evidence.

Most reporter generalizations are:

0	1	2	3	4	5

Unsupported   Well supported
by empirical evidence   by empirical evidence

III. Rating the Newspaper

You should now have one percentage from Part I, and seven averages, one for each characteristic mentioned in Part II. The percentage of substantive news—categories 7-11—is probably the most important. If the newspaper does not address serious topics, it matters little how it treats those topics in Part II's analyses. The percentage of substantive stories should be no less than 70%. Scores below that point indicate a substantial entertainment bias in news selection.

In Part II, average scores on all seven indices should be at or above 3. If not, even though the paper is choosing newsworthy topics, its reporting is shortchanging your understanding of them. Scores below 3 suggest market journalism.

IV. Taking Action

If your analysis suggests that you are reading market journalism, consider:

1. Checking out another source of news.

2. Complaining to the publisher with the specifics of what you found. The rule of thumb in the newsroom is that one letter represents about 100 viewer opinions.

3. Developing alternate sources for the most consequential news. This may mean asking members of organizations such as PTAs or neighborhood associations to attend government or school board meetings and report their events for newsletters.

APPENDIX C:
ISSUES OF VALIDITY
AND GENERALIZABILITY

This book contains two kinds of conclusions. The broader ones outline theories—of commercial news production, of market-driven news production, and of journalistic news production. The more specific conclusions are drawn from a study of local television news. Two questions should be asked of both:

1. How valid are these conclusions?

2. How generalizable are they?

The Theories

Good theories in social science evolve over extended periods of time and lots of research. The theories presented here merely begin analysis of the news as a commodity. They are crude, ugly things in comparison to what I hope will follow in the years to come as others use and refine or revise them. As this was written, these theories seemed helpful in understanding market-driven journalism and contrasting it with normative journalism. Their validity and generalizability are tentative, however, pending further testing and elaboration.

The Empirical Study

VALIDITY

The validity of the conclusions reported about local television news is threatened by at least four major considerations. I'll state each in turn and offer what assurance I can:

1. Observer Bias. Social science has taught us that we have a tendency to observe selectively, looking for what we expect and sometimes what we wish to see rather than what's really there. (All science assumes that there is a reality to be observed and measured, even if we can't logically be certain that there is an "objective" reality or what it's like since we only know it through our own fallible senses.)

Before embarking on the study I read every previous study of local television news I could locate. This research suggested that journalistic norms were often violated in television newsrooms. Therefore, I expected to find problems.

What did I want to find? One could argue that uncovering shocking violations might advance my academic career by making my study more publishable and more important as a warning to society. Of course, one could also argue that my findings would be more publishable in academic journals if they convincingly disconfirmed previous research, that is, were positive. On balance, I think my reward structure is somewhat more influenced by the first argument than the second.

Social scientists have several weapons for combatting observer bias. First, we often randomly select the items—stories, newscasts, and so on—that we study. That prevents picking just those items that confirm our expectations or fulfill our self-interest. Second, the research process requires the researcher to explain the methods as well as the results and submit both to other scientists for critical evaluation. These results, for example, were reviewed and accepted by a university dissertation committee. Third, in this case, the results were reported back to the newsrooms. Although there were charges that I am "a print guy [I identified myself as a former newspaper reporter] beating up on TV," no one questioned the validity of any specific finding reported.

2. Station Self-Selection. Because one station I approached refused to join the study, it's reasonable to ask whether stations that did agree to expose their newsrooms might be different from stations that would not welcome analysis. The news director at the station that refused access said he didn't want his reporters worrying about "journalistic questions" as they performed their jobs. So the possibility that newsrooms visited considered themselves more exemplary than others cannot be ruled out.

3. Reactivity to Observer. A similar problem is the tendency of people to act differently when they know they are being observed than they might otherwise. Although I wrote a letter to each newsroom employee explaining my project and promising confidentiality both to station and individual, such an approach does not eliminate the desire to impress the observer himself. Some journalists may have been on their best behavior.

4. Purposive Selection of Reporting Case Studies. One bias was consciously introduced. Given the negativity of much research on local television news, where I could not follow every reporter as he or she gathered a story, I chose the ones management considered most able. More importantly, I tried to accompany reporters assigned what I considered the most consequential stories. Although the newscasts sampled were in all but one case randomly selected, the reporting case studies were chosen to examine the most normative journalism the stations were producing.

Note that although the first bias, my own as observer, may tend to darken the lens through which I viewed these four newsrooms, all of the other biases act in the opposite direction. Stations and journalists are more likely to be presenting their best selves and my own selection of the best reporters and meatiest stories probably overestimates journalistic quality.

GENERALIZABILITY

The second basic question—how much confidence can we have that these results describe the logic of contemporary local television stations across the U.S.—turns on three considerations.

1. Sample Size. In the formal part of the study only one station was chosen for each of three broad categories of market size—medium, large, and very large. No representative was chosen from the smallest 100 markets, and only four stations—the research design was pretested on a second very large market station—were visited. If there are great differences of journalistic practice among stations, it is absurd to generalize from four newsrooms to the hundreds currently broadcasting local news across the United States.

Perhaps because of the pervasive homogenizing influence of television news consultants, however, the literature of research on local television newscasts is remarkably uniform in the practices it describes (see Chapters 1 and 10). The anecdotal evidence is also surprisingly similar. There was also little difference in the approach taken to news at the four stations visited. This apparent orthodoxy of practice does not assure that the results presented here are representative, but it does strengthen the argument for generalizability.

2. Sample Geography. All four stations visited are located in California. To the extent that California is different from the other 49 states, one might expect differences in television newscasts. Although the present study was conducted in only one state, the research literature is nationally representative. That literature shows no differences important to the present study that researchers associated with state or regional differences.

3. Sample Time. The study data presented here were gathered in 1986 and 1987. Since then, the television industry has undergone change. The FCC has relaxed regulations. An increasing number of households are wired to multistation cable systems, resulting in further fractionation of the viewing audience. Competition for advertising dollars has increased and the overall pool of money has stagnated. Local station profit levels are down from the mid-1980s level, but still well above national averages for other industries, according to the National Association of Broadcasters annual surveys.

Rather than invalidate my research, however, these changes appear to have increased the salience of the collision of profit standards and journalistic standards. Newsroom budgets have shrunk in dollars adjusted for inflation. Many bureaus have been closed and layoffs have become common. The ills of too few reporters chasing too many stories appear to have increased. The cardinal journalistic selection and reporting criteria of explaining what's consequential appears to have lost ground since the mid-1980s to audience-building values. See, for example, Davie, 1992; Eisenberg, 1990; Kaniss, 1991; Lambeth, 1991; Rosenau, 1988; Underwood, 1993; or cover articles in newspaper Sunday magazines such as the *Los Angeles Times Magazine,* January 24, 1988; or *The Washington Post Magazine,* May 13, 1990. Or consider a New York station's decision in 1990 to run Madonna's sexy "Justify My Love" video in its entirety on its local newscast, despite MTV's ban on the video as too pornographic for television. If anything, the data presented here appear to understate the current impact of market logic on local television.

References

Abel, E. (1984). Hutchins revisited: Thirty-five years of social responsibility theory. In R. Schmuhl (Ed.), *The responsibilities of journalism*. Notre Dame, IN: University of Notre Dame Press.

Adams, W. (1978). Local public affairs content of TV news. *Journalism Quarterly, 55*, 690-695.

Adatto, K. (1990). *Sound bite democracy: Network evening news presidential campaign coverage, 1968 and 1988* (Research Paper R-2). Cambridge, MA: Harvard University, John F. Kennedy School of Government, Joan Shorenstein Barone Center on the Press, Politics and Public Policy.

Allen, C. (1992, April). *ABC's news advisory service and local TV news: "Eyewitness" to change in the 1970's*. Paper presented at the Broadcast Educators Association Annual Convention, Las Vegas, NV.

Allen, C. (1993, August). *The "cutting edge" in local television news: Revisiting layoffs, staff reductions and downsizing "mythology."* Paper presented to the annual convention of the Association for Education in Journalism and Mass Communication, Kansas City, MO.

Alter, J. (1986a, September 15). The struggle for the soul of CBS news. *Newsweek*, pp. 52-54.

Alter, J. (1986b, September 15). Taking CBS news to task. *Newsweek*, p. 53.

Altheide, D. L. (1976). *Creating reality: How TV news distorts events*. Beverly Hills, CA: Sage.

Altschull, J. H. (1984). *Agents of power*. New York: Longman.

Anderson, J. A. (1972). The alliance of broadcast stations and newspapers: The problem of information control. *Journal of Broadcasting, 16*, 51-64.

Andrews, E. L. (1991, October 8). "Court lets 'Baby Bells' branch out." *The New York Times*, p. C1.

Antonucci, M. (1993, August 26). KRON's cable channel looks like serious stuff. *San Jose Mercury News*, p. F1.

Atwater, T. (1984). Product differentiation in local TV news. *Journalism Quarterly, 61*, 759-760.

Atwater, T. (1986). Consonance in local television news. *Journal of Broadcasting and Electronic Media, 30*, 467-472.

Audience Research & Development. (1984). *Procter and Gamble spends months on them. You probably spend less than ten minutes on them. What are they? Does P & G know something you don't?* [Consultant's Report]. Dallas, TX.

227

Aufderheide, P. (1990). After the fairness doctrine: Controversial broadcast programming and the public interest. *Journal of Communication, 40,* 3, 47-72.

Auletta, K. (1991). *Three blind mice.* New York: Random House.

Bagdikian, B. (1990). *The media monopoly.* Boston: Beacon.

Baldwin, T. F., Barrett, M., & Bates, B. (1988). [Viewership of local television news in selected markets.] Unpublished raw data.

Baldwin, T. F., Barrett, M., & Bates, B. (1992). Influence of cable on television news audiences. *Journalism Quarterly, 69,* 651-658.

Bantz, C. R. (1985). News organizations: Conflict as a crafted cultural norm. *Communication, 8,* 225-244.

Bantz, C. R., McCorkle, S., & Baade, R. C. (1980). The news factory. *Communication Research, 7*(1), 45-68.

Barney, R. D. (1987). Responsibilities of the journalist: An ethical construct. *Mass Comm Review, 14*(3), 14-22.

Barnouw, E. (1990). *Tube of plenty.* New York: Oxford University Press.

Barrett, M. (1978). *Rich news, poor news.* New York: Thomas Y. Crowell.

Becker, G. S. (1976). *The economic approach to human behavior.* Chicago: University of Chicago Press.

Beniger, J. L. (1986). *The control revolution.* Cambridge, MA: Harvard University Press.

Bernstein, C. (1992, June 21). Feeding an "idiot" culture. *San Jose Mercury News,* pp. 1C, 4C. (Reprinted from The idiot culture: Reflections of post-Watergate journalism, *The New Republic,* June 8, 1992, *206*(23), 22-26)

Bernstein, J. M., & Lacy, S. (1992). Contextual coverage of government by local television news. *Journalism Quarterly 69*(2), 329-340.

Blasi, V. (1977). The checking value in First Amendment theory. *American Bar Foundation Research Journal,* 521-649.

Bogart, L. (1982). Newspapers in transition. *The Wilson Quarterly, 6*(5), 58-70.

Bogart, L. (1989). *Press and public: Who reads what, when, where and why in American newspapers.* Hillsdale, NJ: Lawrence Erlbaum.

Bogart, L. (1991). *The American media system and its commercial culture* (Occasional Paper No. 8, p. 6). New York: Gannett Foundation Media Center.

Bogart, L. (1992). The state of the industry. In P. S. Cook, D. Gomery, & L. W. Lichty (Eds.), *The future of news* (pp. 85-103). Washington, DC: Woodrow Wilson Center Press.

Boorstin, D. (1961). *The image: A guide to pseudo-events in America.* New York: Atheneum.

Bozell, L. B., & Baker, B. H. (1990). *And that's the way it isn't: A reference guide to media bias.* Alexandria, VA: Media Research Center.

Breed, W. (1955). Social control in the newsroom: A functional analysis. *Social Forces, 33*(4), 326-335.

Brennan, T. J. (1991, August). *Economic perspectives on the First Amendment.* Paper presented at the Association for Education in Journalism and Mass Communication Annual Convention, Boston.

Broadcasting Publications, Inc. (1991). *The broadcast yearbook, 1991.* Washington, DC: Author.

Buchanan, B. (1991). *Electing a president: The Markle Commission research on campaign 88.* Austin: University of Texas Press.

Buckalew, J. K. (1969). News elements and selection by television news editors. *Journal of Broadcasting 14*(1), 47-54.

Busby, L. J. (1979). Broadcast regulatory policy: The managerial view. *Journal of Broadcasting, 23*(3), 331-341.

Carey, J. W. (1978). A plea for the university tradition. *Journalism Quarterly, 55*(4), 846-855.

Carey, J. W. (1986). Why and how: The dark continent of American journalism. In R. K. Manoff & M. Schudson (Eds.), *Reading the news* (pp. 109-145). New York: Pantheon.

Christians, C. G., Rotzoll, K. B., & Fackler, M. (1987). *Media ethics* (2nd ed.). New York: Longman.

Ciabattari, J. (1989). Of time & integrity. *Columbia Journalism Review, 28*(3), 27-34.

Code of broadcast news ethics. (1990, January). *The Communicator,* p. 10.

Coen, R. J. (1991, May). Little ad growth: Industry forecaster sees recovery at year-end. *Advertising Age, 62*(6), 16.

Cohen, S. E. (1989, July/August). While S & Ls were robbed, the press watchdogs slept. *The Quill, 77*(7), 21-23.

The Commission on Freedom of the Press. (1947). *A free and responsible press.* Chicago: University of Chicago Press.

Collins, R. K. L. (1992). *Dictating content: How advertising pressure can corrupt a free press.* Washington, DC: Center for the Study of Commercialism.

Compaine, B. M. (1980). *The newspaper industry in the 1980's: An assessment of economics and technology.* White Plains, NY: Knowledge Industry.

Crouse, T. (1973). *The boys on the bus.* New York: Random House.

Darby, M. R., & Karni, E. (1973). Free competition and the optimal amount of fraud. *Journal of Law and Economics, 16*(1), 67-88.

Davie, W. R. (1992, August). *Sex, violence and consonance/diversity: An analysis of local TV news values.* Paper presented at the annual convention of the Association for Education in Journalism and Mass Communication, Boston.

Day, L. A. (1991). *Ethics in media communications: Cases and controversies.* Belmont, CA: Wadsworth.

Dennis, E. E. (1986). *The media and the people.* New York: Columbia University, Gannett Center for Media Studies.

Dhawan, M., & Pellegrino, J. W. (1977). Acoustic and semantic interference effects in words and pictures. *Memory and Cognition, 5,* 340-346.

Diamond, E. (1975). *The tin kazoo.* Cambridge: MIT Press.

Dimmick, J. (1974). The gate-keeper: An uncertainty theory. *Journalism Monographs, 37.*

Document. (1989). *Columbia Journalism Review, 28*(3), p. 25.

Dominick, J. R., & Pearce, M. C. (1976). Trends in network prime-time programming, 1953-74. *Journal of Communication, 26*(1), 70-80.

Dominick, J. R., Wurtzel, A., & Lometti, G. (1975). Television journalism vs. show business: A content analysis of eyewitness news. *Journalism Quarterly, 52,* 213-218.

Donohew, L., Finn, H. S., & Christ, W. G. (1987). "The nature of news" revisited: The roles of affect, schemas, and cognition. In L. Donohew, H. E. Sypher, & E. T. Higgins (Eds.), *Communication, social cognition and affect* (pp. 195-217). Hillsdale, NJ: Lawrence Erlbaum.

Donohew, L., Sypher, H. E., & Higgins, E. T. (Eds.). (1987). *Communication, social cognition and affect.* Hillsdale, NJ: Lawrence Erlbaum.

Dozier, D. M., & Hofstetter, C. R. (1985, May). *Useful news, sensational views: Some sensational observations about local television news and the public interest.* Paper presented at the International Communication Association Annual Convention, Honolulu.

Dreier, P. (1983). The position of the press in the U.S. power structure. In E. Wartella, D. C. Whitney, & S. Windahl (Eds.), *Mass communication review yearbook* (Vol. 4, pp. 439-451). Beverly Hills, CA: Sage.

Ehrlich, M. C. (1991, August). *Competition in local TV news: Ritual, enactment and ideology.* Paper presented to the annual convention of the Association for Education in Journalism and Mass Communication, Boston.

Ehrlich, M. C. (1993, August). *The daily race to see who's best: Competition, control and newswork*. Paper presented to the annual convention of the Association for Education in Journalism and Mass Communication, Kansas City, MO.

Eisenberg, I. (1990, September). TV news at the crossroads. *San Francisco Focus*, pp. 92-110.

Entman, R. M. (1989). *Democracy without citizens*. New York: Oxford University Press.

Entman, R. M., & Wildman, S. (1991, August). *Toward a new analytical framework for media policy: Reconciling economic and non-economic perspectives*. Paper presented at the Association for Education in Journalism and Mass Communication Annual Convention, Boston.

Epstein, E. J. (1973). *News from nowhere: Television and the news*. New York: Random House.

Ettema, J. S. (1987). Journalism in the "post-factual age." *Critical Studies in Mass Communication, 4*(1), 82-86.

Federal Communications Commission. (1973). Editorializing by broadcast licensees (Docket No. 8516). In E. J. Epstein, *News from nowhere* (p. 48). New York: Vintage.

Federal Communications Commission. (1960, July 29). *Report and statement of policy re Commission En Banc programming requirements* (FCC 60-970, Mimeo., 91874). In E. J. Epstein (1973), *News from nowhere* (Exhibit 7, p. 49). New York: Random House.

Ferall, V. E. (1989). The impact of television deregulation on private and public interests. *Journal of Communication, 39*(1), 8-36.

Fishman, M. (1980). *Manufacturing the news*. Austin: University of Texas Press.

Fowler, J. S., & Showalter, S. W. (1974). Evening network news selection: A confirmation of news judgment. *Journalism Quarterly, 51,* 712-715.

Franklin, M. (1982). *Mass media law* (2nd ed.). Mineola, NY: Foundation Press.

Frazier, P. J., & Gaziano, C. (1979, November). Robert Ezra Park's theory of news, public opinion and social control. *Journalism Monographs, No. 64.*

The Freedom Forum Media Studies Center. (1992). *Media at the millenium*. New York: Columbia University, Freedom Forum Media Studies Center.

Gale Research. (1990). *Gale directory of publications and broadcast media* (122nd ed.). Detroit: Author.

Galtung, J., & Ruge, M. H. (1965). The structure of foreign news. *Journal of Peace Research, 1,* 64-91.

Gandy, O. H. (1982). *Beyond agenda setting: Information subsidies and public policy*. Norwood, NJ: Ablex.

Gans, H. J. (1979). *Deciding what's news*. New York: Pantheon.

Gans, H. J. (1985). Are U.S. journalists dangerously liberal? *Columbia Journalism Review, 24*(4), 29-33.

Gitlin, T. (1980). *The whole world is watching*. Berkeley: University of California Press.

Glaser, B., & Strauss, A. (1967). *The discovery of grounded theory: Strategies for qualitative research*. Chicago: Aldine.

Goldstein, T. (1985). *The news at any cost*. New York: Simon & Schuster.

Graber, D. (1990). Seeing is remembering: How visuals contribute to learning from television news. *Journal of Communication, 40*(3), 134-155.

Gunter, B. (1987). *Poor reception*. Hillsdale, NJ: Lawrence Erlbaum.

Hackett, R. A. (1984). Decline of a paradigm? Bias and objectivity in news media studies. *Critical Studies in Mass Communication, 1*(3), 229-259.

Hallin, D. C. (1992). Sound bite news: Television coverage of elections 1968-1988. *Journal of Communication, 42*(2), 5-24.

Harmon, M. D. (1989). Market size and local television news judgment. *Journal of Media Economics, 2,* 15-29.

Lewis Harris & Associates. (1993, August 2). Television is the true mass medium for the news—but not for the college educated. New York: Author.

Helregal, B. (Ed.). (1991). *1991 television financial report*. Washington, DC: National Association of Broadcasters.

Herbert, S. (1992, October 12). Last debate's rating hits 8-year high. *Los Angeles Times*, p. A10.

Herman, E., & Chomsky, N. (1988). *Manufacturing consent*. New York: Pantheon.

Hertsgaard, M. (1988). *On bended knee*. New York: Farrar, Straus, Giroux.

Hilliard, R. D. (1992, August). *The "kept" press? Swedish newspapers balance subsidy, editorial independence*. Paper presented at the Association for Education in Journalism Annual Convention, Montreal.

Hume, E. (1991). *Restoring the bond: Connecting campaign coverage to voters*. Boston: Harvard University, John F. Kennedy School of Government, Joan Shorenstein Barone Center on the Press, Politics and Public Policy.

Iannaccone, L. (1992). Religious markets and the economics of religion. *Social Compass, 39*(1), 123-131.

Iyengar, S., & Kinder, D. R. (1987). *News that matters*. Chicago: University of Chicago Press.

Jamieson, K. H. (1992). *Dirty politics*. New York: Oxford University Press.

Kahneman, D., & Tversky, A. (1973). On the psychology of prediction. *Psychological Review, 80*(4), 237-251.

Kaniss, P. (1991). *Making local news*. Chicago: University of Chicago Press.

Krugman, H. (1965). The impact of television advertising: Learning without involvement. *Public Opinion Quarterly, 29,* 349-356.

Kurtz, H. (1991, January 6). Slicing, dicing news to attract the young, Florida paper aims to buck trend of declining national readership. *The Washington Post*, p. A1.

Lacy, S., & Dalmia, S. (1991, August). *Michigan newspaper competition from 1980 to 1986: Expanding the geographic application of the umbrella model*. Paper presented at the Association for Education in Journalism and Mass Communication, Boston.

Lambeth, E. (1991, June). Gene Roberts: A case for leadership. *The Quill*, pp. 14-24.

Lang, K., & Lang, G. E. (1968). *Politics and television*. Chicago: Quadrangle Books.

Lee, M. A., & Solomon, N. (1991). *Unreliable sources: A guide to detecting bias in news media*. New York: Carol Publishing.

Leff, L. (1993). From legal scholar to quota queen. *Columbia Journalism Review, 32*(3), 36-41.

Lesly, E. (1991, November). Realtors and builders demand happy news . . . and often get it. *Washington Journalism Review*, pp. 20-23.

Lev, M. (1989, July 17). Local news is challenging prime-time shows. *The New York Times*, p. D9.

Levy, M. R. (1992). Learning from television news. In P. S. Cook, D. Gomery, & L. W. Lichty (Eds.), *The future of news* (pp. 69-72). Washington, DC: Woodrow Wilson Center Press.

Lichter, S. R., Rothman, S., & Lichter, L. (1982, December). The once and future journalists. *Washington Journalism Review*, pp. 26-27.

Lichter, S. R., Rothman, S., & Lichter, L. (1986). *The media elite: America's new powerbrokers*. Bethesda, MD: Adler & Adler.

Lichty, L. W., & Gomery, D. (1992). More is less. In P. S. Cook, D. Gomery, & L. W. Lichty (Eds.), *The future of news* (pp. 3-33). Washington, DC: Woodrow Wilson Center Press.

Lippmann, W. (1922). *Public opinion*. New York: Harcourt Brace.

Lippmann, W. (1925). *The phantom public*. New York: Harcourt Brace.

Lippmann, T. W. (1989). *The Washington Post deskbook on style* (2nd ed.). New York: McGraw-Hill.

Main, R. S., & Baird, C. W. (1981). *Elements of microeconomics* (2nd ed.). St. Paul, MN: West.

Major market news growth halts despite added services. (1986, August 18). *Television/Radio Age,* pp. 58-59.

March, J. G., & Simon, H. A. (1958). *Organizations.* New York: John Wiley.

Markle Commission on the Media and the Electorate. (1990, May). *Key findings.* Austin: University of Texas Press.

Massing, M. (1985). The libel chill: How cold is it out there? *Columbia Journalism Review, 24*(1), 31-43.

Massing, M. (1991). Is the most popular evening newscast the best? *Columbia Journalism Review, 29*(6), 30-35.

McClosky, H., & Zaller, J. (1984). *The American ethos.* Cambridge, MA: Harvard University Press.

McManus, J. (1988). *Economic and technological influences on the quality of local television news.* Unpublished doctoral dissertation, Stanford University.

McManus, J. H. (1990). How local television learns what is news. *Journalism Quarterly, 67*(4), 672-683.

McManus, J. H. (1992). Serving the public and serving the market: A conflict of interest? *Journal of Mass Media Ethics, 7*(4), 196-208.

Meeske, M., & Fedler, F. (1993, August). *Checkbook journalism in the electronic media: Alive and flourishing.* Paper presented at the annual convention of the Association for Education in Journalism and Mass Communication, Kansas City, MO.

Meiklejohn, A. (1948). *Free speech and its relation to self-government.* New York: Harper.

Mencher, M. (1987). *News reporting and writing* (4th ed.). Dubuque, IA: William C. Brown.

Meyer, P. (1987). *Ethical journalism.* New York: Longman.

Meyrowitz, J. (1985). *No sense of place.* New York: Oxford University Press.

Miller, D. T., & Kim, H. (1993, August). *Serving the public interest in the absence of ascertainment rules: A survey of Kentucky broadcasters.* Paper presented to the annual convention of the Association for Education in Journalism and Mass Communication, Kansas City, MO.

Mintz, J. (1993, January 2). The battle over a reporter's role. *The Washington Post,* p. C1.

Molotch, H., & Lester, M. (1974). News as purposive behavior: On the strategic use of routine events, accidents and scandals. *American Sociological Review, 39,* 101-112.

Mott, F. L. (1962). *American journalism* (3rd ed.). Toronto: Macmillan.

Moyers, B. (1989, November 22). Illusions of news. Television program, second in the series *The public mind,* Public Broadcasting Service, Washington, DC.

Moyers, B. (1990). High crimes and misdemeanors. Television program in the series *Frontline,* Public Broadcasting Service, Washington, DC.

Mundy, A. (1992). Is the press any match for powerhouse P.R.? *Columbia Journalism Review, 31*(3), 27-35.

Nearly half in U.S. can't read well. (1993, September 9). *San Jose Mercury News,* p. A1.

Neuman, R. W. (1986). *The paradox of mass politics: Knowledge and opinion in the American electorate.* Cambridge, MA: Harvard University Press.

Nielsen Media Research. (1991, January). National audience demographic report, September 1990. In *The broadcast yearbook, 1991.* Washington, DC: Broadcasting Publishing Inc.

Niemi, R. G., Mueller, J., & Smith, T. W. (1989). *Trends in public opinion.* Westport, CT: Greenwood Press.

Olien, C. N., Tichenor, P. J., & Donohue, G. (1991, August). *A changing media environment in the U.S.* Paper presented at the Association for Education in Journalism and Mass Communication, Boston.

Oppel, R. (1992, Summer). Listening to America. *Knight-Ridder News, 7*(2), 1-2.

Owen, B., Beebe, J., & Manning W. (1974). *Television economics*. Lexington, MA: D. C. Heath.

Picard, R. G. (1989). *Media economics*. Newbury Park, CA: Sage.

Pickerell, A. G. (1988). *The courts and the news media* (5th ed.). San Francisco: California Judges Association.

Plumber shocked over instant fame in taped beating. (1991, April 15). *San Jose Mercury News*, p. A1.

Pool, I. (1983). *Technologies of freedom*. Cambridge, MA: Belknap.

Postman, N. (1985). *Amusing ourselves to death*. New York: Penguin.

Powers, R. (1977). *The newscasters*. New York: St. Martin's.

Powers, R. (1977, May/June). Eyewitless news. *Columbia Journalism Review, 20*, 17-23.

Reese, S. D. (1990). The news paradigm and the ideology of objectivity: A socialist at *The Wall Street Journal. Critical Studies in Mass Communication, 7*, 390-409.

Reese, S. D. (1991). Setting the media's agenda: A power balance perspective. In J. A. Anderson (Ed.), *Communication yearbook 14* (pp. 309-340). Newbury Park, CA: Sage.

Renick, R. (1982). The cumulative impact of news consultants after ten years in the field. In M. Barrett (Ed.), *Broadcast journalism* (pp. 195-203). New York: Everest House.

Rivers, W. L., Schramm, W. L., & Christians, C. G. (1980). *Responsibility in mass communication* (3rd ed.). New York: Harper & Row.

Robinson, J. P., & Davis, D. K. (1989). *Informing the public: Is TV news the main source?* Paper presented at the International Communication Association Annual Conference, San Francisco.

Robinson, J. P., & Levy, M. R. (1986). *The main source*. Beverly Hills, CA: Sage.

Robinson, M. J., & Sheehan, M. A. (1983). *Over the wire and on TV*. New York: Russell Sage Foundation.

Rock, P. (1981). News as eternal recurrence. In S. Cohen & J. Young (Eds.), *The manufacture of news* (pp. 64-70). Beverly Hills, CA: Sage.

Roper Organization. (1991). *America's watching: Public attitudes toward television*. New York: Author.

Rosen, J. (1991). Making journalism more public. *Communication, 12*, 267-284.

Rosen, J., & Taylor, P. (1992). *The new news v. the old news*. New York: Twentieth Century Fund.

Rosenau, N. (1988). After the cutbacks: What's the damage to local TV news? *Columbia Journalism Review, 27*(3), 46-50.

Roshcoe, B. (1975). *Newsmaking*. Chicago: University of Chicago Press.

Ross, L. J., & Nisbett, R. (1980). Assigning weights to data: The "vividness criterion." In L. J. Ross & R. Nisbett (Eds.), *Human inference: Strategies and shortcomings of social judgment*. Englewood Cliffs, NJ: Prentice Hall.

Rotzoll, K. B., & Haefner J. E., with Sandage, C. H. (1990). *Advertising in contemporary society* (2nd ed.). Cincinnati: Southwestern.

Runkel, D. R. (Ed). (1989). *Campaign for president: The managers look at '88*. Dover, MA: Auburn House.

Ryu, J. S. (1982). Public affairs and sensationalism in local TV news programs. *Journalism Quarterly, 59*, 74-137.

Sabreen, R. (1985, August 26). News is no longer enough. *Broadcasting*, p. 24.

Salmon, C. (1993, August). *The impact of video news releases on TV news*. Verbal presentation at the Association for Journalism and Mass Communication annual convention, Kansas City, MO.

Sanit, T. (1992, May/June). The new unreality. *Columbia Journalism Review*, pp. 17-18.

Schiller, H. I. (1989). *Culture, Inc.: The corporate takeover of public expression*. New York: Oxford University Press.

Schoenbrun, D. (1989). *On and off the air.* New York: E. P. Dutton.

Schor, J. B. (1992). *The overworked American: The unexpected decline of leisure.* New York: Basic Books.

Schorr, D. (1990, June 10). The show business of TV news. *San Francisco Chronicle, [In This World],* p. 20.

Schramm, W. L. (Ed.). (1949). *Mass communications.* Urbana: University of Illinois Press.

Schudson, M. (1983). *The news media and the democratic process.* New York: Aspen Institute for Humanistic Studies.

Schudson, M. (1987). *Discovering the news.* New York: Basic Books.

Scott, W. R. (1981). *Organizations: Rational, natural and open systems.* Englewood Cliffs, NJ: Prentice Hall.

Shapiro, N. L. (1988). Defamation. In A. G. Pickerell (Ed.), *The courts and the news media* (5th ed.). San Francisco: California Judges Association.

Shaw, D. (1993, March 31). Sizing up the media. *Los Angeles Times,* A16.

Shoemaker, P. J., Brendlinger, N., Danielian, L., & Chang, T. K. (1986, May). *Testing a theoretical model of newsworthiness: Coverage of international events in the U.S. media.* Paper presented at the Mass Communication Division of the International Communication Association, Chicago.

Shoemaker, P. J., & Reese, S. D. (1991). *Mediating the message.* New York: Longman.

Shoemaker, P. J., with Mayfield, E. K. (1987). Building a theory of news content. *Journalism Monographs,* 103.

Sibbison, J. (1988). Dead fish and red herrings: How the EPA pollutes the news. *Columbia Journalism Review, 27*(4), 25-29.

Siebert, F., Peterson, T., & Schramm, W. L. (1956). *Four theories of the press.* Urbana: University of Illinois Press.

Sigal, L. V. (1973). *Reporters and officials.* Lexington, MA: D.C. Heath.

Sigalman, L. (1973). Reporting the news: An organizational analysis. *American Journal of Sociology, 79,* 132-151.

Singer, S. (1991, September). Auto dealers muscle the newsroom. *Washington Journalism Review,* pp. 24-28.

Slattery, K. L., & Hakanen, E. A. (in press). Sensationalism versus public affairs content of local TV news: Pennsylvania revisited. *Journal of Broadcasting and Electronic Media.*

Small, W. J. (1992). A report—the Gulf War and television news: Past, future and present. *Mass Comm Review, 19*(1-2), 3-13.

Smith, A. (1909). *An inquiry into the nature and causes of the wealth of nations.* New York: P. Collier & Son.

Smith, A. (1980). *Goodbye Gutenberg: The newspaper revolution of the 1980's.* New York: Oxford University Press.

Soloski, J. (1989). News reporting and professionalism: Some constraints on the reporting of news. *Media, Culture and Society, 11,* 207-228.

Squiers, J. D. (1993). *Read all about it.* New York: Random House.

Standish, K. (1993, June). More news in the morning. *The Communicator,* pp. 28-30.

Stanley, C. (Ed.). (1986). *1986 television financial report.* Washington, DC: National Association of Broadcasters.

Statistical Abstract of the United States. (1990). Washington, DC: Government Printing Office.

Stephens, M. (1988). *A history of news.* New York: Penguin.

Stepp, C. S. (1991, April). When readers design the news. *Washington Journalism Review,* pp. 20-25.

Stevens, J. D. (1985). Social utility of sensational news: Murder and divorce in the 1920's. *Journalism Quarterly, 62,* 53-58.

Stone, E. (1993, May). Protecting our credibility. *Communicator,* pp. 17-18.

Stone, G., Hartung, B., & Jensen, D. (1987). Local TV news and the good-bad dyad. *Journalism Quarterly, 64,* 41-42.

Stone, V. A. (1993a, April). Cutbacks strike again. *The Communicator,* pp. 32-33.

Stone, V. A. (1993b, April). News stays profitable. *The Communicator,* p. 34.

Stone, V. A. (1993c, May). TV news workforce grows, declines continue in radio. *The Communicator,* pp. 26-27.

Television and video almanac. (1991). New York: Quigley.

Times Mirror Center for The People and The Press. (1989, November). *Times Mirror-Gallup Poll.* Washington, DC: Author.

Times Mirror Center for The People and The Press. (1990a). *The age of indifference.* Washington, DC: Author.

Times Mirror Center for The People and The Press. (1990b). *The American media: Who reads, who watches, who listens, who cares.* Washington, DC: Author.

Times Mirror Center for The People and The Press. (1993). *Jury still out on Clinton's success.* Washington, DC: Author.

Tuchman, G. (1978). *Making news.* New York: Free Press.

Turow, J. (1984). *Media industries.* New York: Longman.

Turow, J. (1992). *Media systems in society.* New York: Longman.

Udell, J. G. (1978). *The economics of the American newspaper.* New York: Hastings House.

Underwood, D. (1988). When MBAs rule the newsroom. *Columbia Journalism Review, 26*(6), 23-30.

Underwood, D. (1993). *When MBAs rule the newsroom.* New York: Columbia University Press.

Underwood, D., & Stamm, K. (1992). Balancing business with journalism: Newsroom policies at 12 west coast newspapers. *Journalism Quarterly, 69,* 2, 301-317.

Verba, S., & Nie, N. H. (1972). *Participation in America: Political democracy and social equality.* New York: Harper & Row.

Ward, W. J. (1967). *News values, news situations, and news selections: An intensive study of ten city editors.* Unpublished doctoral dissertation, University of Iowa.

Weaver, D. H., & Wilhoit, C. G. (1986). *The American journalist.* Bloomington: Indiana University Press.

Weaver, D. H., & Wilhoit, C. G. (1992). *The American journalist in the 1990's* (Preliminary Report). New York: Freedom Forum.

Wenner, L. (1985). The nature of news gratifications. In K. E. Rosengren, L. A. Wenner, & P. Palmgreen (Eds.), *Media gratifications research: Current perspective* (pp. 171-194). Beverly Hills, CA: Sage.

Westerstahl, J. (1983). Objective news reporting: General premises. *Communication Research, 10*(3), 403-424.

White, D. M. (1964). The gatekeeper: A case study in the selection of news. In L. A. Dexter & D. M. White (Eds.), *People, society and mass communications* (pp. 160-171). New York: Free Press.

Whitney, D. C. (1985). *The media and the people: Americans' experience with the news media: A fifty-year review.* New York: Gannett Center for Media Studies.

Williams, R. M. (1963). *American society* (2nd ed.). New York: Knopf.

Williamson, O. E. (1979). Transaction-cost economics: The governance of contractual relations. *The Journal of Law and Economics, 22*(2), 233-261.

Williamson, O. E. (1981). The economics of organization: The transaction cost approach. *American Journal of Sociology, 87*(3), 548-577.

Wulfemeyer, K. T. (1982). Developing and testing methods for assessing local TV newscasts. *Journalism Quarterly, 59,* 79-82.

Zachary, G. P. (1992, February 26). Many journalists see a growing reluctance to criticize advertisers. *The Wall Street Journal,* p. A1.

Zhu, J., Milavsky, J. R., & Biswas, R. (1993, August). *Does the audience learn more about images than issues from televised debates? Effects of the first 1992 Presidential debate.* Paper presented at the annual convention of the Association for Education in Journalism and Mass Communication, Kansas City, MO.

Index

ABC News, 10, 13, 193
Adams, W., 187
Advertisers, 26, 30, 61, 75, 76, 77, 78, 79
  ability to evaluate commodity quality, 75, 76, 77, 78
  bias for, 76, 77, 78
  influence, 34, 193-195
  rationality of, 75
Advertising market, 5, 185
Advertising subsidy, 61
Agnew, S., 32
AIDS, 57-59, 81, 82, 124, 193
Ailes, R., 195
All Things Considered, 69, 206
Allen, C., 6
Altheide, D., 188
Altruism, 204
Altschull, J.H., 32, 159
American Journalism Review, 143
American Revolution, 200
American Society of Newspaper Editors, xiv, 25
Amusing Ourselves to Death, 173
Assignment desk, 92, 101, 103, 112
Associated Press, 101, 104, 179
Associated Press Managing Editors Association, xiv
Associated Press Radio Wire Service, 93
Associated Press Television-Radio Association, 165
A Team, 133
Atlanta Journal and Constitution, 2
Audience fractionation, 202

Audience Research and Development Corporation, 130

Bagdikian, B., 2, 30, 32, 69, 194, 203
Barney, R., 95
Bernstein, C., 1, 2
Bernstein, J., 188
Billygate, 192-193
Boca Raton News, 194, 204
Bogart, L., 7, 61, 189
Bolick, C., 66
Boorstin, D., 74
Brand names, 67
Branscomb, A. W., 2
Brown, H. R., 191
Business norms, 25, 35-37, 47, 82, 95, 112
Buyers/sellers markets, 74
Buying mood, 30

Cable News Network, 28, 69
Cable television, 202
Carmichael, S., 191
Carter, J., 192
Caveat emptor, 62
CBS News, 2, 6, 7, 8, 10, 78, 93, 115, 193
Chains, 22
Checks and balances, 205
Chomsky, N., 32, 159, 193
Christ, W., 116
Ciabattari, J., 193
Clinton, B., 66
Code of Broadcast News Ethics, 24
Cohen, S., 194

Public Broadcasting Service, 174, 206
Public goods, 61
Public journalism, 208-211
Public relations, 66, 73, 74, 88, 97, 101, 104
Pulitzer, J., 200
Pulitzer, R., 134

Quill, 143

Radio-Television News Directors Association, xiv, 10, 25, 181, 203
Rather, D., 93
Reagan, R., 12, 54, 66, 193
Reporter bias, 151
Reporting, 89
  angle, 216
  investigative, 88, 98, 100, 102, 115
Resource dependence theory, 21
Responible investment, 80
Rivera, G., 1
Robinson, J, 174
Robinson, M., 189
Roper Organization, 11
Rosen, J., 170, 210
Rothman, S., 32
Routines, 85
Rowen, H., 194
Ryu, J., 187

Savings and loan scandal, 194
Sawyer, D., 1
Schorr, D., 191
Schramm, W., 17
Schudson, M., 144
Scoops, 70
Scott, R., 63
Search goods, 65, 73, 80
Seattle Times, 3
Securities and Exchange Commission, 79, 150, 176
Sesame Street, 3
Shoemaker, P., 146, 149, 160
Sigma Delta Chi, 209
Silicon Valley, xii
Simon, H., 63
Singer, S., 194
60 Minutes,, 115
Slattery, K., 187
Smith, Adam, 4, 62
Smith, Anthony, 207

Social responsibility theory, 114
Society of Professional Journalists, xiv, 25, 203
Solomon, N., 195
Sources:
  ability to evaluate commodity quallity, 73
  rationality of, 72, 73
Spin, 29
Squires, R., 32
Stamm, K., 190
Star Trek, 124
Stempel, G. H. III, 11
Stephens, M., 123
Stepp, C. S., 7, 190
Stock market, 5, 80
Stone, V., 10
Strauss, A., xiv
Sypher, H., 116

Tabloid TV, 30
Talking back to media, 217
"Talking heads, 82
Technological determinism, 171
Technology, 33, 41, 44-47, 206-208
  differences between TV and print, 48-49, 171-176
Theory vs. reality, xiii
Tichenor, P., 69
Time, 193
Times Mirror Center for the People and the Press, 178
Times Mirror Corporation, 11, 12
Today Show, 133
Topping, S., 6
Truth, 67, 68
Tuchman, G., 183
Turow, J., 21, 27, 29, 32
Tversky, A., 63
TV news consultants, 130

Underwood, D., 190
Unionization, 211
Unreliable Sources: A Guide to Detecting Bias in News Media, 195
USA Today, 7, 23, 69, 178
Uses and gratifications, 116
U.S. News and World Report, 66

Validity of study, 223-225

About the Author

John H. McManus (B.A., College of the Holy Cross; M.A., University of Michigan; Ph.D., Stanford University) is an Assistant Professor in the Communication Department at Santa Clara University. A former newspaper reporter, he conducts research about the social responsibility of news media. His work has appeared in *Communication Research, Journalism Quarterly, Mass Comm Review,* and *Columbia Journalism Review.*